CYBERCRIME

INVESTIGATING HIGH-TECHNOLOGY COMPUTER CRIME

ROBERT MOORE, Ph.D.
DELTA STATE UNIVERSITY

 LexisNexis®

 anderson publishing
A member of the LexisNexis Group

Cybercrime: Investigating High-Technology Computer Crime

Copyright © 2005
Matthew Bender & Company, Inc., a member of the LexisNexis Group

Phone 877-374-2919
Web Site www.lexisnexis.com/anderson/criminaljustice

LexisNexis and the Knowledge Burst logo are trademarks of Reed Elsevier Properties, Inc.
Anderson Publishing is a registered trademark of Anderson Publishing, a member of the LexisNexis Group

Moore, Robert
    Cybercrime: investigating high-technology computer crime / Robert Moore
      Includes bibliographical references and index.
      ISBN 1-59345-303-5 (paperback)

Cover design by Tin Box Studio, Inc./Cincinnati, Ohio

EDITOR Janice Eccleston
ACQUISITIONS EDITOR Michael C. Braswell

Table of Contents

Chapter 3
Identity Theft and Bandits of the Information Superhighway   57

Introduction

Few areas of criminal justice are seeing such increases in recognition as those of crimes involving computers and technology. With computers becoming more ingrained in the lives of citizens around the world, it comes as little surprise that more criminal acts are reliant on the use of computers. In fact, the World Wide Web and the Internet have led to the creation of a virtual reality known as 'cyberspace.' The perceived anonymity of the Internet appears to provide comfort and courage for people to explore their inner desires and personalities. Because of this, many individuals may find themselves more inclined to attempt acts they never would have considered in the physical world.

Electronic commerce, which is often referred to as e-commerce, has also changed the way many people purchase products and services. Readers would be hard-pressed to locate a major national, or especially international, business that does not maintain some form of presence on the Internet. While e-commerce has questionably improved the quality of life for many, there is also little denying that this new form of business has led to the development of several new opportunities for fraud and criminal activity. Take, for example, the crimes of Internet auction fraud, which refers to the fraudulent selling of merchandise on Internet auctions, and Internet prostitution, which refers to the process of soliciting prostitution via the Internet. As these new crimes have developed, so too have the methods for committing traditional crimes through the use of technology. Identity theft, historically a crime of con artistry, has been significantly impacted by improvements in technology. Child pornography is another crime that has been impacted by technological advancements. Today, images of child pornography can be manufactured, copied, and transmitted via computers and the Internet within a fraction of the time historically required.

Unfortunately, while those who would abuse this new technology have been honing their techniques and improving their knowledge of how computers operate, many in the criminal justice community have been unable to keep pace. Few departments are staffed with individuals who are either capable of or willing to handle investigations that involve computers and highly advanced forms of technology. Even departments that are able to find willing investigators must struggle with the never-ending battle facing most law enforcement agencies—funding. The establishment of investigative units that specialize in the investigation of technology-assisted crime is not an inexpensive undertaking, and so even agencies that have the staff to handle such units are faced with determining how to pay for the equipment to handle investigations.

Law enforcement training academies also appear to spend little, if any, time preparing future officers with training on how to handle computers or any other technological device that is encountered at a crime scene. This is despite the fact that in recent years it has been noted by professionals in the field that more cases not involving computer-related crimes are benefiting from evidence obtained from computers located at a crime scene. With this in mind, it would seem incredibly important for law enforcement professionals to understand the proper methods of handling digital evidence. After all, the volatile nature of digital evidence means that failure to properly follow recommended guidelines could potentially result in the damage or destruction of irreplaceable evidence.

There is an incredible amount of literature being circulated today concerning the issue of technology crime and techniques. The problem with the literature is that a majority of the works is written from the standpoint that the reader is experienced with advanced issues in computer science and networking. Few of the works attempt to provide readers with information beneficial to those who have little or no working knowledge of computer technology and technology-assisted crime. It is the intent of this work to provide readers with sufficient information to introduce these complex topics in an easy to understand format that will benefit both those students who are new to criminal justice as well as professionals who are currently working in the field of law enforcement.

To this end, Chapter 1 will introduce readers to the field of technology crime and how the field has developed in recent years. Specifically, this section will provide the reader with information on common terminology encountered by investigators of high-technology crime, and how the definition for high-technology crime has changed in recent years. Chapter 2 will then begin introducing the reader to several high-tech crimes deemed most likely to be encountered by law enforcement personnel. Hacking is the first crime to be discussed, and readers will be provided information on how the crime of hacking has developed and how the Internet has affected hacking and the public's perception of hackers. Chapter 3 will examine the issue of identity theft which, according to most reports, is the number one growing technology-assisted crime in the world today. Information on how the crime is committed will be discussed, as will information on how the crime has changed with increased reliance on the Internet. Chapter 4 provides an examination of digital child pornography and how the Internet is being used today to lure children into sexual relationships. Chapter 5 introduces the reader to financial fraud on the Internet, and explains how law enforcement investigators should handle such investigations, as well as how they should work with consumers to increase awareness. The popularity of online auction sites such as eBay has led to auction fraud becoming one of the more profitable frauds in the United States today. Chapter 6 introduces the reader to several crimes that are emerging in recent years that have the potential to become serious problems for the criminal justice system in the near future. Most prominent of the crimes to be discussed is that of intellectual copyright theft and online peer-to-peer file-sharing software programs.

Chapter 7 introduces several issues associated with conducting investigative operations on the Internet. Foremost are the issues of entrapment and the application of this affirmative defense to prosecutions involving sting operations on the Internet. Chapter 8 introduces the reader to several legal and procedural issues associated with preparing a search warrant for digital evidence. In addition to the requirements of preparing a traditional search warrant, there are several other issues that must be considered; specifically, the issues of particularity and specificity are given incredible weight in the determination of a valid search. The search and seizure of computers and other technological devices also involves several other considerations, including: the number of computers, the types of computers, the software located on and around the computers, and other similar considerations that may not have been previously considered by individuals seeking a search warrant. Chapter 9 provides information on properly securing a crime scene and obtaining digital evidence.

Chapter 10 begins the final section, which is intended to introduce readers to how data are stored on computers and how computer forensics software operates. In this chapter, the reader will be introduced to the basics of how computers handle files, how networks store digital evidence, and how criminal investigators can benefit from knowledge of the techniques. Chapter 10 also briefly introduces some of the more common computer forensics software packages. Chapter 11 examines the legal system's response to computer forensics. Specifically, this section will examine how the courts have ruled in regard to admitting computer forensics evidence into trial. Chapter 12 concludes the work by examining several of the issues sure to become increased topics of concern. Namely, this section will address future high-technology crimes, the evolution of criminological studies, and the evolution of the legal system to address high-technology crime.

It is not the intent of this work to make the reader a professional investigator of high-technology crimes. Instead, the reader should view this work as a starting point for future research and study. To achieve this end, each chapter concludes with a series of review questions designed to highlight the important concepts presented within the chapter. Additionally, each chapter includes a small listing of books and/or articles designed to further the knowledge level of interested readers. If there is to be any chance for the criminal justice field to keep pace with those who are using computers and technology to commit criminal acts then now is the time to begin implementing adequate response plans. It is the hope of the author that this work motivates the reader to become more involved in training that will assist in preparing him or herself or their criminal justice agency to handle investigations involving high-technology crime.

Chapter 1

An Introduction to High-Technology Crime

Prior to this reading, the term high-technology crime may or may not have been heard by the reader. The term "technology" is often used to refer to mechanical or electrical devices that assist individuals in their day-to-day activities, but what does it mean to discuss "high technology"? As this is a work designed for those who are either interested in or currently involved in the field of criminal justice, let us take for example the standard equipment of a law enforcement officer. Today, most all law enforcement personnel carry a firearm of some type, regardless of whether they elect to keep a revolver or a semi-automatic. Is the officer's firearm a piece of technology? Of course. The firearm is a highly mechanical device, with the revolver having been developed by Samuel Colt in 1836. Therefore, the firearm is a piece of technology and one that has been around for more than 100 years. Now, is the firearm a piece of high technology? Some would consider the complex designs and manufacturing components of the firearm to make it a highly sophisticated piece of technology, but does this not make the weapon a device worthy of being termed "high technology"? No. The term high technology should invoke images of highly developed electronic devices. With this in mind, the electronic components involved in the operation of a cellular telephone are better examples of high technology than the components of a firearm.

When discussing the issue of high-technology devices and criminal activities, the issue of computers and crime must inevitably arise. Because of this, it is important to consider that what many individuals believe to be a computer is not the limitation for the technology. People tend to assume that a computer is the large electronic device that we use to type our research papers on and use to check our e-mail. Of course these devices are computers, but the truth is that many other devices meet the level of scrutiny necessary to be considered a computer. Several devices exist that are capable of receiving information, processing the information, and then return-

1

ing results to the user. Not all of these devices come with monitors or keyboards. For example, when we shop at the local convenience store it is not uncommon for many of us to now use our debit card to make a purchase, thereby saving us the time and effort it takes to write out a check. The cashier merely takes our debit card and swipes the magnetic stripe through a small machine, then returns the card to us. Our only input comes in the form of entering our Personal Identification Number (PIN) to gain access to the funds. The small device scanning the debit card has received only minimal information from the user—the PIN—and the only display of information we have received is the readout on the screen telling us whether we were approved or not. The machine that reads our debit cards is a miniature computer and therefore appears to fit the previously discussed concept of a high-technology device. Now that we have a basic understanding of some examples of high-technology devices, the questions that remain are: What is high-technology crime? and Is high-tech crime a serious problem?

What Is High-Technology Crime?

In keeping with the definition of high technology settled upon in the previous section, high-technology crime refers to any crime involving the use of high-technology devices in its commission. These are crimes that involve the use of computers, telephones, check-reading machines, credit card machines, and any other device that meets the previously accepted definition of high technology. There are numerous forms of high-technology crime, ranging from traditional crimes committed prior to technological advances, to newer crimes that rely on high-technology devices for a crime to be committed. In the past, there have been several different ways of referring to crimes involving high-technology devices. Perhaps the two best-known classifications used to distinguish these crimes are *computer crimes* or *cybercrimes*.

Computer Crimes

Traditionally, the term computer crime has been used to refer to criminal activities involving a computer that are made illegal through statute. Casey's (2000) definition is used here because of the clarity of his focus. Accordingly, a computer crime involves a computer in one of the following ways:

> • The computer as an instrument of the crime. Here, the computer is used as a means of engaging in the criminal activity. Under this category, the crime cannot be committed without the computer being turned on and used in the commission of the act. An example here would be the individual who uses a company computer to embezzle funds from a company account.

- The computer as the focus of a crime. Here, the computer is the intended target of criminal activity and is not necessarily used in the commission of the act. The best example of this is the individual who breaks into a computer supply store after hours with the intention of stealing computers and computer peripheral equipment.

- The computer as a repository of evidence. Here, the individual involved in a criminal act has not stolen the computer and has not used the computer as a means of committing the criminal act, but he or she has stored evidence on the machine. A good example of this is the individual who stores their illegally copyrighted music files on their home computer. Note then that, for this category to be applicable, the storage computer could not have been involved in the criminal activity. However, the generalizations are of minor concern because regardless of which of the categories the individual's actions fall under, they are still guilty of a computer crime under this definition.

There is nothing wrong with the definition used here, after all a crime involving a computer could be considered a computer crime. Let us examine one of the most famous computer crimes: hacking. Hacking refers to the unauthorized access of another's computer, and is considered a computer crime under the preceding definition for several reasons. First, the crime involves a computer that was used as an instrument of the crime. For one to be guilty of hacking, they must actually type in commands to penetrate the security of a second computer. Second, the crime has been made illegal through the enacting of a statute. According to 18 U.S.C. 1030, the Computer Fraud and Abuse Act, it is illegal to use a computer in fraud-related activity. Under the Computer Fraud and Abuse Act, it is illegal for someone to intentionally access a computer without the permission of the owner.

Cybercrime

Cybercrime, returning to Casey's (2000) definition, refers to any crime that involves a computer and a network, where the computer may or may not have played an instrumental part in the commission of the crime. The term cybercrime would be used to refer to a criminal act like that of identity theft, which involves the theft of someone's personal information like his or her credit card number or social security number. When an individual commits the crime of identity theft, there are several methods of obtaining a target's personal information. Many of the techniques involve the use of a computer or a network, but many more techniques have nothing to do with computers other than that the information may be stored in text files on a computer's hard drive.

In reading the discussion above it becomes clear that the term cybercrime actually refers to computer-related crime; however, some consider computer crime to be a subdivision of cybercrime that warrants its own definition and understanding. The determining factor between the two appears to be little more than the issue of whether a statute is present to criminalize the use of the computer in the criminal act. Because of the fact that more crimes today are relying on the Internet, there has been a significant effort by legislators to expressly criminalize these acts in the statutes. For example, as recently as five years ago, many states did not criminalize online harassment. Apparently, the reigning thought at the time was that harassment via the computer did not have the necessary impact to harm an individual. Luckily, our legislators and criminal justice professionals today are beginning to understand the danger of crimes involving computers. Prior to the enactment of these statutes, individuals guilty of harassing someone over the Internet were prosecuted under other statutes that were, for lack of a better term, 'stretched out' to include the crime under investigation. Now that more of the crimes are being made illegal through express statutes, the question arises as to whether there is a need to differentiate between the two forms of crime? Should computer crime be considered separately from cybercrime?

Consolidating High-Technology Crimes

A crime is generally defined as an act that violates an established rule or principle that is made known through a statute (Samaha, 1996). Therefore, whether a crime is a computer crime or a cybercrime is merely a trivial distinction. Both activities are crimes and both activities involve technology in the commission of the acts. There is little need to distinguish between the two on the basis of the presence of a network. Hacking, which will be discussed in detail in Chapter 2 and which, historically, has been considered the most recognized computer crime, traditionally relied on direct telephone connections using modems to commit criminal acts. Today, there are a few hacking attacks that involve direct connection via modem; the majority of hacking attacks are now reliant upon the Internet and network connections. Because of this fact, computer crimes are now beginning to blur into the definition for a cybercrime in that a network, the Internet being an example of a network, is now involved in the criminal activity.

If the two are becoming more intertwined, then why not simply refer to all of the aforementioned crimes as cybercrimes? All of the crimes discussed thus far could be considered cybercrimes. However, what if an individual steals someone's cellular telephone information, an act referred to as *phreaking*, and then recodes other cell phones so that the unsuspecting owner is billed for all calls made in the future? Has the individual in the aforementioned example committed a crime? Yes, it is illegal to steal someone's telephone service. Has the individual employed the use of a network? A network was only used in the sense that the call logs are stored somewhere on the phone company's computers, so there was no network involved in the commission of the act. Finally, has the individual involved in this crime used a computer? The answer is an ambiguous yes. To recode the cellular telephone the individual would have had to use electronic equipment that would surely meet our previously used definition of a computer. Under the previous definitions of computer crime and cybercrime, neither properly addresses the act. Perhaps the answer then is to consider this type of activity a crime involving a high-technology device (the computer and the cell phone), and therefore the act should be referred to as a high-technology crime.

In completing this work, the author hopes to provide information on several crimes that may involve only limited influence of computers and networks, as well as acts that rely entirely on the use of a computer and a network. These crimes involve highly developed technology in the commission of the crime, but are used in such a manner as to not strictly satisfy the definition for computer crime or cybercrime. Further, use of the term high-technology crime will separate crimes that do involve technology such as a firearm or an automobile from crimes involving highly developed electronic devices in the commission of criminal acts.

How Serious Is the High-Technology Crime Problem?

Using the term *high-technology crime* we are now referring to many diverse crimes such as: hacking, digital child pornography, identity theft, and online fraud. The rate of each of these crimes has been steadily increasing in recent years and, when examined together as a whole, amounts to a serious problem. It should also be noted that the problem is not isolated to the United States. Problems associated with high-technology crimes have become increasingly serious in every country around the world—even in countries that are not known for their high levels of technology. In fact, the worldwide nature of high-technology crime has developed problems in and of itself, in that jurisdiction for criminal investigations is now sometimes uncertain. For example, an individual living in Russia is capable of transmitting an image of child pornography here to the United States. In this situation, who has jurisdiction? Russia? Perhaps under Russian law the young girl in the picture was of legal consenting age. Was there, then, a crime committed in the eyes of Russian law enforcement personnel? Does America have jurisdiction? It is illegal to transmit images of juveniles, but the individual never touched United States soil when committing the criminal act. Can the use of American telephone lines be considered when examining whether there is jurisdiction for an investigation? These are all important questions that are not easily answered. There is, however, an increasing level of debate and intelligent discussion among world leaders as more international entities are beginning to recognize the dangers of high-technology crimes.

The increasing frequency of the crimes alone is enough to justify a certain level of concern. In the first quarter of 2002, there were more hacking-related attacks reported to the Computer Emergency Response Team Coordination Center (CERT/CC) than in the entire year 2001. At this level of frequency, we are looking at an unforeseeable increase in the frequency of these crimes in the coming years. One has to look no further than their newspaper to find sufficient information necessary to assist in determining how serious the crimes have become. Rarely does a week go by without some form of new computer virus being announced and, as will be discussed in Chapter 2, there are now companies forced to hire individuals to do nothing more than write anti-virus programs.

Hacking is not the only crime seeing an increase in use. Digital child pornography, to be discussed in Chapter 4, is unfortunately seeing an increase in use. Child pornography is a troubling crime if for no other reason than the fact that children are sexually abused in the manufacturing of the materials. According to one federal law enforcement official, as much as 50 percent of all cases involving computers and technology are child pornography cases. Historically, the federal government has handled investigations involving child pornography materials. Today, however, this is slowly beginning to change. Following the terror attacks of September 11, 2001, the federal government has undergone a drastic restructuring of organization and perhaps of focus. Of course, this is not to say that the federal law enforcement agencies will no longer investigate crimes involving child pornography. However, more states are being asked to handle such investigations, and the problem is that many municipalities are currently incapable of handling these investigations.

While hacking is increasing at an incredible rate, the latest reports concerning identity theft have this crime labeled as the fastest growing of the high-technology crimes to be discussed. It is believed that as many as 500,000 cases of identity theft occur every year. Even more upsetting is the fact that many individuals still do not report identity theft whether because of a lack of understanding concerning the crime or because many victims may not realize they are being victimized. Identity theft is perhaps such an attractive crime because it is possible to commit the crime and move on before the victim even realizes they have been victimized. Many times the only way a person realizes they have been a victim of identity theft is when the victim is denied a loan.

The frequency of high-technology crime is also presenting a problem for law enforcement personnel because of the need for training and equipment. Many law enforcement agencies face the same problem year after year—a budget shortfall. The budgetary issues are especially problematic for smaller police and sheriff's departments in rural communities. Criminals retreat to these smaller communities when they want to get away from the larger cities in hopes of being able to stay outside the reach of a law enforcement agency. The funds necessary to investigate high-technology crimes are significant, if for no other reason than the training. Take, for example, the following scenario concerning drug trafficking:

> A major narcotics trafficking operation is believed to be operating out of a county with a population of 22,000. The local sheriff and police chief have worked together to investigate the individuals believed to be involved. However, there has been no communication between the suspects and any buyers. During a routine suicide investigation involving an individual believed to have been a part of the narcotics operation, a deputy encounters a computer.

In the above example, the deputy probably would not consider taking the computer back to the department for examination. Further, if the computer was taken back there is the possibility that the department would not have a deputy capable of examining the computer for evidence; in fact, it is highly probable that the department would not have a deputy capable of forensically examining the computer. What evidence could the computer contain? Remember that no one has been able to monitor a telephone communication concerning a narcotics transaction. The information is obviously being conveyed somehow. Perhaps the individuals are using electronic communications to facilitate their transactions. As foreign as this idea sounds, it is in fact becoming a more common occurrence in the drug trade industry. Because smaller departments either do not think about or know how to monitor e-mail, more narcotics organizations may rely on the technology as a tool for arranging drop times and locations. Even more interesting is the consideration of whether the computer could be used to prove whether the individual was murdered or committed suicide. Perhaps the individual did not commit suicide, and evidence on the computer could be used to corroborate this claim.

In the aforementioned example, it was indicated that the department likely had no one capable of examining the computer for evidence. Some readers may question this assessment by agreeing that most departments would not consider examining the computer but if the computer was seized then anyone could turn it on to look for e-mail. The answer is that anyone could turn on the computer to look for e-mail. However, there are two reasons for this author's statement. First, with the vast number of different e-mail programs available, it is extremely likely that the department may not have someone familiar enough with the different programs to find e-mails because of the different programs available. Second, there are several legal issues associated with searching a computer without proper training. The biggest issue involved in searching a computer? In the present case, the issue would be that of evidence integrity. Without proper training and equipment, there is no way to prove the information was actually on the computer and not added by the investigator.

The proper methods of seizing and examining a computer will be discussed in later chapters, but suffice to say that at this point there are many smaller departments that are not capable of conducting such investigations. Let us also briefly consider the financial issues associated with investigating a crime such as that of the narcotics trafficking example. Because it has been stated that an officer may not merely turn on a computer and examine it for evidence, it must be assumed that there is additional software or hardware required for such an investigation. These software and hardware utilities will be discussed in later chapters, but the majority of these devices and software are very expensive. If a police or sheriff's department can barely afford to pay their officers and provide equipment for their day-to-day operations, then it is hard for them to justify purchasing costly computer equipment.

The Purpose of This Work

There is no way this work can remove the financial roadblocks involved in investigating high-technology crime. However, hopefully the materials presented here can provide a basis for investigators, students, and private citizens who are to come into contact with these crimes in the near future. As stated in earlier sections, the problems associated with high-technology crime are increasing every day. While historically it was possible for an individual to indicate they were not interested in investigating high-technology crimes, today's criminal justice personnel have no such luxury. It is no longer probable that an individual involved in law enforcement will encounter a criminal act involving high-technology devices; it is now undeniable that such an encounter will eventually occur. The goal of this work is to provide readers with information on how some of the more commonly encountered high-technology crimes are committed and what are some basic investigative strategies. The work is not written to make the reader an expert in the area of high-technology crime investigation. There is no work in print today that is capable of making an investigator an expert; however, the foundations for such training are laid within the book. To facilitate this level of understanding the work will be divided into three sections: an introduction to the criminal acts, an introduction to the investigations, and an introduction to computer forensics.

The Criminal Acts

The chapters within this section will focus on introducing the reader to the various crimes considered high-technology crime. The crimes included in this work are not exhaustive, but are instead representative of the crimes predicted to be most commonly encountered by individuals in the criminal justice system. Each chapter will include a discussion on the nature and techniques associated with one or more high-technology crimes. Many of these crimes may be committed either with or without the computer, so a portion of each chapter may be designated to explaining the physical world techniques involved in committing the criminal act. Understanding the physical world techniques is an important aspect of helping to understand how the individuals may apply the information obtained from their physical exploits in furthering their criminal activities using the computer or the Internet. The following sections in this chapter present a more detailed overview (than was presented in the Introduction) of the material that will be covered in Chapters 2 through 12.

Chapter 2—Hacking and Phreaking

Hacking is arguably the most popular and well-known high-technology crime. This should not, however, be taken to mean it will be the most commonly encountered high-technology crime, as the very technical nature of this crime lends itself to being one of the least investigated crimes for non-specialized investigators. Because hacking involves the unlawful access of another's computer without the legitimate owner's permission, the investigation requires a well-rounded understanding of computers and networking, or at the very least an advisor to help with understanding the crime. Phreaking refers to the theft of telecommunications services and is discussed here with the crime of hacking because of the relationship the two have—generally a hacker will also phreak because one activity assists the other in remaining unidentified.

The reader will be provided a brief history of how hacking and phreaking have evolved over the past few decades, as well as how to distinguish between the various types of hackers. The tools and techniques employed by hackers will be briefly introduced in an attempt to provide information on the vast number of attacks possible given the current state of technology. The hacker/phreaker subculture will also be discussed, as the language and terminology employed by these individuals is oftentimes confusing to those who have not been introduced to the style of talking and typing.

Chapter 3—Identity Theft

In this chapter, the reader is introduced to the crime of identity theft, which refers to the theft of another's personal credit identity or physical identity. Identity theft has been labeled as the fastest growing high-technology crime, and is one of the few that still occurs more frequently in the real world than on the Internet. The evolution of physical identity theft techniques will be discussed as a foundation for explaining how the Internet and technology has affected the criminal activity. While the crime still occurs more frequently in the physical world, even the physical activities involve several high-technology devices, and as such, this section will introduce the reader to information on how these crimes are accomplished. The section will conclude with an examination of the techniques used in committing identity theft via the Internet, and with information on identity theft in the future.

Chapter 4—Digital Child Pornography

While hacking is the best known and identity theft is the fastest growing, child pornography is regarded by many as the most physically damaging of the high-technology crimes. Child pornography is an old crime that has merely become modernized with the advent of technology. The Internet has revamped an industry built upon human suffering that had begun seeing a decline in popularity prior to the public release of the Internet. It has already been stated that child pornography is one of the most investigated high-technology crimes, but it is also one of the most debated. Returning briefly to our international crime example, there is a growing argument concerning the illegality of child pornography that is manufactured in a country where such materials are illegal. Is it illegal to view child pornography? It is illegal to download and own child pornography, but what about the Internet user who stumbles across an international child pornography website? Are these individuals violating the law by looking at pictures on their screens? At one point does one own a digital image? These are all questions that are being asked around the world as the problem continues to worsen. Here in the United States, the issue has become even further clouded by recent Supreme Court decisions concerning the nature of privacy and child pornography. Today, it is necessary to not only prove that an individual owns an image of child pornography; it must now be proven that the image in fact depicts an actual child.

Chapter 4 will introduce the reader to this crime, including a brief history on child pornography and children's rights. More specifically, this section will provide the reader with information on what child pornography is used for; many people assume the images are for personal pleasure, if one can consider such viewing pleasure. However, there are far more devious uses for images of child pornography, and these uses will be discussed in detail. The effect of digitization and the Internet will be discussed, as will be information on how the crime is committed today versus just a few short years ago. And lastly, the recent court decisions concerning the investigation of child pornography will be examined as a means of providing guidance for both those who are new to the field and those who have been investigating the crime for years.

Chapter 5—Internet Fraud

The term *Internet fraud* is rather broad, and therefore this chapter will be more of an overview of how the Internet has become the haven for fraudulent behavior in the twenty-first century. There are several crimes that qualify as Internet fraud, and each will be briefly introduced to the reader, with a discussion on how the crimes are committed and what can be done to prevent the crimes from growing in frequency. The first high-technology crime to be discussed here is that of online auction fraud. With the popularity of eBay and other auction websites, it should come as no surprise that fraud has become a popular issue in the past few years. Many individuals are now reporting that they are not receiving the merchandise for which they have paid. Another popular form of Internet fraud is that of adoption fraud; this crime is interesting because unlike auction fraud there may be a child up for adoption. The difference is that ten or fifteen individuals, with each paying upwards of $3,000 or more, may adopt the same child. Finally, the reader will be introduced to one of the latest forms of fraud, the purchasing of wives online and the presence of online prostitution. Prostitution is said to be the world's oldest profession, and it has now moved itself onto the world's newest medium. Here, the reader will be introduced to how prostitution works on the Internet, and how potential 'clients' are being defrauded every day. Each of the aforementioned crimes will be discussed in order that the reader will be familiar with how the operations are conducted. Using this information, in conjunction with information presented in later chapters, individuals will be aware of how to handle a basic investigation involving one of these forms of crime.

Chapter 6—Emerging Crimes on the Net

There are numerous crimes emerging on the Internet as more computers become linked to the system. Almost any crime can today involve some aspect of computers and technology. Chapter 6 will introduce readers to several of the more high profile crimes that are sure to become more popular in the near future. The first crime to be discussed in this section is that of cyberstalking. Stalking itself is a relatively new crime, having only been recognized in the early 1990s, but cyberstalking is still not considered by some states to be a crime. Here, the reader will be introduced to information on how cyberstalking occurs and why the crime is worthy of serious consideration by law enforcement personnel. The second crime to be considered in this section is that of Internet piracy. Child pornography is not the only materials to undergo digitization in recent years. Today, it is possible to store hundreds or thousands of songs or movies on a computer's various storage media. These materials can then be traded via the Internet or via traditional sales methods.

Investigating High-Technology Crimes

In the second section, this work will focus on providing information relating to the actual investigations of the aforementioned crimes. The previous section provided the reader with information on how the crime is committed and the current state of the crime in society. Here, the reader will learn how to actually begin taking steps toward the investigation of cases involving high-technology devices in the commission of a crime.

Chapter 7—Investigating Crime Online

In this section the reader will be introduced to online investigations, and more specifically online sting operations. Much like the investigation of traditional physical crimes, occasionally it will be necessary to conduct a sting operation to ensnare suspects engaged in the commission of one of the aforementioned high-technology crimes. Here, the reader will be introduced to information related to establishing such operations. Additionally, the legal issues associated with online sting operations will be discussed, with special emphasis being placed on the issue of online entrapment. Because there may be little or no face-to-face interaction during the initial stages of establishing an online sting operation, it is necessary that investigators understand how the courts have generally ruled on investigations in general and on Internet investigations specifically.

Chapter 8—Search Warrants for Digital Evidence

The Fourth Amendment of the United States Constitution has ruled that unreasonable searches and seizures by law enforcement are forbidden. As part of this requirement, it is generally accepted that a search warrant be used when seizing evidence. All search warrants must be specific, but this specificity becomes increasingly important in regards to the seizure of digital evidence, which is merely the term used to describe evidence stored on a computer or other magnetic storage media. Here, the reader will be provided with information on drafting a search warrant, establishing the search warrant execution team and pre-planning for the execution of the warrant. Just as the warrant must be more specific, the pre-planning for execution of a search warrant for digital evidence requires the investigator to ensure certain aspects of the seizure will be properly handled during the initial moments following the beginning of the warrant's execution. This section will also include a brief examination of warrantless search doctrines and their application to the seizure of digital evidence.

Chapter 9—Executing the Search Warrant

Unlike many other warrant executions, it is not enough to merely go in and collect the evidence listed on the search warrant. There are numerous additional considerations when the evidence to be seized is a computer or computer-related storage media. In this chapter, the reader will be provided with a step-by-step guide for executing a search warrant involving a computer or other high-technology device. Additionally, this section will include a discussion of how to protect the integrity of the evidence for instances in which the case goes to trial. According to some professionals, the majority of child pornography cases plead out because of either embarrassment or because they know there is sufficient evidence to convict. Protection of the evidence's integrity is instrumental to ensuring that the individual will plead because of the latter reason.

Introduction to Computer Forensics and the Future of Technology Crime

In the third and final section the reader will be introduced to the issues of networking and computer forensics. This section has been included last as a means of providing a cap to the previously discussed issues. Here, the reader will be introduced to common networking concepts and terms, terms that will be beneficial to the investigator of high-technology crimes. Computer forensics is a relatively new field within criminal justice, and is one that is sure to see an increased level of support in the near future. Readers will leave this section with information on how the crimes are committed, how the crimes can be investigated and evidence seized, how networks may contain additional evidence and how computer forensics can help solidify a case.

Chapter 10—An Introduction to Computer Forensics and Software

Computer forensics refers to the process of applying science and computers to the investigation of criminal acts. Here, the reader will be introduced to the field of computer forensics, with specific coverage of how the field has developed over the last several years and some of the more commonly used software packages.

Chapter 11—Computer Forensics and the Law

In this chapter the reader will be introduced to how the field of computer forensics and digital evidence has been accepted by the courts. This section will examine the evolution of both the rules of evidence, as well as case law interpretations related to the admission of scientific evidence. The admission of scientific evidence requires specific criteria be satisfied, and this section will address how adherence to the computer forensics process can result in the proper admission of evidence during a criminal trial.

Chapter 12—The Future of High-Technology Crime in Law Enforcement

In this, the final chapter, the reader will be provided with information concerning where the author believes high-technology crimes are heading in the near future. Many experts argue that it will be hard to ever eradicate high-technology crime through legal efforts because the crimes can change so fast and those who are committing the crimes always stay one step ahead of the law enforcement aspect; this leads some to speculate that the future to high-technology crime fighting lies in the education of youngsters who have the potential to commit these crimes or in modifications to the technology itself. This chapter will also include a discussion on the future of criminological research involving technology-assisted crime, including a brief discussion on how three theories could be applied to high-technology crime.

Review Questions

1. What is meant by the term *high technology*? What is high-technology crime?

2. Is the high-technology crime problem serious enough to begin reevaluating the way in which the criminal justice field handles such investigations?

3. Historically, what was the difference between a computer crime and a cybercrime? Is there a need to continue differentiating between the two?

4. Discuss three methods by which an individual could commit a criminal activity through the use of technology, but not involve what we historically consider a computer.

Online Resources

The Computer Emergency Response Team—provides information related to the frequency and types of attacks against personal computers. Available at www.cert.org.

High Technology Crime Investigators Association—professional association designed to provide training and information for individuals who investigate high-technology crimes. Available at www.htcia.org.

Chapter 2

Hackers, Crackers, and Phone Phreaks

When the term *hacker* is first mentioned, it is not uncommon for people to conjure up an image of a small, fragile, nerdy looking teenager who is sitting in front of his computer, playing video games. Not only is this appraisal of hackers inappropriate, it is troubling because it indicates that many people believe only teenagers and children are engaging in acts of hacking. The truth, however, is that there are many adults who engage in hacking on a day-to-day basis, and many times these older transgressors are as guilty as their younger counterparts, possibly even more guilty when it comes to malicious acts involving computers. There are several possible reasons that would explain why individuals would conjure up the image of a teenager. First, when computers were originally released, it may have seemed to some that the devices were reserved for teenagers or those who were among the intellectually elite, a scenario that would explain the nerd-like apparition for our imagined hacker. Additionally, many teenagers did devote countless hours to learning how to operate computers when they were first released. Several of these individuals foresaw the potential role that computers could play in the future of society. With this in mind, many teenagers were intent upon learning more about computers as a means of ensuring that they would have a secure job when computers eventually began to catch on with businesses and corporations.

The addiction these individuals maintained for their computers was certainly a factor in the development of the aforementioned misconception. The truth, however, is that Hollywood most likely played almost as an important role in the ingraining of the image. There was a point at which Hollywood movie studios began releasing films that provided images of a teenager using his or her computer to wreak havoc on America; often the level of mischief was so great that the safety of Americans was threatened. Sadly, if individuals are not informed and trained in regard to understanding the term 'hacker', then they will assume that the individuals in movies such as *Hackers* and *Wargames* are representative of the entire hacker population. Of course there are individuals who fit this image, but it is generally accepted that the image is nowhere near representative of the entire population.

The Evolution of the Term Hacker

Understanding of the term *hacker* is further complicated because there are many different definitions available for hackers. Perhaps the best method of understanding the connotations related to "hacker" is to briefly examine the history and development of the term. Interestingly enough, the definition for the term has undergone many dramatic changes since its inception. Today, individuals who claim to be hackers argue that true hackers are interested in furthering computer security and that those who do not conform to this belief system are not hackers in the truest sense of the word. It is these individuals who do not care to aid in improving computer security that are benefiting, albeit occasionally in a negative sense, from the aforementioned emphasis in Hollywood and media reports.

The origin of the term hacker can be traced back to the Massachusetts Institute of Technology (MIT), which was one of the first institutions to offer computer programming and computer science courses. The term is believed to have first been used in a computer context by the members of the Artificial Intelligence Lab at MIT. These individuals were not criminals. In fact, they were a highly devoted research team (Levy, 1994). This is not to say that these individuals did not violate the rules of the university. Many of the team members were constantly in violation of university rules and procedures concerning the number of hours a computer could be used by a student or faculty member. The members began referring to themselves as hackers because they were able to take computer programs and make them perform actions not originally intended for use by the software. The term was developed on the basis of a practical joke and a feeling of excitement because the team members would "hack away" at the keyboards for hours at a time.

Prior to the use of the term by the A.I. lab members, the term "hack" was held to refer to any practical joke that was imbued with creativity, extreme style, originality, and technical virtue (Levy, 1994). The term was originally used in the early 1950s, and it is commonly held to this day that many, if not all, students will eventually perform a hack before graduating from MIT. The catch is that the hacks must not only be high-profile and original but must also be committed anonymously. For more information concerning the history of hacks and practical jokes at MIT, readers are encouraged to visit the MIT website and order one of the university's official publications concerning the history of hacks at the university.

The term hacker lived a life of relative obscurity until computer crimes began gaining more publicity in the media. It was at this time that the term became associated with individuals who were using their personal computers to gain unauthorized access to other individuals' and businesses' computers. Those individuals associated with the Artificial Intelligence lab at MIT immediately expressed their discontent with the use of the word in relation to a negative and criminal act (Denning, 1990). The term *cracker* was recommended to replace hacker in the media reports; this term is a combination of hacker and criminal that refers to a criminal hacker. Unfortunately, the term cracker was not as accepted during the early years of media coverage, and with the release of the aforementioned Hollywood films, the term hacker has become even further ingrained into the vocabulary of society. It would be extremely hard, perhaps even impossible, to completely distinguish between the two terms today.

Cracker is a recognized term today, but according to Casey (2000) it refers to one who violates copyright protection and cracks password protected files and services. The issue of copyright protection has become an extremely hot topic in recent years with the advent of peer-to-peer networking and the sharing of music and video files via the Internet. Within the computer science community, and more specifically within the hacking community, the difference between hacking and cracking is still recognized today. Outside of these communities, however, the two terms have come to mean almost the same thing. If the terms arise in conversation it is important to examine the context with which the term is used. It is possible that the user is intending to talk about one aspect more than the other and is merely misusing the terminology. Further, many times, individuals most likely do not realize that there is a difference between the two and therefore will make no attempt to properly apply the terms.

The Introduction of Hacking to the Public

Threats associated with computer crime existed long before technology evolved to a point where two or more computers could link up and share information and resources. It was, however, this initial linking that has ultimately led to computers becoming an instrument of mass harm and nuisance. Linking of computer resources has raised the level of potential harm to the point where computer-related attacks can impact national, as well as international, security. The foundation for this principle was first laid with the development of the ARPANET, which stands for the Advanced Research Projects Agency Network. The ARPANET was developed when four sites around the United States were linked together as a means of sharing information and resources. In this respect, the ARPANET could be considered the birth of the Internet; although it should be noted that there have been several additional developments in computer technology that has led to the current state of networking and the Internet.

When the original researchers launched the ARPANET in 1969, each of the original team members reportedly commented on the potential the new technology had for research and the sharing of information around the world (Denning, 1990). It was commonly held that the future of networking and the potential impact of the ARPANET would alter every individual's life. What is ironic is that technology developed as a means of improving research, education, and training, has developed into one of the most used criminal tools in existence.

Several events would occur during the decade of the 1980s that would introduce the public to the potential dangers associated with hacking. These events began in early 1983 with a series of rather serious computer break-ins. During the course of investigating these break-ins, it was discovered that at least 60 computers belonging to the Memorial Sloan-Kettering Cancer Center and the Los Alamos National Laboratory were compromised. News media began covering the case and, before long, the Federal Bureau of Investigation (FBI) launched an investigation. As a result of the FBI's investigation it was determined that the break-ins were committed by a gang of teenagers that referred to themselves as the 414 Gang; the gang received their nickname because of the area code in which they were committing their crimes (Trigaux, 2000). The public began demanding better protection from high tech youths and interestingly enough the public automatically associated the offenders' ages with the crimes involving computers. This misconception was, of course, only further reinforced because similar reports surrounding the incident all involved the age of the individuals responsible for the acts.

Following the events surrounding the Los Alamos Research Facility, and several additional incidents involving computers, Congress began work on legislation that would curtail the incidence of computer-assisted crime. In 1986, the legislation was finally approved and labeled the Computer Fraud and Abuse Act (CFAA). The CFAA made the unauthorized access of a federal interest computer an illegal act. While the CFAA was designed with the best intents, the truth is that the legislation only addressed hacking into federally controlled computers unless the incident occurred across two or more different states. Several states followed the suggestion of the federal government and began implementing similar legislation concerning the use of computer technology in criminal activity.

It would be only a few more years after the passing of the CFAA that the public would once again be introduced to a high profile crime involving computers and technology. On November 2, 1988, Robert Morris, a Cornell University graduate student, inadvertently released a computer program that would come to be known as a worm program.[1] Morris was working on a graduate degree in computer science with an emphasis in computer security. The program he wrote was allegedly a practice program that he

---

[1]   A worm is a computer program that, unlike a virus, is not usually written as an attempt to damage a computer system. Instead, a worm program will usually replicate itself repeatedly and then resend itself back out over the Internet. This constant duplication and re-mailing can slow down a network to the point of collapse, as was the case of Robert Morris' worm program.

intended to use as a test and then remove from the systems he infected. The program was to be installed on a computer within the MIT computer lab. Once installed on the first computer the program would copy itself onto the other computers in the lab and then remain hidden until Morris could remove it from the system. Unfortunately, due to an error in coding the program began replicating itself at unforeseen speeds. By taking advantage of a security defect in the network, the program was able to copy itself onto somewhere between 2,000 and 3,000 computers; this rapid copying resulted in the computers shutting down due to a loss of memory and processing capacity. Many of the companies whose computers were infected lost hundreds of thousands of dollars because of down-time and the costs of repairing the damage (Hafner & Markoff, 1991).

On November 7, 1988, the FBI became involved with the case, and in a strange series of circumstances, Morris' father became involved in the investigation of the case. Many speculate whether Morris would have ever been discovered had he not contacted authorities to inform them that it was an accident and that he was sorry. Once Morris was located there arose the problem of how to press charges. On the basis of information provided by the investigation there was no legal statute under which to charge Morris. Eventually, it was determined that by stretching the Computer Fraud and Abuse Act of 1986 it would be possible to prosecute Morris (Hafner & Markoff, 1991). The results of Morris' being charged under the CFAA were interesting. Officially, this was the first time an individual had been charged under the newly enacted legislation, and there was still debate as to whether the charges were properly filed in the case-at-hand. Because of this, Morris gained extreme notoriety for being the first person charged under the CFAA; the result of this recognition leading to Morris being inducted into several of the hacker halls of fame. It is undetermined whether Morris would have received these honors had he not been the first to receive prosecution under the new computer crime statutes. Apparently Morris is not remembered for much beyond his prosecution and inadvertent discovery of the worm program.

Because of the unique circumstances surrounding the case of Robert Morris, the Cornell Commission was developed and charged with the task of investigating the incident and making recommendations on how to prevent future occurrences. It was the opinion of the Commission that Morris' actions were indeed accidental in nature and that as a result of his actions there were several security deficiencies in the computer systems detected. Further, the results of the investigation indicated that there was a positive result from the act in the form of improved computer security. The Computer Fraud and Abuse Act required that the prosecution prove that Morris "intentionally and without authorization accessed federal interest computers." It was the Commission's determination that, during the course of the trial, the prosecution did in fact prove that Morris' actions were intentional because he released the worm into the computer lab with premeditation; this belief was based upon testimony that indicated Morris took advantage of several holes in the UNIX operating system during the process of implanting the worm program. Despite the fact Morris had not intended for his program to be loosed upon the world, he was still convicted on January 22, 1990, and on the recommendation of the Cornell Commission it was determined that Morris should not have his punishment reduced. Morris was ultimately sentenced to three years probation, was fined $10,000, and was ordered to perform 400 hours of community service. Therefore, despite the Commission's determination that Morris' act was nothing more than a juvenile act that ignored the potential consequences, Morris began serving his sentence (Denning, 1990).

The cases involving the 414 gang and Robert Morris initiated the process of highlighting hacking in the media. However, the two crimes involved only limited media coverage when they occurred. The 414 Gang had brought attention to the citizens of Minnesota and the surrounding states, but overall the majority of the nation remained unaware of the problem. Over the next few years the entire nation would slowly become aware of the perceived power a hacker could possess, as well as the publicity such acts could generate.

During the late 1980s and the early 1990s, individuals around the world were introduced to the escapades of a young man named Kevin Mitnick. As a teenager in the 1980s, Mitnick was constantly in trouble with authorities because of his activities involving computers and criminal acts. In the early 1990s, however, his name became very well known when a computer engineer whose computer he had illegally accessed tracked him cross-country. Mitnick witnessed the engineer on television discussing a new technique for converting a cellular phone into a digital receiver. Wanting the information for himself, Mitnick hacked into the engineer's computer and took the plans associated with the technique. Because of this act, Mitnick was forced to live life

Computer-hacker-turned-author Kevin Mitnick poses for a portrait June 27, 2002, in Las Vegas. Barred by the terms of his probation from tampering with computers, ex-convict hacker Kevin Mitnick turned to writing about them, baring the tricks of his former trade in his book, "The Art of Deception." Mitnick was given permission to use a computer to write his book. (AP)

on the run. Mitnick was the first computer-related criminal to be featured on the television show "America's Most Wanted," and a book titled *Takedown* was written that chronicles his chase and capture.

Mitnick's escapades are generally considered to have brought the issue of hacking to the forefront of the nation's attention. Further, his activities are credited with scaring the government into believing that hacking could be dangerous. When Mitnick was finally captured, his sentence was more severe than some manslaughter sentences at the time. Over the course of his criminal career, Mitnick managed to gain access to some of the most guarded computer systems in the country; this was accomplished by employing a combination of computer programming skill and social engineering skills. Social engineering is a term used by hackers to describe the process of using communication skills to trick computer users into revealing information necessary for the hacker to gain access to the computer system (Hafner, 1991; Mitnick, 2002).

So great was Mitnick's reputation for working on technological devices that many of the prison administrators feared the possibilities should he gain access to electronics equipment. For example, Mitnick was once placed in solitary confinement because prison officials were afraid he was attempting to turn his Walkman radio into a bugging device. Allegedly, he was planning to place the homemade bug in the warden's office. Mitnick was also reportedly denied access to unsupervised phone calls because of a fear that he could dial into the defense department's computers, which he reportedly was able to do several times over the course of his career; a fact that has never been confirmed by an official source (Penenberg, 1999).

Kevin Mitnick's story is of special interest because of the impact his arrest had on others in the hacker community. As a result of his incarceration, Mitnick became arguably the world's most popular hacker. Numerous websites in almost all languages sprang up on the Internet arguing that Mitnick had to be released. The common cry became "Free Kevin." There has been numerous Internet articles discussing the 'Free Kevin' campaign, and a documentary was made by the company that publishes the hacker magazine *2600*. After Mitnick's release, he was not allowed to touch a computer but was able to provide expert assistance in cases involving computer crime through the use of a proxy typist. Since his arrest and time in prison, Mitnick has reportedly gone straight and relinquished his life of computer crime. In fact, he has formed his own computer security company, which incidentally had its web page hacked on the day of its public release, and has written a book detailing how companies can prevent persons from gaining access to data through social engineering.

The Types of Hackers

There has been a growing amount of literature concerning the evil nature of hackers. However, the original hackers were intellectual programmers who were interested in determining how far computer programs could be taken; these individuals had little, if any, interest in criminal activity. Many in the computer security field maintain a similar view today, and view themselves as hackers because they have an appreciation for computer technology and the capabilities of the machines. Because of this there are generally four categories of hackers recognized in the hacker/cracker community: black hat hackers, white hat hackers, gray hat hackers, and script kiddies (Wang, 2001). In this work, there will be two additional types of hackers discussed: the hactivist and the cyber terrorist.

Black Hat Hackers

The black hat hacker is the epitome of all that the public fears in a computer criminal. These are individuals who violate computer security for little reason beyond maliciousness or for personal gain. This form of hacker writes programs to damage computer systems and networks. It is because of this category of hackers that computer security and anti-virus manufacturing have become full-time enterprises that cost businesses around the world millions of dollars to develop protected computer networks and operating systems.

White Hat Hackers

These individuals are the exact opposite of the black hat hackers. The main objective of the white hat hacker it to provide computer security programs that will protect systems from being illegally and maliciously penetrated. White hat hackers may publish their computer security programs on the Internet or via software companies as a means of protecting others from computer security vulnerabilities they have discovered. These hackers will still search out target computers and then attempt to hack into the systems. Once they are successful, however, they will normally cease their activities and alert the owner of the computer system to the vulnerability.

Gray Hat Hackers

These hackers are a combination of white hat and black hat. Perhaps the best way to describe this class of hackers is to call them opportunistic. If a gray hat hacker is searching the Internet for a target and successfully gains access to a computer system, then they will notify the system's owner. However, instead of offering to tell the administrator how the system was exploited the gray hat hacker will normally elect to offer to repair the defect for a small amount of money. Many hackers associate themselves with hacker groups such as L0pht or the infamous Cult of the Dead Cow. These groups work together to develop hacker utilities programs for release via the Internet or at the annual hacker convention, DefCon. One member of the group may illegally gain access to a computer system and then recommend to the system administrator that one of their friends be hired to secure the system. While this may appear to be a form of blackmail, in the business world such decisions may be a matter of cost-benefit analysis. If it truly is cheaper to hire the individual than to lose the data or the use of the computer networks, then the business may extend a position to the individual. Recently, the practice has witnessed a decrease in use as more businesses have elected to prosecute individuals who attempt these acts.

Script Kiddies

These individuals are the lowest on the hacker ladder, and are oftentimes not considered hackers at all. The debate over whether these individuals should be considered under the heading hacker has to do with the average technical ability of the script kiddy. Generally, these individuals have little or no computer programming skills. Script kiddies earn their names from their abilities to surf the Internet looking for hacker utility programs and then launching the programs at a target computer system. The script kiddy is the most dangerous of the hackers because this is the individual who has no idea how the program will affect the computer system the attack is being launched upon. Some of the more notorious hacking attacks that involve the shutting down of websites like eBay and Amazon.com have involved the use of generic computer programs launched by script kiddies.

Hactivists

Categorizing hackers into the hactivist category is a risky and perhaps odd distinction. After all, the acts these individuals engage in is the equivalent of hacking, the same as the above categories of hackers. These individuals, however, are distinguishable from the other categories in regard to their motives. The majority of the above attempt to hack as a means of gaining illegal access to a computer network or system—access that will allow them to either fix a problem or create damage and mischief. The hactivist, on the other hand, is an individual who hacks as a means of spreading their political message. The majority of hactivist attacks involve web page defacement, which refers to when a hacker gains access to the server that is storing a web page and then modifies the page to display their own message. In regards to the hactivist, these defacements involve modifying web pages to reflect the hacker's political messages. Many extremist organizations employ hactivists to overtake popular web pages and replace them with information on the cause of the group.

Cyber Terrorist

The term cyber terrorist is a relatively new term that refers to an individual who uses their hacking ability to instill a sense of fear into the public. It is important to distinguish between someone who is merely using the Internet and hacking ability as a means of harassing someone and one who is using their abilities to attack a portion of the critical infrastructure. By critical infrastructure, it is meant utilities such as water purification, electricity, and nuclear power plants. The cyber terrorist is one who would break into a computer system or network and then in someway manage to cause damage or death because of the loss of the service. Cyber terrorism is a relatively new concept and has only gained recognition in the last few years. As more computers are connecting to the Internet everyday, it is becoming increasingly easy to locate critical targets that could inflict terror into the general public. Because of these facts, it is a personal belief that this form of hacking is certain to become more discussed in the coming years (see Chapter 12 for a more detailed discussion on cyber terrorism).

Hacker Technique and Modus Operandi

An understanding of how hackers operate, as well as the tools they employ in their trade, will be beneficial in the mission to prevent the proliferation of high-technology crime. Many people are under the assumption that all activities related to hacking are conducted from the safety of their home and involves only the computer and the Internet. The truth, however, is that many times the hacking incident will be preceded with an investigative stage that has been termed the pre-hack stage. The pre-hacking stage is the term used by the Knightmare (1994) in describing the process of physical techniques that precedes the actual act of hacking into the computer.

Targeting is the first step in the pre-hack stage. It is here at this step that the hacker will first determine which computer system or network they will attack. There are numerous factors considered during this stage, and the factors have been modified in recent years as more companies have moved to the Internet. Historically, the majority of businesses maintained all of their network connections via the telephone lines. If a hacker was able to gain access to the phone number and a password, with the phone number normally being sufficient, then the computer system was easily exploited. Today, the method of selecting an actual company or network may involve one of two methods. First, the hacker may physically select a target that is of interest to them. For example, the hacker may be interested in crippling the online services of a retail store that has offended them in the past. The second method, which is becoming increasingly popular, involves the use of a port scanner. Port scanners are software packages that scan computer networks to determine if any computers have open port settings. A port is the opening through which the computer receives data via the network. Because these open ports allow for information to pass into and out of computers, it is also a primary method for hackers to gain access to a computer; and, once the computer is controlled the network is also available to the hacker.

The second stage of pre-hacking is known as the researching and information gathering phase. It is during this stage that the hacker will physically visit or contact the target in hopes of gaining information that will assist in penetrating the system. Researching will normally involve one of two different techniques. First, there is the use of social engineering, which is employed when the hacker contacts the system administrator under the auspice of being a legitimate user who is locked out of the system. One of the more commonly used social engineering tricks involves the hacker calling the night security system administrator and convincing the individual that they work for the company on the day shift and need access to the computer network. In the process of providing assistance to the hacker, the administrators will accidentally, or perhaps even intentionally, provide enough information for the hacker to infiltrate the network. While for some it would seem ridiculous that a system administrator would give out important information over the phone, it is unfortunately an all too common occurrence.

Hackers who have written on social engineering have recommended some of the following as successful techniques. Mitnick reportedly enjoyed contacting system administrators and convincing them that he worked for the company and was having trouble accessing the network. At the time Mitnick was applying this technique it was common for companies to keep default passwords installed for just such instances in which an unskilled operator inadvertently caused a problem with their account (Hafner, 1991). The reliability of this technique could be questioned today, but it is still incredibly common for universities to provide user information over the phone if the individual can convince the help desk operator that they are a student. A requirement of this approach is of course that the individual who is answering the phone has not been sufficiently trained to handle such requests for information. Because universities often employ students to work at their technology offices, it becomes apparent why universities are targeted with such frequency.

If the target is a business then it has been recommended that the hacker pretend to be a new temporary employee who is having trouble accessing the system (Mitnick, 2002). Larger companies that maintain high volumes of temporary help may have default passwords installed for situations in which an employee will only be with the company for a brief time and needs access only to a limited amount of space on the network. The problem is that once a hacker has any access to a network, it is only a matter of time before they gain root level access that will allow them to adjust the system. These adjustments may include adding a higher-level account with greater access to files and resources or the adjustment may be nothing more than a program to damage the entire computer system. Many hackers will also use this opportunity as a means of installing a backdoor password that will allow them to return the network at their convenience.

One final social engineering technique offered by the hacker literature involves the use of the angry supervisor approach. Here, the social engineer will call the help desk or the system administrator and pretend to be angry if the individual begins to question the hacker's right to access the system. The hacker will at all times maintain control of the conversation by never pretending to be disappointed, never begging, and never complaining if the administrator or help desk refuses to help. In place of displaying anger, the hacker will get louder and louder while making threats against the administrator's job if he or she continues to be of no assistance (Knightmare, 1994).

Along with social engineering there is also a technique known as reverse social engineering, which is when the hacker will let the system administrator or a network user contact them for assistance. When this assistance is granted the hacker will obtain information related to the user's network access information. The initial contact may take the form of a letter to the system administrator or user, or the contact may come via a forged e-mail. The communication will inform the user that the hacker is the new system technician and that any questions should be e-mailed to a certain e-mail address, which is of course only used long enough to obtain network access information.

Law enforcement agencies must be especially careful when it comes to contacting individuals for assistance, or when it comes to providing information to individuals over the phone or e-mail. The information accessible via a law enforcement network is of great financial and personal benefit to a hacker. While there have been few, if any, incidents involving the compromising of a law enforcement agency's network, the potential for harm is sufficient for concern. Although attitudes are changing there are still many law enforcement personnel who have little or no interest in computers and may therefore feel as though there is no danger associated with computers. Therefore, when they are approached for information they may be inclined to release sensitive information such as passwords, if the storyteller on the other end of the phone is skilled enough. Agencies must ensure that their personnel understand the dangers associated with releasing such information.

The second method of researching a target is referred to as dumpster diving. Dumpster diving refers to the act of literally climbing inside a trash dumpster and searching for information that could be of benefit to the hacker when he or she attacks the computer network. Manuals related to the software programs or operating systems running on the company computers are popular items sought out during these escapades. Additionally, the hacker may search for scraps of paper that contain passwords or network access information.

Because the act of dumpster diving is a physical act, it is possible that individuals engaged in the activity may encounter law enforcement personnel or private security officers. If an individual is encountered who appears to be engaged in the act of dumpster diving, then a search should be conducted whenever possible for the presence of a G.I.R.K. The term "G.I.R.K." was developed by the Knightmare (1994) and is used to describe the tools used by a potential hacker during the course of dumpster diving. While the work by Knightmare is almost 10 years old, dumpster diving is still employed today, and whether the tools are still referred to as a G.I.R.K. is irrelevant because there remain important tools necessary for successful dumpster diving. A typical kit will include the following items: rubber gloves, step device, flashlight, garbage bags, and empty soda cans. The items are used as follows:

- Rubber gloves—used to prevent dirt and grime from being picked up during the diving process

- Step device—because the individual cannot carry a ladder, this will allow the individual to get in and out of the trash dumpster

- Flashlight—used in the search of the dumpster; the majority of these incidents will take place at night

- Garbage bags—normally dark brown or black, these are used in conjunction with the empty cans to convince unwitting passersby that the activity is a can collecting outing

Once the researching stage has been completed, the hacker will begin the actual hack of the computers or network. The hacker will at this point either attack the target via the telephone line, which is admittedly becoming a less frequent target, or the Internet, which is the emerging target of choice. Upon beginning the hack attack, the potential hacker will resort to their hacker tool kit. The hacker tool kit is a collection of software that a hacker will need to gain entry-level access, or higher level root access if entry-level access has already been obtained. There appear to be several variations of the hacker tool kit, but the majority appear to contain very similar items. According to Dr. K. (2000), a self-proclaimed hacker and e-zine publisher from the United Kingdom, any hacker tool kit must contain the following items: password grabbers and key loggers, blue boxing programs, war dialers, encryption software, program password crackers, BIOS password crackers, security vulnerabilities scanners, packet sniffers, and UNIX vulnerabilities scanners.

Password Grabbers and Loggers

These programs can be planted on a target computer and can run in the background without the computer owner's knowledge. There are few differences between key loggers and password grabbers, as both programs are installed on a computer as a means of recording each key that is pressed by the user of the target computer. The keystrokes are recorded into a special text file established by the hacker and hidden somewhere on the target computer's hard drive. Recent releases of these software programs have enabled the feature to e-mail the text file to the hacker at fixed intervals. These programs are of course mentioned here because of their use by hackers to gain access to secured portions of a computer or network. However, it is worth noting that these programs are also seeing an increased use in the business world. Companies that are concerned about the work habits of their employees are now using these programs to ensure that workers are not performing personal business on the company's time. Even the FBI has been accused of applying this software to recent investigations, but there is little information beyond the mention of software referred to as "Magic Lantern" in two or three news articles.

Blue Boxing Programs

These programs have been traditionally used in the hijacking of telephone services. Originally, the devices were small boxes capable of accessing telephone lines through the emission of a 2600-megahertz tone. This tone opened a connection on the phone line and thereby allowed the user to make free calls (Draper, 2001). Today, however, there are software programs that emulate the blue box and open phone lines. Because of recent advances in technology, these software programs can be run from laptops, personal digitial assistants (PDAs), and pocket PCs. If an individual does not have a PDA or a laptop, then it is possible to record the sounds emitted by the computer program onto a portable tape player and then played back into the phones to open the lines. Interestingly enough, while there remains support for the use of these programs and Internet message boards still contain discussions of the devices, many of today's telephone lines are not susceptible to attacks from these devices.

War-Dialers

The term war-dialer refers to a program that will scan a predetermined range of phone numbers to determine if there is a computer enabled to receive telephone connections. The movie *WarGames* made this program famous in the early 1980s. In the movie, (it is worth noting that the movie has always been considered one of the more accurate depictions of hacking with only a few misrepresentations) a hacker used the program to dial every number within his local dialing area. This information was later used in an attempt to gain illegal access to a computer. A war-dialer program will provide its user with a list of numbers that successfully contacted computers. Once the list is provided to the hacker, then they will begin attempting to contact the numbers in order to determine if any of the computer systems are worth the effort associated with hacking into the system. Along with locating computers, some war-dialers may locate a PBX, which is a public branch exchange that controls telephone calls and would allow the hacker to monitor or control incoming and outgoing phone calls. There are several variations of war-dialer programs, but the program Tone-Loc is still considered today to be one of the more popular programs. However, much like blue boxes, these programs are not as useful today for at least two reasons. First, phone companies can now trace war-dialers, should they decide to put forth the effort, and second, the majority of computers is now connected to the Internet and therefore require less direct calling for network access; the exception being of course Internet service providers that still require dialing in to access services. The individuals who develop these software programs are aware of these limitations and have begun generating programs that allow users to stagger the redial attempts in an effort to confuse the phone company. There have been reports by professional computer security companies that dialing in has been useful in gaining access to fax machines that are connected to a network and have not been properly secured.

Encryption Software

Encryption software was originally designed for use by the government as a means of protecting files from being seen by those without proper security clearance. Phil Zimmerman, a computer programmer who determined that his encryption software should be available to the public, released a version of the software known as Pretty Good Privacy (PGP). PGP was released to the public free of charge, and is today not recommended for use by those who are unfamiliar with computers and how they operate. Encryption is a very complex subject that has been the subject of numerous books written on the various encryption algorithms. For simplicity's sake, it should be noted that encryption assigns new letters to represent the letters already in the file and will then scramble the letters to make interpretation significantly more difficult. Files are encrypted using a public key or a private key, which must be provided to individuals by whoever encrypts the file. Once its intended recipient receives the message, the opposite key must be used to open the file. Mathematical applications of encryption algorithms are extremely powerful, and while not invincible to attack, files encrypted are significantly harder to decrypt. To ensure maximum encryption, some hackers may triple or quadruple encrypt their files. In situations such as this, it is quite difficult to crack the encryption without the proper key. Currently the encryption software Pretty Good Privacy (PGP) is still considered one of the best encryption programs around and is available free on the Internet.

Password Recovery Software

Password recovery software is used to satisfy one of the driving forces behind hacking motives—the belief that information should be free. These programs normally consist of utilities designed to crack the internal passwords of programs such as Microsoft Word, Microsoft Excel, and other commercial software programs. Many of these programs work by brute forcing the passwords stored within the aforementioned programs. The attacks will consist of either dictionary attacks, which cycle through entire dictionaries trying to break the password, or name attacks, which cycle through entire databases of names forwards and backwards. There is little consensus among those on the Internet as to what is the most efficient password cracker. Part of the reason for this is because typically password recovery software is utility specific, meaning that the password recovery programs will only recover passwords from one software package. If the hacker is attempting to crack passwords from both Word and Microsoft Windows Screensaver, then the activity will more than likely require two software programs.

BIOS Password Crackers

These utility programs are designed to hack into the BIOS passwords stored on the motherboard of a computer. BIOS password crackers are necessary to gain access to computers belonging to more sophisticated users. Many individuals rely on the Windows Operating System for their password protection. There is, however, a more secure method of preventing unauthorized access. Whenever a computer is started up the BIOS is where the system checks to ensure that all hardware and software is operational. Additionally, there is a password feature that will prevent this system check absent the correct information. Originally, these cracker programs were designed for legitimate uses such as when an individual purchased a used computer that contained a password stored on the motherboard. Absent these programs the new owner would have been forced to physically open the computer and disengage the BIOS password settings. These programs were kept on hand by individuals who purchased large quantities of used computers and did not want to invest the time necessary for physical resetting of the system's passwords. Hackers, however, have since turned these utility programs into a means of gaining unauthorized access to personal computers.

Security Vulnerability Scanners

Security vulnerability scanners are programs that have little purpose beyond scanning a network to determine whether there are known security vulnerabilities present in the network that have been reported in the database. The databases for these programs are rather large as there are dozens of exploits published each month, and as a result of this constant change these programs have to be updated frequently. Over the years there have been few security scanners that have withstood the test of time. Perhaps the only program that has maintained its popularity and warrants discussion is that of SATAN, which stands for Systems Administrator's Tool for Analyzing Networks. A computer security expert named Dan Farmer wrote the SATAN software. Farmer was working to develop a tool that could be used to secure networks from potential hackers when he was terminated by his employer for the creation of the SATAN software. Farmer still maintains his work with the SATAN vulnerability scanner; and incidentally, most systems administrators do own a copy of SATAN, which was Farmer's original target audience.

Packet Sniffer

A packet sniffer program is computer software designed to sniff packets of data as the information is moved across a network. When an individual sends out an e-mail, or even a request for a web page, the information sent back to the computer is normally too large to be shipped at one time. The data is therefore broken down into smaller packets of data that allows for faster transfer of information. Once the entire collection of data packets reaches the destination computer, the original file is reconstructed using information stored in the header section of each of the smaller packets. A packet sniffer is installed on a network and programmed to examine all packets that pass through the network. Individuals who are attempting to steal passwords or perhaps credit card information from commercial websites generally use these programs. Numerous packet sniffers are available via the Internet. The reader who is interested in testing this belief should merely type the phrase "packet sniffer" into an Internet search engine and the result will be a listing of both commercial and free utilities. Of course, as is the case with most searches conducted today there will be a number of worthless hits; however, in the end the software will be located.

Operating System Password Crackers

The final tool to be discussed is that of a password cracker designed for a computer's operating system. These programs are similar to password cracking programs designed for software programs, but are designed to crack passwords on the various operating systems. Much like the password crackers designed for software the attacks can be dictionary based or brute force attacks, with brute force attacks referring to situations in which the software will launch multiple combinations of words until a password is discovered. There are numerous commercial and freeware password crackers available on the Internet if one is willing to spend the time wading through the blind and dead links. It should be noted that the programs are operating system specific, meaning that a password cracker for the Windows operating system will not normally crack passwords on the UNIX/Linux operating system. If one is interested in cracking a UNIX operating system, then the software cracker program CRACK is considered the appropriate program. John the Ripper is the program most favored for attacks against Windows Operating Systems and L0phtcrack is the program of choice for those who are attempting to crack passwords on a Windows NT operating system.

Every effort has been made to make the previous list as accurate as possible. However, there are new software programs written everyday by computer programmers who are interested in computer security and hacking. Many of these programs may no longer be considered acceptable programs by the time this work reaches print. For the most up to date information, readers should take advantage of Internet search engines and the information available on the Internet. By typing in the above software descriptions an individual should be able to discover the latest programs available for download or purchase. As with any form of research conducted on the Internet the reader must work to ensure that websites containing information on these software programs contain accurate information. The best method of ensuring this is to obtain information concerning the programs from legitimate Internet security web sites, which are easy enough to find if one is willing to devote the time to the search.

Hacker Attack Techniques

The aforementioned tools are used to gain access to a target computer or network. The question that remains is what a hacker will do once they have gained access to their target system. Will they merely browse around to see what information is available on the system, will they steal data from the system, or will they merely damage or destroy the system without thought of the consequences? The answer to these questions depends heavily upon the type of hacker that has intruded into the system. The white hat hacker may merely look around the system in order to discover what information is insecure and then exit to alert the owner of the potential danger. The black hat hacker does not normally stumble upon a compromised computer system, so it is possible that they are there for information. With that in mind, the black hat hacker may be the one who compromises the system in order to steal data. The lowly script kiddy is the one who port scans networks for targets and then enters the systems unaware of the effect their presence has on the system; this is the individual who will most likely damage the computer system either because they are unfamiliar with how to handle the situation or because they are merely attempting to show how powerful they are to other hackers.

There are several different types of attacks used by hackers once they have access to a system. The attacks can range from annoyance attacks that launch data across the Internet in an attempt to force a computer offline to computer viruses that destroy valuable work data and costs thousands or millions of dollars for companies to combat. In the early 1990s, Peter Denning referred to many of these attacks as crimoids, which he considered a crime that creatively applied technology and received extensive coverage in the news media. Even Denning admitted that not every crime involving a computer should be considered a crimoid. However, he did believe that the majority of computer-related crimes could be classified under his new terminology. Several of the crimes discussed by Denning as a crimoid have fallen into disuse because of changes in computing and networking. There are a few of these crimes that are still popular today, with some even being considered perhaps the most costly of computer-related crimes. The more commonly encountered of Denning's crimoids that are still discussed today are: data manipulation, Trojan horses, and viruses. All of which can be launched on a computer system after compromise by a hacker.

Data Manipulation

Data manipulation rarely poses a physical danger to the owner of a computer system. The term refers to the process by which an individual manipulates data or deletes the data from a computer system as a means of causing harm to the computer's owner. Harm that is almost always intellectual or financial in nature. For example, this attack could be used in a situation where a hacker has gained access to a reputable computer software company. By gaining access to their secured server, it would be possible for the hacker to destroy any existing research on an upcoming software system. As a result, the company could lose thousands of hours of work and millions of dollars in research expenses.

Another possibility for this attack is the former worker who uses their security codes to gain access to bank records and then transfers funds into their personal banking account or a bank account offshore where it cannot be detected. The rounding down technique, or salami technique as it is sometimes referred to, is an example of data manipulation involving financial information. The instructions related to the program are secretly inserted onto the network or computer system and when changes to bank accounts occur, the program will round down deposits and transfer the excess funds into a separate account. Once the account has reached a certain level the money can then be transferred to a separate account. Built into these programs is coding that will alert the owner of the program when the account has reached a pre-specified level. This technique has even appeared in Hollywood films such as *Office Space*. In the movie, three friends angry with their employer, determine to insert a rounding down program onto their network. However, because of an error in coding, the program continues to round down deposits long after the desired amount of money is deposited into their account. Within a short period of time the amount of money collected in the account is so great that the friends believe they cannot hide the money without being caught.

While the film is a comedy designed to entertain, there are serious financial consequences involved in the use of this technique. Because the technique holds such potential in cases involving financial fraud, individuals responsible for the security of networks that handle money should be aware of the technique's existence. This ability to transfer funds without notification to a bank or financial institution could be of immeasurable use by organized crime groups and other like-minded associations. Law enforcement personnel, or even internal investigators, who encounter the presence of rounding down programs may find their investigations somewhat easier if they begin by attempting to determine if recently dismissed or disgruntled employees have had access to the system and could be responsible for the attack. This is not to say that the perpetrator will always be an employee, but it is believed that the majority of cases involving this technique are inside jobs committed by angry personnel.

Trojan Horse

The Trojan horse attack is so named because the instructions for the program are secretly inserted onto a computer system or network without the owner's knowledge and in much the same manner that Troy warriors snuck inside a compound using a wooden horse. These programs are commonly sent to a target computer system via e-mails to legitimate users of the system. Trojan horses may be programmed to activate upon a number of given situations. For example, the commands could be activated when an execution command is given to start a particular computer program. There is also the possibility of programming the Trojan horse to install upon being introduced to the computer network or operating system, such as when the user receives the attachment in an e-mail and unwittingly activates the file. A hacker may enjoy releasing a Trojan horse onto a computer system for a number of reasons. First, the individual may wish to sabotage the computer network in order to gain access to other computers on the network. Second, the user may merely wish to see how the introduction of additional programs will affect the entire system's operations. Two of the more common Trojan horse programs are Back Orifice and SubSeven. Both programs begin by accessing stored passwords on an individual's computer and then e-mailing the password list to the owner of the Trojan program. The programs will also open ports on the target computer in order for other programs to be transmitted to the computer or network. Today, many hacker forums look down upon individuals who employ either Back Orifice or Sub-

Seven, but there are still many people who download and run these programs on a regular basis.

Another program closely related to a Trojan horse, which is not used as frequently today, is that of the time bomb. Occasionally, this program is referred to as a logic bomb. These programs are secretly inserted onto a network or a computer operating system. Unlike the normal Trojan horse program, however, the logic bomb is designed for damage and sabotage. Once the program is inserted onto the network or operating system, the time bomb can be set to activate on a specific date, time, or condition. When the program is initiated, the time bomb will begin erasing certain records or files and thereby cause the system to become unstable and possibly even cause the system to crash. The time bomb program is rarely read about today. Perhaps this is because of the popularity of Internet worm programs. Today, individuals who desire revenge on a computer system belonging to an individual or company that has committed a wrong in the eyes of the attacker employs the few time bombs that are used. Much like rounding down techniques, this program can many times be traced to someone within the victimized company who has been terminated from their position. Weeks after they have left the company the time bomb may activate and destroy sensitive and important data on the network.

Computer Viruses

A computer virus is any computer program capable of damaging a victim's computer, and is replicable. Viruses are quite possibly the biggest and most expensive problem facing computer users today. There is hardly a day that goes by without some new virus or derivative of an older virus being discovered. The leading anti-virus computer software manufacturers, Norton and McAfee, now maintain a team of anti-virus computer programmers whose job consists of analyzing emerging threats and writing anti-code to prevent infection of subscribers' computers and networks.

Viruses come in several different formats and are capable of varying amounts of destruction. One of the more common targets for a computer virus is the boot sector of the target computer's hard drive. Viruses are deposited on the boot sector so that each time the computer is booted up the virus will load itself and run its program. The first reported incident involving the use of such a virus was the Pakistani/Brain virus, which received its name from the fact that the company that wrote the virus was Brain Computer Services in Pakistan. The owners of the company, a pair of brothers, became infuriated at the number of bootleg copies of their software that was available on the streets. As a form of retaliation, the brothers programmed their software to launch a boot sector virus any time a copy of the software was made. Ironically, the two brothers had a side business themselves—the selling of bootleg American software for word processing and data analysis. At one point the two even began installing the boot sector virus on each copy of the bootleg American software that they sold (Wang, 1998). Apparently, the two justified their behavior on the belief that they were punishing users for purchasing illegal copies of software. For a short period of time the Pakistani/Brain virus ran rampant; however, the virus lost the majority of its power several years ago. This is not to say that there are not versions of the virus still in existence, because there most certainly are some remaining versions. However, the spread of the virus has been dramatically slowed because of the change in disk drives. The original virus was designed to run on the 5-1/4 inch floppy disks, so as more individuals converted to the 3.5-inch floppy disk, the virus has become less of a threat to computer users.

There are several additional acts that are involved in the act of hacking, but they are less dependent upon computer software to be accomplished. These are techniques that have been in use for many years. For example, there is the presence of piggybacking activities. There are two forms of piggybacking: physical and electronic (Van Duyn, 1985). Physical piggybacking refers to when an individual gains access to a computer by following someone into a secured room. A commonly encountered method of accomplishing this is for the individuals desiring illegal access to wait outside the door to the building until someone who is authorized to enter the building comes along. Traditionally, this form of piggybacking was used to describe activities for breaking in to business computer rooms. Today, however, many universities appear to be experimenting with self-regulated computer labs that require student identification cards to grant access. University networks are very valuable to computer criminals, so it is not unreasonable to suspect that an unlawful user may use this technique to gain access to a secured building that houses computers. The second form of piggybacking is digital in nature and involves the illegal user waiting until a legitimate user neglects to sign off and then taking control of their account. The use of this technique is still common in larger businesses, especially retail operations. A former employee who is familiar with the operation of the computer system may wait until they see a manager leave a computer terminal logged on, and they will then begin manipulating prices for merchandise or they may modify other settings for the system. If this sounds farfetched, it must be remembered that, more and more, large retail companies are placing computers on the sales floor as a means of increasing customer service. The next time a reader is visiting their local Wal-Mart or Barnes & Noble, notice should be paid to the fact that there are often a number of computers activated and within reach of shoppers and those who could abuse the computer network.

The crimes discussed above are still encountered today, but advancements in technology surrounding computers, and especially networking, have led to the development of new techniques and programs involved in hacker-related attacks. Denial of Service (DOS) attacks and brute force attacks are seeing increased use against computer networks; and, techniques such as Internet Protocol spoofing and web spoofing are also becoming increasingly used by spammers, pornographers, and identity thieves that wish for you to buy into their fake websites—for you to give out your credit card number, for you to visit their website or for you to support their website.

Denial of Service Attacks

These attacks are often referred to as DOS attacks for short, and should not be confused for Disk Operating System, which was the required operating system for earlier computers. The term refers to an attack where an Internet website or network server is flooded with enormous amounts of data that will, in essence, consume the entire resources of the target computer system; this overload will normally then result in the target computer crashing or shutting down. The goal of a DOS attack is not to gain access to a secured computer system but is to prevent legitimate users from accessing the computer. These attacks were made famous in 2000 when an attack managed to shut down several high-profile websites. After an intense investigation, it was discovered that the individual responsible was none other than a 15-year-old boy who used the online handle of mafiaboy. According to mafiaboy, the act was designed to impress a girl in one of his classes (Dube & Ross, 2001). Recent advances in computer technology have resulted in computer systems that are able to handle more amounts of data requests. Additionally, the system settings of various networks allow an administrator to limit the number of requests to accept from a certain computer. As a result of these advances, there appears to be a growing acceptance for the use of dDOS, which are distributed denial of service attacks. When activated, dDOS attacks allow for multiple computers to launch data at a target computer system; this allows for a heavier flood of data that can therefore shut down the more powerful computers (CERT, 1997). The most remarkable thing about the dDOS attack programs is that many allow for such attacks to be launched without the owner of the computer realizing they are taking part in the activity. The dDOS software can be installed on a computer or network without the system administrator's permission and may shut down its desired target before many individuals realized their computer has been used in a denial of service attack.

IP Spoofing

IP spoofing refers to when an individual will forge their Internet protocol address. There are generally two reasons an individual will attempt to accomplish this activity. First, if the individual is going to be sending out a massive mailing list then the use of IP spoofing software is a good investment.

Spammers often use this technique because it becomes harder for the spam to be traced back to the actual owner (Wang, 2001). There are programs capable of helping someone spoof their IP address, or an individual can use an anonymous re-mailer, which is a service that will hide the IP address of the original sender before forwarding the message on to the intended recipient. While the IP address of the original sender may be missing, this is not to say that an officer cannot still obtain information on a suspect from the e-mail. The re-mailer service will generally keep a log of the e-mails they have received and forwarded. The problem with such logs is that they are not kept for long periods of time, so therefore haste is of extreme importance when handling a case that involves an anonymous re-mailer.

Web Spoofing

The act of web spoofing involves the redirection of an Internet browser to a given website when the computer user types in a similar URL address; this technique is often used by pornography websites to lure visitors to their sites. Once within the grip of these sites it is sometimes hard to back out because of the sheer number of pop-up ads to launch. Perhaps the most popular of web spoofing accounts is that of Internet pornography site, Whitehouse.com. Numerous individuals have visited this pornography site during the course of attempting to locate the official web page of the White House and the President of the United States of America which, incidentally, is located at Whitehouse.gov. Individuals attempting to obtain official information on an Internet browser could use web spoofing. For example, suppose we are looking to purchase a book on Amazon.com; however, during the course of typing in the web address Amazone.com. The addition of the "e" to the URL will result in the browser being directed to the fake website where the financial information entered will be used as a means of committing identity theft. It is worth noting that this technique is rather complex, and the majority of individuals engaged in the act of identity theft will probably find it far more efficient to select another means of obtaining credit card information, such as hacking into a bank's credit card records.

Web spoofing should not be confused with cyber squatting, which is becoming a more popular form of Internet deception. Here, an individual will wait until an official website neglects to renew their annual registration for the domain name, and then they will purchase the domain and begin putting in their own information. The benefit of this technique is that some of the more popular websites are linked to thousands, more than likely hundreds of thousands, of other web pages. Therefore, the individual purchasing the lapsed domain name will find that they have obtained a website that requires little or no advertisement to attract visitors. Senator Orin Hatch recently experienced this when a pornography company purchased one of the web pages that was linked to his home page. Visitors that used the link's section were treated to a website full of pornography.

It is important to remember that there are certainly more techniques and hacker attacks available for computer criminals that wish to find such items. However, the aforementioned section has provided the reader with an introduction to several of the more commonly encountered tools and techniques. Understanding of these attacks and the methods through which they are often employed should allow the reader to better understand how computers and networks are often used in the commission of criminal acts against other computer systems.

The Crime of Phreaking

The crime of phreaking has been added to this section because of its close relationship to hacking. The term, phreaking, which should be noted is intentionally spelled with a "ph," refers to one of the oldest computer crimes around—theft of telecommunications service. The "ph" is used in place of the "f" to represent the phreaker's tool of choice, the telephone (Wang, 2001). Statements regarding the age of this crime have to do with the fact that the first reported case of phreaking, even though no one termed the activity phreaking at the time, occurred in 1870. Several teenagers were denied access to the newly established telephone system after they managed to tap into the phone lines and redirect outgoing phone calls for their area. Today, the term phreaking refers to any activity resulting in the individual gaining use of a telecommunications service without paying for such services. While this form of computer-related crime still occurs today, it is significantly less publicized than hacking. Part of the problem with this could be the fact that few media reports cover the phreaking aspect of hacking attacks, and even the Hollywood films previously discussed take the act for granted and treat it as merely a minor part of the hacking attack. Phreaking is an important part of hacking, albeit not as important since the telephone does not play as great a role as in the past, but it is also an activity that stands alone. Today, phreaking is commonly encountered when a telephone subscriber receives their bill and there is an abundance of calls not made by the subscriber. It has been stated that the North American continent could lose more than $500 million a year to phone phreaking incidents.

While a primitive form of phreaking was discovered in 1870, it should be noted that the incident failed to garner sustained media attention. Certainly there were more cases of phreaking to occur during the late 1800s and early 1900s, but it was not until the 1970s that phreaking began to receive attention again. An article in *Esquire* magazine, published in 1971, detailed the exploits of an unnamed blind boy who was reportedly able to make free phone calls by mimicking the sounds of the phone system. The boy was able to mimic the phone system sounds through whistling. Apparently, he had become very interested in sounds because of his visual deficiency and had begun memorizing the sounds made during telephone calls. After a little practice he discovered that he could in fact whistle similar tones that would open the telephone lines. Before long the boy had told several of his friends, who were incidentally blind as well, and before long there were numerous children attempting to learn about the telephone system and how the various sounds affected the types of calls that could be made (Draper, 2001).

One of these young men introduced the technique to an engineering student, John Draper. Draper, who was not blind, became interested in learning the technique so he and his friend began spending untold hours learning about telephone routing and the sounds the system made during these transactions. Draper would go on to become one of the more famous and influential phone phreaks of all time when he earned the nickname Captain Crunch by opening telephone lines through the use of a whistle he obtained from a cereal box. Draper would phreak the phone lines using the whistle and his friend would whistle into the telephone receiver, thereby making free phone calls around the world. After repeated warnings by law enforcement personnel concerning their activities, and their refusal to stop, the two were arrested and charged. Immediately the duo became celebrities.

Draper's escapades influenced several individuals who could then have been classified as up-and-coming phone phreaks. Two of the more well-known phreaks are Steve Jobs and Kevin Poulsen. Both individuals would go on to successful careers in the computer industry, although each would take drastically different routes. Readers who are familiar with the evolution of computers will probably remember the name Steve Jobs. Jobs was a co-founder of Apple Computers. Before he was a computer entrepreneur, however, he made his living in college selling blue boxes, which were the small electrical devices that emitted a tone capable of controlling the telephone lines. These devices were extremely popular among college students because they allowed users to call family and friends back home anytime they desired with the only cost being that of purchasing the blue box from Jobs and his partners.

Kevin Poulsen took a completely different route through the computer industry. Unlike Jobs, who played with phone phreaking before moving on to a professional career in the computer industry, Poulsen spent the majority of his early life in trouble with the law because of his activities. At the age of 13, Kevin discovered that he could use his braces to gain access to the telephone lines. Early on his obsession with the telephone system, which led him to read manuals on the telephone system as a hobby, appeared to be one of curiosity and not mischief. Poulsen would entertain his friends by going to the mall and using one of the pay phones to make prank phone calls where he would jump around through several telephone exchanges before ringing the pay phone next to him. Unfortunately, as he got older his phone capers got more serious and more outrageous. At one point Poulsen was routinely breaking into one of the main headquarters for his local telephone company. Once inside the building he would steal manuals and various other forms of training documentation that provided him with insight into how the company's main computer worked. The computer was of immense interest to Poulsen because it controlled all incoming and outgoing telephone lines. Control of this computer would, in essence, allow him to tap into anyone's phone line and listen in to their conversations. Because Poulsen was an equally impressive hacker and phreaker he would eventually gain access to one of these computers, an event that led his closest friends to fear talking on the telephone. Apparently, Poulsen once commented in their presence that it was not cool how they made fun of him and his obsession with the telephone systems when they were talking to each other on the phone (Littman, 1997).

Poulsen was known by several different handles over the course of his hacker/phreaker career. Early on in life he reportedly went by the handle Dark Dante, which incidentally is the handle used to refer to Poulsen in the hacker halls of fame. During the time period when he was routinely monitoring telephone communications in his area, he also reportedly took on the handle The Watcher. Poulsen was eventually arrested for abusing the telephone system. However, before his arrest he was able to accomplish several remarkable feats using his computer hacking and phone phreaking abilities. Some of his more notable feats include:

- Reportedly he was able to once tap the telephone lines for one of the foreign embassies in Los Angeles. Many suspect that this was the activity that truly led to his demise because of the government's recognition of his abilities. As of this date, there have reportedly been investigations into this area but nothing has resulted from the inquiry. Poulsen himself has refused to confirm or deny that he was able to tap the embassy, but if he was then many speculate that he was privy to extremely classified information.

- He once rerouted a local pimp's competitors' entire phone numbers so that whenever any one of the rival pimps would receive a call it would ring at the one pimp's office. Poulsen claimed that his act was originally intended as a joke to prove to a friend that he was capable of accomplishing the feat. The pimp, however, reportedly enjoyed the increased profits and wanted to keep Poulsen, and his phone rerouting abilities, on payroll indefinitely.

- Perhaps the most notable accomplishment of Poulsen's was his rigging of a telephone call-in contest. Poulsen and a friend were able to tap into the phone lines to the radio station. From a nearby apartment the two were able to monitor the number of phone calls being placed to the radio station.

> When the appropriate number of phone calls had been made, Poulsen would then reroute the incoming phone calls. Next, Poulsen or his friend would call the radio station and win the prize being offered. Over the course of a one-week radio contest Poulsen and his friend were able to win twice, an act that resulted in a pair of matching Porsche automobiles (Littman, 1997).

Poulsen did attempt several times to clean up his life by getting a legitimate job in the computer security field. Ultimately, however, he was unable to refrain from returning to the "dark side" of computing. Perhaps it was Poulsen's constant return to the illegal and high-profile aspects of both hacking and phreaking, despite numerous lucrative offers from computer firms, that has led many to consider him one of the most influential individuals in hacking/phreaking history. It should be noted that after Poulsen's last arrest he has been leading a life that is apparently free from criminal activity. He is currently the editor of SecurityFocus.com, an online information security website.

How Phreakers Operate

Traditionally, an understanding of phone phreaking would have required an advanced level of understanding in regards to how telephone systems work. Unfortunately for criminal justice professionals, such in-depth understanding is no longer required. Today, there are computer programs written to recreate the tones and activities of many phreaking activities. Add in the easy distribution available via the Internet and it becomes easy to see how little technical ability is actually required. While use of computer software is quickly becoming the chosen method of committing telecommunications fraud, there remain individuals who employ other methods. Phreak boxes, while nowhere near as popular as they once were, are still routinely discussed among phreaks. Originally, the boxes were purchased by phreaks, but plans for building the devices are now available on the Internet. Combined with the decreasing cost of electronics to manufacture these phreak boxes, the availability has created a situation in which almost anyone with minimal technical ability can manufacture a phreak box.

A phreak box's function is often discernable by its color, with there being several different colors of phreak boxes. An online entity going by the handle of Elf Qrin (2001) appears to be regarded as an expert in this area, as one of his websites contains an in-depth discussion on phreak boxes and their functions. The following are some of the more popular phreak boxes. The list is by no means exhaustive as there are at least 100 different colored boxes available for manufacture, depending upon the time one wishes to spend tracking down the blueprints on the Internet. Examples of phreak boxes are:

- **Aqua box.** The use of this box presents a problem for law enforcement investigations because the device is capable of preventing the proper application of a Lock-in-Trace device, which is a device that generates sufficient electricity to hold open a phone line after the call has ended but before the call has been traced. Proponents of the device have been hard-pressed to argue a legitimate claim to the boxes use, as it appears to provide nothing but protection from criminal investigation. The device works by lowering the voltage level on a phone line, thereby preventing the Lock-in-Trace device from holding the line open.

- **Beige box.** Phreaks use this box as a means of listening in on other people's phone conversations or making free long distance phone calls at someone else's expense. The operation of this box is similar to that of a lineman's handset, which is issued to workers by the telephone company. The box is applied to one of the telephone company's metal boxes that are located near the street.

- **Red box.** Defrauding pay telephones is the only use for this phreak box. The device replicates the sounds made by coins when they are dropped into a pay phone. Traditionally, pay phones worked by recognizing the tones that are emitted when an individual inserts a certain combination of coins. The proper amount of coins will open the phone lines and thereby allow the user to make their phone call. Today's pay phones operate on a more advanced technological level and therefore there is question as to whether the red box still works on any older model telephones.

- **Blue box.** Invented by John Draper, also known as Captain Crunch, after he discovered that the whistle he was using to open telephone lines was emitting a 2600-megahertz tone. Using this information, Draper designed and built a small box that was capable of recreating this tone. The box was used by Draper to keep in contact with friends around the world. Jobs and his friend came to meet Draper and from there developed the idea to sell the blue boxes to college students. Draper's design of the first phreak box lends additional credit to some of the arguments that Draper was one of, if not the most, influential driving forces in the development of phreaking.

- **Rainbow Box.** The rainbow box generates electricity through the telephone system and is normally used as a means of damaging an adversary's phone system. By generating a high volume of electricity through the phone line, all phone systems within a given area can be damaged.

It is worth noting that in examining the aforementioned phreaking devices, there are few devices designed to cause physical harm to individuals. The majority of phreakers justify their use of phreak boxes to steal telecommunications services on the basis that Ma Bell, the name given to the telephone companies, has been overcharging users for years. Many of the phone phreaking devices have seen a decreased level of use attributable to the advances in telecommunications that have outdated the devices. However, the decrease in the use of phreak boxes should not be taken as an indication that phreaking is dying out as an activity. In much the same manner as society has begun relying on cellular telephones, phreakers are now looking toward digital techniques and new creative applications for phreaking abilities.

Cellular Phone Phreaking

When a cellular telephone is first activated it is assigned an Electronic Serial Number (ESN) and a Mobile Identification Number (MIN) that is used by the cellular provider to direct any incoming phone calls. Using the proper equipment, which normally consists of a radio scanner and a data-capture tool, the ESN and MIN numbers can be captured as they are transmitted. Once a phreaker has all of the necessary numbers, he or she will reprogram their cellular telephone to emit the stolen ESN and MIN numbers. With the reprogramming completed, any calls made from the cellular telephone will be billed to the registered owner of the ESN and MIN numbers (Wang, 2001).

This photo illustration shows some of the possibilities of altering telecommunications instruments—a laptop computer and software capable of modifying a cellular phone. Hackers from San Francisco to San Diego gather regularly to display their latest gadgets and share tips on how to alter equipment. (AP)

Cellular telephone phreaking appears to have become a very popular pastime for phreakers; this is despite the widespread use of encryption used by cellular telephone providers. Paul Luehr, cybercrime investigator for the Department of Justice, has reportedly offered a plausible reason for the popularity of the technique—the inability of law enforcement agencies at the municipal level to properly investigate these crimes. It is Luehr's contention that the secret to reducing the problem is to increase training for individuals within law enforcement agencies who are willing to undertake advanced training. Funding is of course a consideration in every law enforcement agency, but the problem is sure to worsen as reports are now indicating that more handheld phones using cloned information are being used to assist in the Internet-related crimes.

Calling Card Fraud

The commission of calling card fraud is another form of phreaking that has seen an increase in use in recent years. Calling card numbers are stolen from unsuspecting consumers via any number of different techniques. There is the traditional method of stealing card numbers—shoulder surfing the information over the legitimate user's shoulder. Here, a phreak will wait behind someone who is using a calling card and when they begin to input the numbers for the card the individual will memorize the numbers. Incredibly, there are individuals who train themselves to remember long strings of numbers such as calling cards, credit cards, etc. Once the number is memorized, the phreak will transcribe the number on a piece of paper or even a log book. It is also not uncommon for two or more individuals to work together, as this requires each to remember fewer numbers. Phreaks who no longer desire to employ shoulder surfing techniques can also use the services of calling card generators, which are computer programs written to generate random calling card numbers (Dr. K, 2000). These programs will print out entire lists of calling card numbers that the phreak will then systematically attempt to dial until one is found to be active.

Call Sell Services

The call sell service involves the use of traditional phreaking activities, calling card fraud, and cellular phone cloning. Call sell service is the term used to describe an operation where phreaks will charge individuals anywhere from $5 to $15 for the unlimited use of a telephone system (Teledesign, 2002). Normally, these operations are based out of homes or buildings in poorer neighborhoods; although there is little doubt that they exist in better, more secure neighborhoods. Individuals are allowed to use stolen calling card numbers or cellular phones that have been cloned. The fee then allows individuals to call loved ones around the world for a fraction of the normal cost. When an individual receives their phone bills and then refuses to pay for the calls they did not make, these activities begin significantly contributing to the $500 million a year lost on telecommunications fraud.

There is little doubt that phone phreaking will continue to see use in the future. Regardless of how far technology develops there will always be someone who is willing to attempt circumvention of the established techniques or equipment. Phreaking is commonly encountered in serious hacking cases because the ability allows a hacker to better hide their true identity and the location from where they are connecting to the computer network or system. Another potential use for phreaking involves the use of the techniques in organized crime operations. The ability to make untraceable calls, or at least calls that would require advanced training to trace, would be of immense benefit in protecting the crime group.

The Hacker/Phreaker Subculture

The profiling of any criminal can be an arduous and time-consuming task; however, the profiling of a hacker or phreaker is perhaps more difficult than any other crime. There have been few studies conducted on hackers and phreakers, but there has been at least one study to determine whether there exist any common traits among these high tech criminals. Neil Hibler and Jim Christy conducted one such study, the results of which were presented at the Department of Defense Computer Crime Conference in Monterey, California in 1993. As part of the research project, the two men interviewed several hackers and phreakers soon after they were arrested and charged for their alleged crimes. The two found that in almost all of the cases they encountered, the subject was found to be a quiet, almost introverted, individual between the ages of 14 and 30, who spent very little time with friends and family. Instead of interacting with other human beings, the research seemed to indicate that the individuals spent the majority of their time with the computer and the telephone system. Subjects included in the study were found to be extremely intelligent, some were even considered borderline geniuses, and were substandard performers at school. One attempted explanation for such behavior could be that the individuals were too smart for their own good, and therefore, they became bored with the subjects being taught. Each of the subjects was deemed intelligent and skillful enough to have obtained well-paying jobs in the computer industry.

Unfortunately, advances in technology have dramatically changed the information that could be gleaned from the study by Hibler and Christy (1993). The Internet had only just been made public when the two completed their study, so there were few individuals not previously interested in computers who were using the technology. Today, however, script kiddies can download information and programs from the Internet and launch them without any understanding of what they are doing to their targets. The wide-scale availability the Internet 'brings to the table' means that no longer can those involved in investigating these crimes assume that the individual committing the crime is an intelligent person. For all we know, the individual may be an 8-year-old kid who has learned how to install a computer program and activate the commands. There are numerous stories involving young kids who have disabled popular websites by launching preprogrammed computer attacks on the servers of the companies. A few of these individuals may fit the characteristics presented by Hibler and Christy, but the majority of the individuals may also not appear to fit the profile.

The Hacker Ethic

Briefly returning to our earlier classification of hackers into six primary groups, there are many individuals who violate computer systems but do so without removing any data from the system or causing any damage to the system. In the past it was commonly held that individuals who would maliciously attack computer systems would do so against company computers. As we have already discussed, there are so many hacker attacks and techniques today that focus on individual computers, that this assessment no longer holds merit. In 2000 the Cult of the Dead Cow, one of the hacker groups mentioned earlier, released their Trojan horse software, Back Orifice 2000. The functions of the software lead this author to believe wreaking havoc on another user is one of the primary reasons for the software's development. Some features of the software are the ability to remotely reverse the left and right mouse buttons, open and close the compact disc drive, and the ability to launch websites without the legitimate user's permission. The software does allow for the transfer of files, which could be used in an attack against a company or large business, but the majority of the features lend themselves to attacks against individuals.

The question that remains is if the majority of individuals who hack are not attempting to be malicious or cause harm, then why hack? The answer lies in understanding how individuals who claim to be true hackers think. To a hacker there is no such thing as secured information. Any computer that is connected to a network, with the Internet being the most common network, is susceptible to attack. The only certain method of preventing computer-based attack is to land-lock the computer, which would involve the computer having no outside access to other computers. Even in this situation there is the possibility of physical intrusion. Further, not only do hackers believe that information is not secured, the majority appear to believe that it should not be secure. According to these individuals, all information should be free. Take for example the following segment taken from a text file circulated via the Internet, and via bulletin board systems before the popularity of the Internet:

> This is our world now . . . the world of the electron and the switch, the beauty of the baud. We make use of a service already existing without paying for what could be dirt-cheap if it wasn't run by profiteering gluttons, and you call us criminals. We explore . . . and you call us criminals. We seek after knowledge . . . and you call us criminals. We exist without skin color, without nationality, with-

out religious bias . . . and you call us criminals. You build atomic bombs, you wage wars, you murder, cheat, and lie to us and try to make us believe it's for our own good, yet we're the criminals.

Yes, I am a criminal. My crime is that of curiosity. My crime is that of judging people by what they say and think, not what they look like. My crime is that of outsmarting you, something that you will never forgive me for. I am a hacker, and this is my manifesto. You may stop this individual, but you can't stop us all . . . after all, we're all alike.

The text above was written by the hacker, Mentor. In his statement, Mentor is attempting to argue that hackers are perhaps better than other people in society. He argues that unlike others in society, hackers view people on the basis of their abilities and their statements and not their color or ethnicity. Intelligence is used by Mentor to explain why others in society are afraid of hackers. He argues that because hackers are smarter than others they fear that which they cannot effectively stop.

The reasoning behind the Mentor's early statement concerning the freedom of services that are ran by greedy individuals or governments appears to be that hackers value the creation of something great far more than they value the destruction or damage of a computer system. By sharing information and resources, theoretically by making all information free for everyone, then all hackers can work together to great a wonderful and powerful world. Evidence of this belief can be found in examining open source computer coding in operating systems such as the Linux operating system. Anyone who is interested in the code may obtain the original source code for Linux. These individuals can then modify the software in whatever way they deem necessary for their use. Many users of the Linux operating system claim that this freedom to modify is what makes Linux superior to other operating systems like Windows and Macintosh. Unfortunately, the Mentor is right in one respect—human nature precludes everyone from participating in these activities. There are some whose greed will not allow them to share their code, for to do so could result in a loss of revenue or even worse someone developing a better computer program. There are also those who would maliciously seek to damage the hard work of others. While the idea of a free information society is interesting, it is unfortunately not possible at this point in time or in the foreseeable future.

The Hacker Language

There are so many various cultures involved within the hacker and phreaker community that entire books could be written on each. Individuals who are going to handle activities involving the hackers and phreaks should have a cursory understanding of the language used by those engaged in the activity. An individual who cannot read or write the language faces the possibility of being labeled either a "lamer," which is one who believes himself to be a hacker but is in fact a loser, or a "suit," which is the term used to refer to law enforcement officers. Occasionally, an individual will also be labeled as a "neophyte," which refers to one who is new to the hacker community. There are positives and negatives to being labeled as a neophyte. On the positive side this means that perhaps the individuals in the chat rooms will understand if you misuse terms or appear lost when it comes to discussions. On the negative side, many of the more experienced hackers may refuse to discuss anything with a neophyte, so this label may end up getting the individual removed from the conversation.

To assist individuals who are new to this area of technology, the following section will attempt to briefly discuss the issue of hacker language. The use of this language does not necessarily indicate that you are dealing with a dangerous and deadly hacker. After all, remember that not all hackers are out to commit criminal acts and there may be others in the chat room that have the same problem we do—they want to fit in with the hackers when they know very little. The visiting of hacker chat rooms can prove beneficial as it is here that the latest exploits may be discussed, as are the solutions to preventing these exploits from happening to you. There is what could be termed national chat rooms for hackers to meet and discuss their national and international exploits, and then there are local chat rooms where hackers from within smaller areas gather to discuss their activities.

Eric Raymond and Guy Steele Jr. are two of the better-known individuals in the area of hacker language. The two individuals are responsible for updating and maintaining the Hacker's Jargon Dictionary. The dictionary is a compilation of hacker terminology, as well as information related to the language. It is worth noting that while this author refers to the hacker language as an almost separate language, it is not a new or officially recognized dialect. The terminology is, however, drastically different from the acceptable English that is spoken on a daily basis around the world. Raymond and Steele attribute many of the differences in the way hackers speak while they are online to the introverted type personalities that originally developed in the spoken part of the hacker language. These individuals were not adept at conversing with fellow human beings so they felt more comfortable creating new words to express their ideas and feelings.

One of the first differences involves the issue of spelling. Hackers have a great respect for what was once a required tool of their trade, the telephone and the modem. With this in mind, it is not uncommon for words containing an "f" to have the "f" replaced with "ph." For example, instead of stating the following, "yeah, it was fun," a hacker might state, "yeah, it was phun." The reverse for this grammatical rule is also true, the "ph" is occasionally replaced with an "f." Another common substitution involves the replacing of the letter "s" with the letter "z." When a hacker writes about "hacks" he or she will state, "hackz." There has been no written explanation for such substitutions, but it appears that the use of such language is merely another means of separating the hacker from the rest of society. Numbers are routinely replaced with letters and letters replaced with numbers. So, the word Lophtcrack will be spelled as L0(o)phtcrack and the word "goals" will be spelled as "goa1(l)s." Notice that with some words the differences are minute, hence the justification for including the actual letter in parenthesis. Understanding of this similarity is important because this similarity has affected investigations in the past where the investigator mistakenly requested a search warrant for the wrong username because of the use of a letter instead of a number.

The next area of difference is that of sentence formation. Hackers routinely type in all caps, which is commonly considered shouting on the Internet. Use of such sentence structure perhaps gives the hacker a sense that they are in control of the chat session. Should a word be used in a discussion that warrants emphasis, it is not uncommon for the hacker to repeat an expression. For example, suppose that a hacker loses an important file from a disk, he or she may type a statement such as "file is lost! Bang, Bang." While important expressions are doubled, unimportant expressions are shortened as much as possible. The word "without" becomes "w/" whenever possible. Finally, there is the use of asterisks around a word to indicate an expression. For example, if a hacker sighed during the course of typing a response, then the response might read, "I am tired of this *sigh* crap."

There are literally hundreds of slang words and possible sentence combinations available to the hacker. It is recommended that readers who are interested in learning more about this emerging issue visit the Hacker's Jargon dictionary, located online. The web version of the dictionary is constantly being updated and should have the latest information on hacker language trends. For the reader's purposes however, the following is a collection of basic terms that should be understood:

- **Warez D00dz**—these are individuals who crack software and set up fserves on IRC chat rooms to distribute the software. Fserve is a feature of IRC that allows one user to set himself up as a server where others in the chat room can download files from the individual.

- **Warez**—these are cracked tools. Warez usually consist of hacking tools and games that previously were copyright or password protected.

- **Appz**—these are cracked application software packages. Usually these programs are software that has had the registration codes removed so that multiple copies can be made.

- **Exploitz**—these are successful attacks by hackers on websites or servers. Most hacker websites will have a section entitled "exploitz." This is where you can go and read about the different servers and web pages the group has successfully hacked.

- **Suit**—this is the term given to law enforcement officers. If members of an IRC chat room suspect that an individual is a suit then he or she will be booted from the chat and denied access to fserves, which could potentially contain large amounts of evidence.

- **Lamer**—this is the same thing as a "loser." This is an individual who thinks he or she is a real hacker when they are really just a beginner or a copycat.

- **Neophyte**—this is an individual who is new to hacking and phreaking. A useful tactic for law enforcement officers would be to pose as a neophyte in a chat room. There are positives and negatives to this approach. The positive is that a neophyte is not expected to know all of the hacker terminology. The negative is that sometimes the sources of the best information are the most experienced hackers and they will have nothing to do with neophytes. Experimentation will determine which methods work best in what circumstances.

- **Newbie**—another term for a neophyte.

- **Leech**—this is the term assigned to an individual in an IRC chat that is not sharing files or information with others in the chat room. Law enforcement officers may either place "fake" files in their shared folder or they may simply be forced to be careful and not hang around for such lengthy times that they could become labeled as a leech and booted from the IRC chat room.

Hacker Conferences

Just like a legitimate company or an organization, hacker groups travel from all around the country, and occasionally the world, to attend trade conferences. If an individual wishes to see how true hackers and phreakers behave it is recommended that he or she visit one of these conventions. One of the more famous conventions is that of DEFCON, which is held in Las Vegas, Nevada every summer. It is at DEFCON that the very best and brightest of the hacking and phreaking community will come together to discuss the latest developments and techniques in the hacking community in an almost conference like setting. There are topics on almost any imaginable topic with sections ranging from paper presentations on computer security to demonstrations of the latest hacker utilities written by the larger hacker populations.

Hackers are not the only ones to attend these types of conferences. Many computer security professionals and federal law enforcement personnel will also attend to learn the latest tricks and techniques. However, while many federal law enforcement agencies will attend a hacker convention, these individuals should not expect a warm reception. One of the more common games played by conference participants is the game "spot the fed." According to the rules of this game, all hackers and phreakers will attempt to spot the federal law enforcement officers as they are making attempts to contact potential informants or informational contacts. An agent that has been spotted will then be publicly embarrassed.

People attend these conferences for a variety of reasons. Some may come because they are curious about computer security and want to learn more about the topic. Others may come merely as a means of scouting out potential employees. Remember that not all hackers set out to violate criminal laws. Many set out to gain access to computers out of a sense of security, and could therefore be properly motivated to work on the proper side of the law. Further, businesses may desire someone who is experienced in breaking into computers to secure their system, because these are the individuals who have taken advantage of the system in the past and therefore are aware of where the weaknesses lie and how to repair the problems.

Conclusion

Neither hacking nor cracking are new crimes. Both are, however, seeing increased modification as technology continues to advance. Hacking, which began to receive extensive media coverage in the 1980s is set to explode into the twenty-first century. Today there are more computers connected to the Internet than ever before. Hacking utility software and techniques developed in the early days of the crime's beginning are still seeing use today, along with new and improved techniques and software. Understanding of the how is but one part of the equation necessary for proper investigation of these types of crimes. In order to continue mounting a fight against hackers it is important to also understand the who and the why. Remember that technology changes almost too fast for most people to keep up with today. The key to preventing these types of crimes lies in education and understanding of how to convince these individuals to reflect inward on the why. There are some in the hacker community who do not share the belief that their skills should be used for mischief; unfortunately, there are still far too many who believe that their skills require that they continue to violate systems as long as they can get away with the act. Investigators called upon to investigate these crimes should be aware of the various types of attacks available to the hacker and should understand the basics of the culture that have been presented here.

Phreaking, while not as high-profile as hacking, is a financially devastating crime that costs the United States and other countries millions of dollars a year. Because of the reliance hacking has on the computer and access to networks, actions that normally involve the use of telephone services, it is not surprising that many hackers are also interested in the crime of phreaking. The ability to hide one's location and identity is instrumental to avoiding detection and arrest following the commission of a criminal act. Phreakers use a variety of techniques and devices to assist them in their activities, and while many of the phreak boxes no longer work on the telephone system there are new technologies that are taking the place of the older boxes everyday. Computer software and the portability of computers and handheld personal data assistants are making the use of such new technology easier every day. Additionally, there are several physical techniques involved in the commission of the crime of phreaking that require understanding. Phreaks often train themselves to memorize long calling card numbers that they obtain via looking over victims' shoulders or via computer-generated programs designed to guess legitimate users' numbers. Just as in the case of hacking, the solution to the problem may rely on education and training of investigators who must track down and convince individuals who violate the telephone system that their futures are nothing without focus toward legitimate work in the field of telecommunications.

Law enforcement, and private security, personnel who are beginning to investigate computer-related hacking and phreaking attacks are going to have to develop at a minimum a basic understanding of how these individuals communicate and why they behave the way they do when they are on the computer or the telephone. Admittedly, the crimes of hacking and phreaking are probably to be the least investigated of the high-technology crimes discussed in this work; this statement being due to the belief that hacking and phreaking involve largely technical investigations that may be beyond the investigative abilities of those who are unfamiliar with some of the intermediate and advanced level information concerning computers, networks and the telecommunications system. However, understanding the basic language and cultural habits may assist investigators who so choose to handle these investigations. Understanding is, after all, the key to detection and prevention.

Review Questions

1. Briefly discuss the evolution of hacking. What role did the founding members of the Artificial Intelligence lab at M.I.T. play in the development of hacking?

2. List and discuss the six types of hackers discussed in this chapter.

3. Phreaking has been labeled a financially threatening crime with little physical danger associated with the act. Should the crime then be given lesser consideration? Why or why not?

4. Colored boxes, known as phreak boxes, provide for users the ability to wreak havoc on the telecommunication lines. What are some of the more commonly encountered phreak boxes? Why is it still important to understand the operation of these devices?

5. How have changes in technology impacted the profiling of hackers and phreakers today?

6. Discuss the hacker subculture and language. What are some of the influences on each?

Further Reading

Bequai, A.. (1987). *Technocrimes*. Massachusetts: Lexington Books.

Judson, K.. (1994). *Computer Crime: Phreaks, Spies, and Salami Slicers*. New Jersey: Enslow Publishers.

Littman, J. (1996). *The Fugitive Game: Online with Kevin Mitnick*. Boston: Little Brown and Company.

Meinel, C. (2000). *Uberhacker! How to Break into Computers*. Washington: Loompanics.

Parker, D. (1976). *Crime by Computer*. New York: Scribner.

Power, R. (2000). *Tangled Web: Tales of Digital Crime from the Shadows of Cyberspace*. Indianapolis, IN: Que.

Zaenglein, N. (2000). *Secret Software*. Boulder, CO: Paladin Press.

Online Resources

Hackers Dot Com Website—information on hacking techniques and text files. Not a how-to guide for neophytes. Available at www.hackers.com.

2600 Magazine—a magazine devoted to updating subscribers about the latest events and news in the hacker and phreaker world. Available at www.2600.com.

Hacker's Jargon Dictionary—the electronic version of the Hacker's dictionary. Information on terminology and language used by hackers and those in the computer industry. Available at www.jargon.8hz.com/jargon_1.html#SEC1.

Chapter 3

Identity Theft and Bandits of the Information Superhighway

Identity theft has been defined as the theft of someone's identity through the use of personal identifying information (Eliot, 2002). Put simply, this is the theft of someone's identity using their name, social security number, or birth information. There are generally two types of identity theft, although one is significantly less discussed than the other. The first form of identity theft is the lesser known case, where an identity thief assumes the life of a victim. Perhaps this version of identity theft is rarely encountered because taking over someone's life is significantly harder to accomplish. However, there are potential uses for this form of identity theft, especially in regards to organized crime activities. The ability to leave a trail that leads to someone else who has no actual ties to the organization would be of benefit to any criminal operation. This form of identity theft has been used in a small number of high-profile celebrity cases. One of the more famous incidents involved a gentleman by the name of Anthony Taylor, who used this form of identity theft to live life as Tiger Woods. Apparently, Taylor believed himself to be one of Tiger's biggest fans. He further managed to obtain Tiger's social security number and was able to obtain official identification such as a driver's license. The ploy was uncovered when the young man attempted to secure a room at a local hotel and the clerk recognized that the individual was not Tiger Woods.

The second type of identity theft is the theft of a victim's credit identity, which is more of a financially devastating criminal act. An individual is a victim of credit identity theft when someone obtains their social security number along with a small amount of other identifying information and then begins applying for credit in the name of the victim. There are a number of ways in which a social security number may be obtained by an identity thief. Take, for example, a recent case of identity theft that involved an office of the Internal Revenue Service. A clerical error in the local IRS office resulted in people receiving the wrong tax information; as a result of this mistake, hundreds of people received sufficient information that could have been used in identity theft.

There is a third form of identity theft that is beginning to develop, but it is one that receives little attention because of a lack of either financial or physical harm incurred by the victim. The current level of electronic communication has led to the development of virtual identities, which are equivalent to what are known as online handles. Because of the number of people on the Internet, it is almost impossible for someone to choose a screen name consisting only of their true name. Today, it is almost a necessity to use combinations of letters and numbers, and to get creative in the creation of a screen name. Many people use the screen name as a means of expressing an inner attitude or personality. In recent years there has developed a growing number of people who will hijack a user's screen name, either as a means of harassing people, or as a means of using the account to spam other users. The theft of one's screen name—virtual identity theft would perhaps be a better term—was documented in a recent case involving America Online. A young girl had her screen name stolen by an unknown individual who then changed her profile to indicate that she enjoyed sex with older men. Every time the girl went online for the next few weeks she was bombarded with perverse requests. The father unsuccessfully attempted to file a lawsuit against America Online, claiming that the company failed to protect his daughter.

The commission of identity theft requires information that can be obtained in a variety of manners, ranging from traditional techniques of stealing credit card carbons to newer methods involving computers and software. Each of these techniques will be discussed in an upcoming section, but it is first necessary to briefly examine the problem of identity theft and how the crime has developed.

The Growing Problem of Identity Theft

Identity theft is an interesting crime in that it is rarely a dangerous crime, but is instead an extremely damaging financial crime. Victims of identity theft often find themselves in a remarkably embarrassing situation when their credit is denied because of the crime. Even more serious is the situation where the victim of identity theft will also encounter legal problems as the identity thief used the stolen identity to provide anonymity during the commission of criminal activities. There have been several cases where unknowing victims of identity theft discovered they had been victimized only after a court of law contacting them concerning outstanding warrants and fines. Consider the following examples:

- In the case of Christian Richards, a young man was sent more than 20 speeding tickets and tickets for moving violations, along with summonses for failure to appear in court. When Richards informed the court that he had never owned a driver's license, it was determined that someone had stolen his identity and registered a car in his name. Whenever the individual was stopped while driving the illegally registered automobile he would claim he did not have his license with him and the officer would ticket him on the basis of the vehicle's registration.

- It was recently reported that an inmate with the Florida Department of Corrections was operating an identity theft ring from inside the confines of the prison. By using a combination of outside prison contacts and telephone communications services within the prison, the ring was able to commit somewhere around $200,000 worth of fraud and identity theft. It is believed that the ring could have continued operations for an unknown time had one of the victims not complained when they were served a summons for failure to appear in court concerning a rental vehicle.

- Finally, there was the case of Donald McNeese, a former employee of Prudential Insurance Company, who recently stole a personnel listing with over 60,000 individuals' names, social security information, and other personal information such as addresses. The list was then sold via numerous online chat rooms and Internet relay chat sessions. It is unknown how many of the personnel listings were sold before law enforcement were able to put a stop to McNeese's activities.

According to information released by the Federal Trade Commission, identity theft now accounts for more than 40 percent of all consumer fraud complaints, with somewhere between 500,000 and 700,000 reports of identity theft collected each year by the various law enforcement agencies. It has been speculated that identity theft continues to rise because of the very nature of the crime and the fact that victims can easily come from any social or racial class (Doege, 2002). Regardless of the victim's age, financial status, living conditions or other factors, if the identity thief can gain access to the necessary personal information then the individual is susceptible to identity theft. One argument often made here is that this makes identity theft not only the fastest growing of the high-technology crimes but also the easiest.

In recent years the financial damages associated with identity theft have continued to grow exponentially. It is now believed that claims of identity theft cost the United States more than $1 billion in lost revenue (Hopper, 2002); of course, this figure does not take into account the fact that identity theft is not only a U.S. problem but is a worldwide problem. Further, the $1 billion does not include the thousands, or even hundreds of thousands, of people who may not discover that their identities have been stolen until months after the thefts occur and never report the crime to their local law enforcement agency. There develops an interesting question as to why these individuals do not report the crime. Do many believe they made the charges? Do others believe that there is no need to report the crime because it will never get solved? There have been no specific reasons provided for why individuals do not report some cases of identity theft, but it is the belief of this author that many individuals may believe that the crime will not be solved and therefore they are wasting their time. Or perhaps these individuals may have the perception that their local law enforcement agency cannot handle such an investigation, and they are unaware that under federal law they are only responsible for a small percentage of the any illegal transactions conducted using a victim's credit card.

Misinformation in regards to how identity theft operates is also a serious problem and is one that must be addressed in the near future, whether it is law enforcement personnel who are to provide this education or if the education is to come from commercial entities. One piece of false information that is circulating around the Internet is the belief that identity theft is a result of placing a credit card number on an Internet pay site. While it is possible for this to happen, the truth is that this form of identity theft is extremely unlikely. According to past studies on the frequency of identity theft and the source of the personal information, it has been reported that less than three to five percent of all identity thefts involve the Internet in any form (Verton, 2001). Of course, the information contained here is always subject to change as more companies move toward the Internet, and online targets are certainly becoming more attractive to identity thieves. However, there is also the consideration of effort that must be factored in to the equation. It is rather difficult and time consuming to set up an operation that allows for the theft of credit card information via the Internet. The time spent in accomplishing such a task may better be spent employing a hacking attack to penetrate a database containing thousands of credit card numbers. Put simply, it is just not economical to steal credit card numbers from the Internet.

The mere fact that more crimes are certain to involve the Internet in the future is currently scaring many individuals who believe that law enforcement is not adequately preparing to fight the oncoming wave. One insurance company has viewed this belief as an opportunity to take the initiative and offer a service that can only be termed ridiculous. In April of 2002 a Virginia insurance company reportedly began selling identity theft insurance in the amount of $25,000. In an article by Bonisteel (2002), representatives of the company indicated that they do not argue that credit card companies and law enforcement will not work with victims of identity theft. However, it is the insurance company's contention that the hardest part, and the most expensive, is the completion of paperwork necessary to get a victim's credit rating restored. The policy is intended to take some of the financial burden off of victims who are engaged in the process of repairing their credit rating.

How Identity Thieves Operate

It was stated in the previous section that only a small percentage of identity theft involves the Internet. How then does the crime occur? Identity theft can be committed through a variety of techniques consisting of those that employ the use of computers, those that employ other high-technology devices, or those that employ just old-fashioned physical thievery. The Internet has affected several of these techniques, but there are many more that have remained constant throughout the years. Several of the more traditional identity theft tactics will also be discussed because they provide a glimpse into the mindset of the individuals who commit these types of crimes.

One of the original forms of identity theft involved financial fraud in the form of check fraud. The materials necessary for the commission of financial fraud would begin with blank checks either being stolen, which was a common technique, or being manufactured. Manufacturing checks was not as commonly encountered merely because of the work involved in the activity and the money to set up the operations. Today, it is not uncommon to find individuals who are capable of manufacturing checks on a computer. In fact, through the Internet it is now possible to download driver's license information and/or checks. These materials can then be printed out using a high end color copier. When check forgery's popularity was at its peak, there was little understanding of how high-technology devices could benefit the craft.

Once a check was drafted, the perpetrator would cash the check at one bank, while drawing the money from a fake bank across the country. The distance between the two locations was normally enough for the check to clear after the forger had left the area. By the time the bank realized there was a problem with the check the individual had disappeared. It is important to remember that at the time this was developing there was no Internet or advanced networking of computer systems. Today, such transactions may seem ridiculous because the computers are all networked together; however, at the time the crime was in use there was no networking and the people were not informed of financial transactions except by mail, which almost anyone will attest to as being slow at times.

Beginning in the early 1990s, there were thousands of documents traded over the Internet via bulletin board services that discussed the issue of identity theft. When a user would dial into the bulletin board service, they would be allowed to chat with other users, upload files from their own collection, or download files made available from others' collections. Hundreds of these documents traded in the early days discussed the issue of identity theft, which incidentally was referred to as "carding" in these manuscripts. Carding was a catch-phrase to identify the theft of someone's credit card. Numerous authors provided information on this area of identity theft, albeit they operated under pseudonyms. Three of the better-known authors on carding were Avenger, Video Vindicator, and Masood. Each individual had their own writing style and included small nuances that separated them from the others, but they each shared much of the some information. It is this shared information that was used in developing the following section.

What Is Carding?

Carding refers to the theft of an unknowing victim's credit card information, and then the use of this information in shopping sprees for electronics or other goods. The early text documents circulating the Internet contained a vast number of ingenious methods of stealing a victim's credit card information. For example, along with the techniques discussed below there were documents detailing how to create your own credit card number using only a mathematical equation and information related to the type of credit card desired. The mathematical equation was reportedly developed by a 10- to 12-year-old boy. While the equation is unnecessary today because of advances in computer programming and the release of software that computes calculations for us, it is still impressive and indicative of the potential held by those who are capable of developing such formulas.

Individuals who advocated carding stressed that while obtaining the card information was fun, it was only half of the act. To complete the act of carding you had to go shopping with the information obtained from the act. Early techniques involved ordering the information and then structuring the delivery time to where the actual owners of the address were not at home. Here, experienced carders also dabbled with phreaking techniques to hijack answering machines in order to inform the delivery service of when would be the best time for a delivery to be made to the residence. This was possible because the delivery services in the past would comply with a carder's request to phone before delivery. The carder would then wait until after the delivery person had left the package—either at the front door or around back depending upon the instructions provided by the carder. According to the text files this technique was abandoned, or at least less frequently used, because of the danger associated with the technique and the potential for getting caught. Of course, changes in the policies of delivery companies that for-

Dan Clements, CEO of Cardcops.com, poses for this photo in the Sherman Oaks section of Los Angeles on September 1, 2005. Card-Cops monitors Internet chat rooms and other hacker communications for stolen credit card numbers, then notifies merchants and consumers to block bad purchases (AP)

bid the dropping of packages without signatures more than likely played at least a small role in the paradigm change.

Carders then moved their deliveries to official delivery spots where anyone could open a fake account with minimum effort. These places would collect deliveries for customers and then hold them until it was convenient for the owner of the package to come by the office. While carding is not as frequently addressed, nor applied, in the realm of identity theft, there remains the issue of the technique's use. Individuals who have chosen to employ this technique have discovered their own methods of modifying the technique. Today, companies such as Mailboxes ETC, the UPS store, and other similar stores are being used to store these materials. The item, or items in many cases, that appears to be illegally purchased with the greatest frequency? None other than top-of-the-line computers and computer hardware.

Dumpster Diving

All forms of identity theft begin with the theft of personal information. Many times this information is straightforward and consists of credit card numbers belonging to potential victims. Additionally, there are social security numbers, names, addresses, and employment information. Most professional thieves, and the term professional is used loosely here, do not agree with brute force attacks like those of purse snatching or armed robbery. While each of these methods is capable of providing the necessary information, each also presents a problem for the identity thief. If an individual is mugged or robbed at gunpoint, then what are they immediately aware of? The theft of their credit card or driver's license. This means that the identity thief will not have time to even enjoy the card before it is deactivated and reported stolen. To avoid this problem, one technique that has survived the test of time is that of dumpster diving.

Dumpster diving was previously discussed when examining the pre-hack stage of hacking. In regard to identity theft, however, the focus is not on manuals but on credit card carbons or other identifying information. Preapproval forms for credit cards are popular items to search for during this activity, as are letters from official government agencies that contain social security numbers and addresses. Some have questioned whether dumpster diving will continue to be used because there are fewer companies using credit card carbons. Unfortunately, this technique is poised to remain for quite some time, although it may see a slight decrease in use over the coming years. Smaller retail stores located within strip malls still use the traditional credit card slider device that creates carbon copies of the entire credit card's information. It is therefore possible that some of these receipts may be obtained from the dumpsters of such malls. Even in the absence of these devices, however, there is still a great deal of information that can be obtained from the newer receipts. Examine a recent credit card receipt and notice that only the last four digits of a card are showing. However, the receipt also provides the owner's name and the type of credit card used. All of this is information that is of benefit to the identity thief.

Further, there is a new development in the art of dumpster diving—the use of university unions. To understand this, a reader must only move over to the central location of their local university. The majority of universities provide a postal service within the main building. On any given day an individual can notice 100 or more pre-approval notices being received and discarded by college students, and on some days it is possible to see 1,000 or more during a mass mail out. Credit card companies recognize that college students represent a good potential market. Numerous studies have shown that college students earn more money over the course of a lifetime than their high school equivalents. By latching on to students while they are still in college and providing them with small balances it is the hope of the credit card company that they will develop life-long customers. In fact, the companies want the business so much that they will many times fill out the form for the student so that all the student has to do is sign the card and return for approval. The problem is that many students merely take the pre-approval cards and toss them into the trash. At the end of the day it is possible for an identity thief to come along, collect several of these cards, and assume the credit life of any of the students. The thief merely has to sign the pre-approval form but indicate that they are graduating and need the address changed. The victim may not realize they have been victimized until they are denied credit at a later date.

Credit Card Skimming

The use of credit card skimming devices was labeled by Massood to be the easiest technique in use by identity thieves. As more companies are moving away from the use of slider devices that create credit card carbons, the new industry tool is an electronic card reader. The device allows retail clerks to scan into memory the credit card's information that is stored within the magnetic strip on the back of the card. Information received from the card is then sent to a credit card verification service via a direct call made by the machine. If the card is accepted, then the device will store the authorization numbers in a separate digital file. It has been recommended that individuals who are serious about committing identity theft should obtain careers in the retail industry. Becoming a cashier or clerk in a store that uses this system will guarantee that the identity thief has constant access to credit card files. Because the data files are stored in a computer file, the technologically sophisticated user can transfer the data files to a separate disk at the end of a shift. These verification files contain the credit card numbers scanned for the day, the expiration dates of the cards, addresses, and phone numbers for all purchases.

Another technique employed by insiders engaged in identity theft is to use an actual credit card skimmer. A card skimmer is a small, often handheld, device that can store up to 200 or more credit card numbers, cardholder names, and expiration dates. In essence, the device provides the same service as the electronic device used in retail stores to confirm the use of a credit card. The only difference being that the card skimmer does not dial into a central computer and confirm the authenticity of a credit card. Instead, the information from the credit card is copied into a file within the memory of the skimmer. The device is used in the following manner. The retail store clerk will take the customer's credit card and prior to running the card through the verification computer he or she will run the card through the card skimmer. Normally, the card skimmer is kept directly beneath the register or next to the actual verification device.

Once the card numbers are collected, the credit card skimmer is connected to a separate device that will encode the stolen numbers onto fake manufactured credit cards. There is no limit to the type of card that can be falsely generated. If the card maintains an electronic stripe on the back, then the card can be skimmed and recreated. The technique has been used numerous times to defraud larger corporations that have sold their own store credit cards or gift cards. In an effort to curb these activities, several states have recently made advances toward criminalizing card skimmers. California was one of the first to consider moving for such sanctions. As of today, however, the devices are still considered legal, despite the fact that there is no known legal use for the devices. Credit card skimmers can be purchased for around $100 and are available from various online electronics companies.

Shoulder Surfing

In much the same manner as dumpster diving, shoulder surfing conducted by identity thieves is similar to shoulder surfing conducted by hackers and phone phreaks. When a user takes out their credit card to pay for their merchandise, either in preparation for the payment or after payment has been made and the user is waiting to sign the credit card slip, the identity thief will peer over the user's shoulder. Within a few brief seconds an experienced shoulder surfer can memorize all 16 or more numbers associated with a credit card. So, how can a human being memorize so many numbers so fast? Do only geniuses become identity thieves?

Of course not all identity thieves are geniuses, but the majority are fairly creative and innovative in their approaches. Further, it is not necessary to memorize the entire card most of the time. Experienced identity thieves will probably own a list of each of the major credit card issuers and the first eight numbers associated with the card. These listings contain information on all of the major credit card companies, and even go so far as to separate the listings for subcategories of credit cards. For example, one listing indicated that the fact that gold VISA cards began with a different eight-number sequence than a regular VISA card. Therefore, the identity thief only has to shoulder surf half of the credit card and the expiration date. The memorization of eight numbers for a short period of time until the number is written down is not that hard for an individual who has devoted their life to dealing with numbers all day, every day. Further, due to the prevalence of cellular telephone communications, it is now possible that one identity thief could wait behind a potential victim and then call out the numbers and expiration information over a cellular phone. A second identity thief could then be located outside writing down all information received. Every so many hours the two could switch roles so as to throw off suspicion of their activities.

Retail Scams

The previous sections have dealt with several techniques that have involved occasional interaction with retail operations, but each could be accomplished outside the retail arena. Here in this section, the reader will be provided information on several of the more common identity theft scams designed to work in large scale retail outlets. If any retailer were asked about security for their customers, they would respond with a canned answer indicating that they do everything in their power to protect the private information of consumers. Oftentimes, however, it is impossible to prevent everything, as is the case with the two identity theft techniques to be discussed here.

The first technique is a rather ingenious combination technique that involves the use of an unwitting store clerk in the commission of the identity theft. In using this technique, an identity thief will get at the end of a long retail line, hide behind a display near the cash registers or position themselves in the front of the store where they are hardly noticed. The identity thief will then wait for an attractive mark to come along. As the cashier completes the transaction of an individual deemed appropriate by the identity thief, a phone call will be made to the cashier. On the phone is the identity thief, who is pretending to be a member of the company's loss prevention or security division. Next, the cashier is informed that the customer is a potential suspect in a check cashing, or credit card, scheme. In many cases, the cashier will believe the person on the phone and will begin examining the customer's identification, check, and/or credit card. The clerk is then instructed to inform the customer that the next actions are routine and are designed to protect the company and the customer from problems. The clerk will then be asked to read the check or credit card numbers over the phone while the identity thief writes down all of the information. The clerk is then told everything is alright, at which time he hangs up the telephone believing that they had just taken part in an everyday security check when in reality someone has just used him or her to steal the customer's identity.

The next retail scam requires the identity thief to be a slightly more computer savvy operator. Many retail companies have begun offering credit cards that are used by shoppers only at the store issuing the credit card. As a means of speeding up the application process, thereby allowing for a quicker return to shopping, the application is now available via various miniature computers located in different areas of the store. The computers allow the potential customer to enter their social security number and name into the computer just as they would on a paper application. However, when the application is completed, the user will indicate they are done and the computer will run a check on the social security number to determine the legitimacy of the request. If the social security number is real then the customer will be issued a paper slip with an account number printed on the front. The slip of paper can then be used as a temporary shopping card until the actual card is mailed to the residence of the applicant.

The problem with the use of the computer verification service is that many times it only verifies the existence of the social security number and does not verify the actual identity of the owner of the social security number. With this in mind it is possible for an identity thief to shoulder surf someone's social security number and name and apply for a temporary shopping card that would be charged to the victim's social security number. Further, some of these devices only require a social security number. Anyone's name can be used on the application. The victim would never know that they were victimized until they were tracked down by a credit collection service attempting to clear out the account, on which the identity thief has never made payments.

In recent years there has been a new retail scam to see increased use. Utilizing an employee within a target company or store to assist them, the identity thief will approach a clerk or cashier and ask them to sell a copy of the credit card listings for the day. This means that at the end of the day an individual can gain access to hundreds of credit cards receipts containing card numbers and user identification information for one price. Normally, this price will range from $20 to $50. In the eyes of those involved the deal is a win-win situation. The identity thief gets easy access to credit cards and the store clerk makes an easy $50 or so per night. The reader should not go out immediately and begin destroying their credit cards, as this technique has only been encountered in a few convenience stores and therefore warrants consideration but not fear.

Internet Scams

The Internet may not play a significant role in identity theft as of yet, but networks are sure to play a larger role in the coming years. It is with this in mind that the following section will discuss two of the more potentially damaging Internet scam techniques. The first is the use of a packet sniffing program, which is used to intercept credit card information while the data is en route to a website (Wang, 2001). Packet sniffing programs are normally used in conjunction with a commercial website to commit identity theft. For a better understanding of how packets operate, refer back to Chapter 2's discussion on packet software and packet sniffing. Packet sniffers, in regard to the crime of identity theft, read the headers of packets containing credit card information and then make a copy of the information and forward it to the packet sniffing software's administrator. The individual in control of the software then collects all of the information and will begin making purchases on the credit card numbers as they were received. The software is infrequently used because it takes a great deal of effort to come away with a few credit cards. Time spent carrying out this technique is believed by many to be better spent obtaining mass lists of credit cards. Additionally, the technique is normally reserved for use by individuals within a company's ranks, as it is easier for them to gain access to network servers and implant the software.

The second type of Internet scam is that which is referred to as "subscriber account update" scams. This is where an individual will be tricked into giving out their subscriber account information. Unsuspecting users will be asked for this information because of a "computer failure" or a need to update the "official records." The frightening thing about this technique is that it requires little or no technical skill. The subscriber information requested by the identity thief will consist of a credit card number, name, address, and password to the Internet service provider's service. Many of the larger internet service providers have begun implementing steps to prevent the use of these techniques. However, as the service providers have begun making changes to their policies, so have the identity thieves been making changes to their techniques. America Online is one of the largest Internet service providers, and now tells its customers not to respond for such requests for information unless they receive an official request from the company itself. Users are told that they will recognize an official communication from the company by the use of a blue icon next to the sender on the main e-mail screen. However, there is software developed by an anonymous programmer called AOHell, which is capable of assisting users in committing several pranks.

The true danger in the use of the software is the ability of the program to generate an official looking e-mail and instant message requesting the subscriber renew his or her credit card billing information in order to continue using America Online's services. Despite the warnings from America Online, people are once again giving out their credit card numbers in response to these types of messages and identity thieves are using the information to go on extravagant electronic shopping sprees (Wang, 2001). Another technique that has recently developed is the use of questionnaires to receive bonus prizes offered by America Online. Here, users are informed that they have won some prize and must merely complete a questionnaire. As part of the questionnaire, the user is asked to enter their America Online screen name and password. Few users take the time to examine the website on which the questionnaire is being offered, and fewer still realize that they are giving out information that America Online does not officially request from customers. While America Online is one of the most popular Internet services to be attacked by identity thieves, all service providers are potential targets. Users must understand that giving out personal information at the request of an e-mail or an instant message is dangerous and unnecessary.

Government Assistance

The title for this section may be confusing to some, as no one wants to believe that the government is assisting identity thieves. Does the government aid identity thieves? Well, the answer is yes, but not intentionally. The truth is that because of relaxed security and procedures it is sometimes possible that a government agency may inadvertently assist an identity thief in the commission of an identity scam. In other situations, the government may merely be made to appear as a co-conspirator. Take the following situations involving identity theft and government agencies:

- Recently the Internal Revenue Service released a report indicating that an unknown individual had managed to forge a set of fairly realistic looking IRS and bank documents. The materials were believed to be used to convince individuals to send out their credit card and checking account information. According to the documents, the IRS would use the information to examine an individual's checking account to determine whether or not they were exempt from federal withholding tax on the interest paid on their financial accounts. The presence of the fake report was uncovered when someone realized that all interest is reported to the IRS.

- The California Department of Motor Vehicles was recently audited after it was discovered that hundreds of fake driver's licenses had been issued from several offices around the state. The audit was initially launched as a means of tying up the loose security issues present in many government operations leading up to the events of September 11, 2001; a situation that was believed to have contributed to several terrorists being able to obtain fake identification that allowed them to take part in such activities as flight training classes.

- Finally, there have been recent reports concerning the theft of credit reports. Here, an individual's credit report is stolen while being transported via the traditional mail carrier. The use of this technique is still under investigation, but it has been reported that over 800 in 2002 reported that they had requested a copy of their credit report from Equifax, one of the largest credit consumer agencies in North America, and never received the document.

The aforementioned examples provide further proof that identity theft is one crime that is sure to continue, and those who employ the technique are extremely opportunistic and will always continue seeking to improve their methodologies. Identity theft will continue as long as there are individuals such as those above who are willing to give out their information for easy money or rewards, or as long as there are individuals who continue to manipulate governmental and private business enterprises to assist themselves in the commission of a criminal act.

Responses to Identity Theft

It was only recently that many law enforcement agencies began to deal directly with the investigation of identity theft complaints. Historically, when an individual complained that he or she was a victim of identity theft, the department would merely mail out a victim's statement packet. Generally, the packet would be received within a week, but there were at least two serious problems with this procedure. First, by the time the victim received the packet, completed the questionnaire and returned the materials to the police department, the identity thief would be long gone. Second, not only did this procedure slow down the investigation, but victims cannot begin repairing their credit until they have received an official copy of their complaint filed with the law enforcement agency. It could take several weeks to accomplish all of the steps, and this was considered unacceptable by both victims and investigators.

Procedures such as those discussed above are slowly beginning to change. California, which was especially plagued with problems related to the policy, is now requiring law enforcement officers to take timely reports concerning incidents of identity theft. The law was developed by Representative Susan A. Davis as an attempt to aid citizens who have become victims of identity theft with repairing their credit in a timely manner. Law enforcement agencies now provide copies of the final reports as soon as possible after completing their initial investigation. Since the passage of the new law, representatives of the Los Angeles Police Department have reported that their identity theft claims have increased to more than 100 claims a week (Tran, 2001).

The process of investigating identity theft depends upon whether the crime is committed in the physical or the cyber world. Crimes occurring in the physical world are investigated much like any other physical world crime, with the added complication of handling evidence obtained from high-technology devices. It is the necessity for properly handling such devices that complicates such investigations. If the crime involves the use of the Internet or some other network, then there is the issue of following the digital trail of evidence—a procedure that is still unknown to many in the criminal justice field.

There is a growing trend toward the development of trained computer forensics experts to handle investigations involving digital evidence, but there are several limitations. Digital evidence, which will be discussed in detail in later chapters, involves any evidence stored on an electronic medium. Without proper software and equipment, this form of evidence can be easily destroyed and a case lost. The increasing number of identity thefts occurring through the use of the Internet is leading some to argue that the criminal justice system is facing a time when a majority of crimes will involve high-technology devices, and there must be someone there to investigate. Some of the better financed law enforcement agencies have begun training officers in computer forensics. Investigators who are trained in this field have been instrumental in solving several cases of identity theft. For example, a New York City investigator trained in computer forensics recently arrested Abraham Abdallah. Abdallah was a 32-year-old high school dropout, who managed to collect personal information on more than one-half of Forbes' top 400 richest men. He accomplished this entire crime using nothing more than his cellular phone and computer. Despite having less than a high school education, Abdallah's skills were good enough that it took the New York police department more than two months to track him down. Along with the credit card information he obtained, Abdallah was also able to gather bank codes and brokerage accounts for individuals such as Oprah Winfrey and George Soros. Because of the bank transactions, an investigator was able to trace two e-mails back to Abdallah's account.

So, is the criminal justice field ready for a period in which larger numbers of crimes are being committed through a combination of old-fashioned ingenuity and high tech bravado? The answer is no, the field is not ready for such a large number of high-technology crimes, but there is hope. Preparing for the future of these crimes will involve a combined effort between law enforcement agencies, the government, and citizens. Investigators who notice an increasing number of identity theft claims within their jurisdiction may find that, by simply spending a little time speaking to civilian groups, the problem can be lessened. Perhaps not removed completely, but reduced considerably. What information should investigators provide these groups? The information does not have to involve any more than a general overview of the basic strategies for handling personal information that contains sufficient data to assist an identity thief. For example, it is recommended that an individual do the following to falling victim to identity theft:

- Do not give out personal information like a social security number or bank account number over the phone.

- Delete e-mails asking for banking information to help someone who is in need of assistance. Often the desire for easy money will motivate people to fall prey to tricks that would not have normally affected them.

- Shred all papers containing social security numbers, names, addresses, and similar information before throwing them out into the trash.

- Be careful with credit card receipts and carbons. Do not allow the materials to be thrown away at the ATM machine or the gas pump. Destroy the receipts and trash them at another location.

Corporations are now beginning to provide their own protections against identity theft. Through the use of innovative technology, credit card companies are now trying to protect individuals from having their credit destroyed with online purchases from a stolen credit card number. Visa recently released their Verified by Visa program, which requires online consumers to select a password that will be required whenever the credit card is used at particular websites (Goldstein, 2002). The problem is that the technology is new and not all online retailers require the use of the Verified program.

Government regulations are also being used to protect consumers from cases of identity theft. Within the past eight years there have been an increasing number of legislative acts passed concerning identity theft. Many states are moving toward legislation aimed at limiting the amount of personal information that is printed on credit card receipts. Further, the legislation would allow for law enforcement agencies to penalize credit agencies that do not take adequate precautions to protect consumers from becoming victims of identity theft. According to Stamberg (2001), the State of California has also begun restricting the sale of state birth and death records because reports indicated that sales were not being verified to ensure that identity thieves were not purchasing the records. The federal government has also passed legislation aimed at penalizing those who would use personal information to steal someone's identity.

An example of such legislation would be the Identity Theft and Assumption Deterrence Act, passed in 1998 to amend the United States code, Title 18, to account for identity theft. This legislation decrees that identity theft is committed by anyone who, "knowingly transfers or uses, without lawful authority, a means of identification of another person with the intent to commit, or to aid or abet, any unlawful activity that constitutes a violation of Federal law, or that constitutes a felony under any applicable State or local law." As noted by the broad wording of the statute, identify theft occurs when someone uses another's identity for any purpose that is illegal. This legislation then covers the act of using another's identity to hide one's true identity when committing another crime, while also covering the act of stealing someone's identity with the intent to commit financial fraud (credit cards, bank accounts, etc.). While the above legislation deals with federal offenses, the majority of states have also passed similar legislation in the wake of increasing numbers of identity theft claims. Those states that have not are certain to begin the process shortly.

Conclusion

Identity theft is not a new crime, having been committed for decades. In the early stages of the crime's development, identity thieves employed techniques involving old fashioned techniques of impersonation and con artistry. One of the more popular original criminal acts involved the act of check washing. From washing checks the crime moved to the age of plastic. By applying a variety of new techniques, identity thieves moved to the commission of crimes involving credit cards; crimes that were referred to at the time as carding. Through carding credit card information perpetrators were able to go on electronic shopping sprees the likes of which had never been imagined before. In the early 1990s, the Internet began to gain notoriety and the information concerning how to commit the crime of identity theft became more easily accepted. A new generation of con artists was born and the foundations for the development of future technological techniques were laid.

Today, identity theft still occurs with greater frequency in the physical world than in the cyber world. There is no doubt, however, that the crime will see a greater reliance on the Internet in coming years. Already, the techniques used in the physical world have moved beyond check washing and simple forgery, although both techniques are still in use. Identity thieves now rely on a combination of physical techniques (shoulder surfing and dumpster diving) and electronic techniques (credit card skimming and Internet scams). Carding has been defined as the theft of another's credit card information that is then used to purchase materials. While the technique has seen a decrease in recent years because of improved security and procedures for delivery services, there is still a strong presence for the technique present on the Internet. Of course, the technique is not obsolete as there are still some who commit the crime of carding as a means of purchasing high-end electronic items. An investigator tasked with investigating these crimes must understand how the crime is committed in both worlds, before they can begin attempting to investigate crimes involving identity theft in either of the worlds. Failure to understand these basics could result in massive confusion arising during an investigation, or even worse the inability of a law enforcement agency's to even begin an investigation. At this point and time it is still possible to begin formulating plans to counter this trend, but agencies must begin considering the issues as soon as possible.

Society is continuously becoming more and more "connected" through electronics. Legislation and administrative policies are each very important to the combating of this crime; however, the real strength once again lies in education and making citizens more aware of the potential dangers associated with allowing information to be too free. An agency that were to invest a small amount of time into educating citizens about the danger of identity theft and how to protect themselves would certainly not find themselves regretting such an investment. Fewer cases of identity theft will result with an increase in caution from the public, and despite the large number of newspaper, television and magazine articles concerning the issue, there are still many who did not realize the dangers and how to avoid becoming a victim. Through a combination of education and enforcement it will be possible to reduce, although probably never eradicate, the crime of identity theft. The failure of law enforcement agencies to adequately prepare for these crimes will result in identity thieves continuing to outpace law enforcement in much the same manner that they have done up to this time.

Review Questions

1. What is identity theft and how is the act conducted?

2. Discuss 'carding.' What is it and how is it accomplished by identity thieves? Do individuals continue to engage in activities deemed as carding?

3. What are some of the various techniques employed by the identity thief in obtaining the personal information of victims?

4. The Internet is said to be minimally involved in the commission of identity theft. This does not mean that identity theft does not employ high technology in the commission of the crime. What are some of the technological tools employed in identity theft?

5. How has the attitude of law enforcement and the government changed over the years in regard to identity theft?

6. Should the crime of identity theft be handled in a manner different from that of more physically threatening crimes? Why or why not?

Further Reading

Newman, J. (1999). *Identity Theft: The Cybercrime of the New Millennium*. Port Townsend, WA: Loompanics Unlimited.

Wang, W. (2001). *Stea\puter Book 2: What They Won't Tell You About the Internet*. San Francisco, CA: No Starch Press.

Online Resources

Better Business Bureau—here readers will be provided with information on how to handle identity theft if you are victimized. Available at www.bbb.org.

National Fraud Center—provides information related to the crime of identity theft, how to protect yourself from becoming a victim, and how to begin repairing your credit after being victimized. Available at www.nationalfraud.com.

National White Collar Crime Center—provides information related to the crime of identity theft and how to avoid becoming a victim. Available at www.nw3c.com.

Chapter 4

Digital Child Pornography and the Abuse of Children in Cyberspace

It is commonly held that children possessed fewer legal rights in the 1800s than they do today. Minors were often considered nothing more than the property of their parents and were therefore largely excluded from the safeguards of American Constitutional law. Many times children were used as workers by their parents in an attempt to supplement family income. Examples of work included laboring in factories or fields, but occasionally the child was also subject to prostitution; this was especially the case for younger girls who fetched a premium among clients of such services. It is believed by some researchers who have studied this phenomenon that men have always had fantasies relating to sexual relationships with virgins; and because few women who worked as prostitutes were of virginal character, parents were able to get good money for the prostitution of their daughters and even, occasionally, of their sons.

Over time, the desire of adults to have sexual relations with children has come to be known as pedophilia, defined as the attraction of an adult toward the affections of a child. Normally, this attraction consists of nonviolent sexual contact with a child. Contact includes acts such as: genital viewing or fondling, oral-genital contact, penetration, and other forms of sexual contact. In recent years the crime of pedophilia has come to be considered one of the most common victimizations of children around the world. Recent media coverage of criminal activities involving suspected and convicted pedophiles has brought forth even more discussion and consideration of this affliction.

With an increasing desire to view and engage children in sexual situations, individuals began manufacturing and distributing child pornography. In this instance, child pornography is used to refer to videos, books, magazines, or photos depicting children in various sexual activities. The first recorded instance of child pornography is believed to have come from China in the late 1400s when a sex manual titled *The Admirable Discourses of the Plain Girl* was released (Flowers, 1994). Since the time of this book's release, child pornography has undergone dramatic changes. Children have more rights under the law, but the production and distribution of child pornography has increased. Over the last several decades the production of child pornography has risen dramatically. In the 1960s and 1970s, Europeans began mass producing images of child pornography. The material, which was circulated mostly from Denmark and Holland, was distributed in such large amounts that even today much of the child pornography manufactured during this time is still in circulation. In recent years, Denmark and Holland have reduced their manufacturing levels, while it is believed that Japan has emerged as a leader in the production and dissemination of child pornography.

Advances in technology have also been responsible for an increase in child pornography manufacture and distribution. Images can be manufactured, copied, and delivered in a fraction of the time it previously took for similar activities. Individuals involved in the child pornography industry now find that through the use of technology the time required to manufacture materials has decreased, while the variety of child pornography has increased. Traditional movies and pictures have been commonly replaced with the use of the following file formats to depict children engaged in sexual acts:

- **.mpeg**—stands for motion picture expert group. The .mpeg format allows for better compression but not as good a picture as the .avi format

- **.avi**—stands for audio-video. The .avi format has less compression than the .mpeg format but normally results in a better picture quality

- **.jpeg**—stands for joint picture expert group. The .jpeg extension denotes a picture format that allows for better compression than the majority of other picture file formats.

The .mpeg and .avi file formats are video formats. Web pages use the .mpeg format because the compression creates smaller file sizes and is better suited for the possibility of being downloaded via slower Internet connections. The .avi format is used by individuals who want higher video quality but also are willing to deal with larger file sizes. Because of the large file sizes associated with .avi files, many individuals will transfer these video files via CD-ROMS and DVD-ROMS, which can hold larger files. The .jpeg files are highly compressed picture formats commonly used for picture files that are going to be transmitted via the Internet. These electronic formats are superior to their physical counterparts in that copies can be mass produced at a speed ten times faster than physical copies, and the images never lose quality, regardless of how many times the image or video is copied. For these reasons, it is entirely possible that both users and traders of child pornography will soon prefer the electronic formats. It should be noted that the above file types are not exclusive and there are other formats that could be used. For example, movies files could also be compressed with Apple's QuickTime software and bear the extension .mov or could be compressed into the .asf format. However, at this time the use of .mpeg and .avi are believed to still be used more frequently. Additionally, picture files can be compressed in the windows bitmap format, which is labeled as a .bmp, or in an animated image file, which is labeled as a .gif, but the .jpeg is still likely the most commonly encountered. Recently, the issue of pornography and children has gained increased recognition with the release of studies indicating that 80 percent of all pornography (both adult pornography and child pornography) will eventually find its way into the hands of children (Buford, 2002). How are these materials used? In a process referred to as grooming.

The Grooming Process

According to many researchers, as well as law enforcement officers, pedophiles share and swap their collections of child pornography with others who share their desires. As a means of providing some sort of sexual gratification, these images are shared among collectors via message boards, chat programs, or web pages. While even maintaining such materials for personal gratification is viewed as unacceptable by many, the use of the materials in grooming children is even more unsettling. When a pedophile encounters a child they believe to be susceptible to a sexual relationship, they begin a process designed to gain a child's trust. In essence these individuals are breaking down the child's defenses and then manipulating the child into performing a desired sexual act. This is the process now referred to as grooming (Freeh, 2002; Weber, 2002; Wolf, 2001). Drawing upon the work of previous scholars, the following are the phases in the grooming process.

Friendship Phase

The grooming process will normally begin with an attempt by the pedophile to foster a pseudo-friendship with the child. Child victims of pedophiles are selected from a variety of areas; but schools, shopping malls and playgrounds are popular because of the large number of potential victims. Children targeted as victims will also often come from homes in which the child believes that he or she is not loved. Pedophiles often attempt to convince the child that he or she respects, understands, and even loves the child. Once the child becomes comfortable with the pedophile, and a relationship has been established, then the child is moved to the next level of seduction.

The Secrecy Phase

With a growing sense of trust developing between the child and the pedophile, the child will then be convinced by the pedophile that the relationship is secret. To assist in this deception, the pedophile will convince the child that their parents would be upset if they knew the child was having fun with an adult. Another variation of this deception may involve the pedophile providing gifts to the child, then attempting to convince the child that the parents would be upset if they discovered the child was receiving gifts. It is at this level that the pedophile may occasionally go so far as to convince the child that talking could result in someone being hurt, whether it is the child or the child's parents.

Physical Contact Phase

At this point, pedophiles will examine their relationship with the child and attempt to determine whether there is an emotional bond established between them. If the pedophile determines that there is a bond developing, then the physical contact may begin. The first few physical contacts will normally consist of very light touching or rubbing. In fact, many children may not even realize that their adult friend is touching him or her in a negative manner. Many pedophiles will attempt to represent these first few touches as accidental contact. Regardless, once the physical contact begins, it is normally only a matter or time until the child becomes engaged in the commission of a sexual act.

The Pornography Phase

Pedophiles may begin using their pornography in the grooming process around the same time physical interaction with the child begins. While child pornography is most often used as a means of convincing the child that sexual contact is normal, there are also instances where adult pornography has been used. Regardless of whether the materials are of adults or of children, the purpose remains the same and the delivery of the pictures will follow a preset pattern. Of course, as we will see below, the use of child pornography is preferred because of the very nature of the grooming process. The pattern for grooming a child through the use of pornography is as follows:

- The first pictures consist of images showing children merely standing around in various states of undress. Eventually these images will be of nude children. These images may consist of one or more children, but each child in the image is nude and separate from the other. These images are used to convince the child that being naked in the presence of others is an acceptable behavior.

- The next level of pictures consists of images of nude children touching each other. These pictures are, of course, used to convince the child there is nothing wrong with children who are nude touching each other. Once the pedophile believes the child has become accepting of these pictures, the victim will be sent the final series of pictures.

- These final pictures will consist of children having sexual intercourse with an adult. Generally, it is after this stage that a pedophile will begin attempting to initiate a sexual relationship with the child.

Traditionally, the grooming process has been used in the sexual entrapment of children, but unfortunately a new technique is becoming increasingly popular. Law enforcement personnel have recently seen an increase in pedophiles circumventing the children. Some pedophiles have decided that the process of gaining a child's trust can be sped up if he or she first grooms the child's parents. Under this form of grooming, pedophiles attempt to convince parents that he or she has a genuine interest in the well-being of the child. Once the parents are accepting of the relationship between the perpetrator and the child, then the pedophile will begin to groom the child. This speeds up the grooming process because the secrecy phase is eliminated. Pedophiles normally tell children that his or her parents are aware of their physical contact, or try to convince children that their parents would not believe them if they tattled. Because the parents are removed from the child's life as a possible means of escape, this is an extremely dangerous development in the grooming process and is one that warrants increased education for parents of young children. Few parents understand the grooming process and therefore do not discuss the potential dangers with their children. For this reason, one recommended solution for controlling the problem lies in involving both parents and law enforcement in a process of education that provides children with the necessary skills to detect situations where they are being groomed. Once discovered, then adults and parents are alerted to the situation (Burstow, 2002).

Child Pornography and the Internet

In much the same manner as the Internet has influenced other criminal activities; the Internet has increased the various problems associated with child pornography. According to reports from various federal law enforcement agencies, almost all of the government's remedial campaigns from the 1980s were undone within two years of the Internet's public release. During the 1980s federal law enforcement agencies cracked down on the manufacture and distribution of child pornography. As a result of these efforts, the government managed to stem the flow of child pornography to a point where it was considered a controllable problem. The ease of transportation that the Internet brought forth, however, led to an increase in child pornography that has made the problem worse than ever. Indeed, some law enforcement officials have been quoted as stating that the Internet has reduced the campaign against child pornography to an almost half-hearted effort (Kaplan, 1997).

Part of the problem may lie in the fact that the pornography industry has been well established for centuries, with many believing the Internet to be merely another method of obtaining the materials. According to a recent study, one-third of respondents to a survey indicated that downloading child pornography was acceptable behavior. These findings came despite the fact that more than 90 percent of the respondents indicated they knew child pornography was illegal (McCabe, 2002). It was McCabe's contention that the reason for this discrepancy lies in the fact that some adults view juvenile sexuality as a necessary part of the maturation process. Further, the respondents that indicated support for child pornography were predominantly white males who maintained gainful employment. McCabe further theorized a correlation between acceptance of child pornography and the general acceptance of pornography by adult males.

Additional problems have also been created by the Internet. For example, thanks in part to the Internet, individuals not generally known for having enough freedom to obtain such illicit materials are reaching the child pornography industry. According to one report, inmates in state and federal penitentiaries are now capable of collecting and distributing child pornography via the library computers. Because many correctional officers and other prison personnel may not be familiar with computer technology, it is possible that no one would understand what the inmates were doing with the computer. While this one report is an isolated event, there is the possibility that a correctional institution could become part of a child pornography distribution network. This is especially true if the computers are running some form of distributed peer-to-peer network, which will be discussed in later sections. Correctional institutions are not as insecure as other institutions. After all, correctional officers in general will monitor any computer access by inmates. There are other government institutions and public facilities that provide clients with greater opportunity to engage in criminal activity. Take, for example, public libraries or Internet cafés. Each of these institutions maintains computers connected to the Internet and could be used in the distribution of child pornography if the computers are not properly monitored.

In the 1980s, bulletin board services (BBS), which today are referred to as web forums, became used in the transmission of child pornography. The story of Helena became the most popular child pornography series on these BBSes. Helena was a little girl who appeared to be 8 to 10 years old. A series of photographs depicting Helena having sex with a boy her age and an older man, who was assumed to be her father, became the most traded images on BBSes. Helena became known as "Hel-Lo," a call-name by which individuals could locate these photographs online (Jenkins, 2001). Hel-Lo apparently stood for Helena-Lolita, with Lolita being a term often associated with pornography featuring little girls. The Lolita call name is believed to be associated with the classic novel *Lolita*, which was the story of a pre-pubescent girl who became the love interest of an older man. The adventures of Helena are apparently still one of, if not the most popular child pornography series on the market. In early 2005 Florida Department of Law Enforcement agents arrested an individual for the possession of child pornography. Their investigation turned up that the individual was looking for Hel-Lo pictures.

Today, BBSs are not as often used. Instead, there are several commonly encountered methods of transmitting information over the Internet. One method involves the use of websites devoted to child pornography. It has been asserted in recent years that as much as 69 percent of all profits for websites are generated through the sale of pornography. Further, of the 40 million sites available on the Internet, there are more than one million pornographic pictures of children available at any one time during the day. A second method involves the use of electronic mail (e-mail). E-mail is now the chosen method of communication for almost all Internet users in their day-to-day communications and children are no exception. In fact, it is entirely possible that children use e-mail and the Internet more than some adults, because many older people appear to have little or no desire to learn about computers unless their jobs require the use of a computer and the Internet.

Pedophiles are fully aware of the popularity of electronic mail among children. The grooming process does not change significantly when a pedophile uses the Internet and e-mail instead of physical interaction. The only real changes are the changes in contact. Rather than physically visiting schoolyards, playgrounds, and other child-related hangouts, pedophiles now stalk chat rooms designed for children. Most pedophiles will enter child-topic chat rooms and strike up discussions with the children, with the adult normally being well versed in the latest in children's television and movies.

While most of the individuals involved in these activities are adults, some reports have found that an increasing number of those trying to prey on minors in chat rooms are children the same age as the victims. Regardless of the age of the sexual predator, however, the victim is normally desensitized via e-mailed adult and child pornography. The process of grooming via e-mail works in much the same way as grooming works in the physical world. The first pictures are of naked children, and these are followed by others that progressively reveal more sexual contact between the children. Once the child is fully desensitized, the perpetrator arranges a meeting with the victim. When this occurs, it is common for a "traveler case" to develop; that is, the pedophile travels across state lines to the area in which the victim lives.

Just as the introduction of the Internet undid the work federal law enforcement had accomplished in the 1980s, the introduction of peer-to-peer networking has affected the work accomplished by law enforcement in the 1990s. Peer-to-peer networking is commonly referred to as P2P networking and involves the linking of two computers in order to share files, whether the files are music, video or picture formats. Peer-to-peer networking software has provided new challenges to law enforcement officers who are investigating the distribution of child pornography. Because of the technology behind current peer-to-peer programs, it is almost impossible to track all users. This is especially true because there is now one piece of software serving two million registered users at any given time during the day. Each piece of software works the same, with only minor differences in how files are transferred. For example, Music City Morpheus allows users to download any file format, and even allows users to download from multiple users. By downloading from multiple users, the transfer of a file is sped up as the program pulls bits of the data from several different users who have higher transfer speeds. Once the file is completed, then the file is assembled and is ready to be opened. This is especially helpful for distributors of child pornography because they can download videos up to six times faster than other peer-to-peer software users.

The fact that transfers of video files may take considerably longer to transfer than music files does not appear to have greatly affected the transfer of child pornography via these peer-to-peer networks. According to recent research conducted by a representative of the U.S. House of Representatives, these peer-to-peer networks are used by a large number of children and are resulting in children swapping images of child pornography. In fact, three of the top ten most requested search terms on one of the peer-to-peer networks related to child pornography terms. This is evidence that the trading of videos depicting child pornography may be becoming more rampant than the trading of child porn pictures.

Law Enforcement's Response to Digital Child Pornography

Law enforcement has traditionally been slow to respond to advances in technology, and while there have been numerous efforts to stem the flow of child pornography, there are several groups that feel these agencies are not doing enough. As a result, several vigilante hacker groups have begun targeting those who manufacture and distribute child pornography. In fact, an informal contest has developed among several hacker groups with each trying to outdo the others in shutting down websites containing images of sexually abused children. Two of these organizations, cyberangels and condemned.org, have even established websites through which citizens may report child pornography. Once the groups are made aware of a possible website with child pornography, they notify the FBI and local law enforcement, as well as the offender's Internet service provider. Many ISPs claim that any individual caught transmitting child pornography will be banned, but there are some who doubt the existence of such a punitive policy (Platt, 1997). If remedial action is not forthcoming, the groups may take matters into their own hands, gaining access to the suspect's computer and erasing all of the child porn located on the hard drive or other connected storage media (Radcliff, 2000).

According to some of these organizations, law enforcement has rarely responded despite the fact that they were alerted early on about the problem. The fact that these cyber vigilantes are in operation has met varying response from individuals in the law enforcement community. Many law enforcement officers appear to believe that child pornography is such a horrible crime that they have no problem with hackers violating the sanctity of a suspect's computer. Others believe that to allow the cyber vigilantes to continue would merely encourage the existence of physical vigilantes, which almost all would agree to be an unacceptable action. Another problem law enforcement agencies face with the increase in vigilante hacker groups relates to evidentiary procedures. When hacker groups attack a website, the normal procedure is for the hackers to delete the contents of the drive storing the materials. Deleting information does not mean that the information is gone forever and cannot be retrieved; however, it does make it considerably harder for law enforcement to garner evidence against the alleged perpetrators.

One possible explanation for the failure of some agencies to respond could be trained personnel. Recognizing that many law enforcement agencies are not able to hire computer technicians to handle the investigations of high-technology crimes, several software companies have begun offering new tools that aid in the investigation of electronically distributed child pornography. VisualRoute is one such tool and works off the same concept as Traceroute, with Traceroute allowing one individual to track the location of another individual's computer. Visual-Route is another program that works in a similar manner and simplifies the location of a suspect by displaying an actual map and pinpointing on the map the exact location of the user's computer (Moad, 2001).

Bob Leazenby, special agent with the Wyoming Division of Criminal Investigation, scans information taken from the hard drive of a computer confiscated in a suspected child pornography case, March 1, 2002, in Cheyenne, Wyoming. Leazenby is a member of a Wyoming task force that has been recognized by law enforcement peers for its work in combating Internet child porn distribution around the world. (AP)

Another technique used in the past by law enforcement agencies involves the establishment of a "honey pot" to attract potential child pornography addicts. A honey pot is commonly used in the field of computer security to describe a website that is established solely as a means of being attractive and luring perpetrators to the site. Law enforcement officers working for the U.S. Customs Service have applied this technique, establishing a fake child pornography website. The website attracted more than 70,000 hits in the course of the first two months (Kaplan, 1997). By offering users access to child pornography, and then requiring them to sign up to swap child pornography with others visiting the website, law enforcement personnel were able to locate thousands of child pornographers by either their subscription information or their computer's identifying information. The main draw in this operation was of course access to a large porn collection. Of course the individuals did not realize that such a large collection belonged to federal law enforcement, and therefore did not realize they were being deceived until it was too late.

While tools for law enforcement use are getting easier, there still remain several non-technical problems for law enforcement officers. A private investigator in Canada uncovered proof that several supposed child pornography "investigators" were actually pedophiles who were using their job as a means of viewing child pornography at their discretion. To combat this problem, legislation has been introduced in Canada that would prohibit investigators from viewing child pornography even when they are on the job. There appears to be no documentation that supports the belief that this is a widespread problem, but it also does not appear to be merely a Canadian phenomenon. Representatives from both United States Customs and the FBI's Operation Innocent Images have each indicated that several pedophiles under watch are either active military or law enforcement (Ko, 2002).

Anti Child Pornography Legislation

18 U.S.C. 2252A regulates the possession, manufacture, and distribution of child pornography. The Act provides for a punishment of up to 15 years imprisonment and/or a fine for the manufacture and distribution of child pornography, while providing for a prison sentence of up to 5 years for the possession of such materials. The statute expressly covers the manufacture of videos, images, and documents containing children engaged in sexually explicit activity. Further, the statute specifically mentions that the use of the computer to manufacture or distribute child pornography will result in the same punishment discussed above.

While today it might seem obvious that child pornography is both inappropriate and illegal, it was only during the early 1980s that the courts upheld statutes banning the manufacture and distribution of such materials. In the case of *New York v. Ferber* (1982) the United States Supreme Court was asked to determine whether child pornography could be banned by a New York statute. At issue was whether the First Amendment protected an individual's right to manufacture and possess images and videos of child pornography. The Supreme Court ruled that the regulation of child pornography did not violate the First Amendment because there is such a great need to protect the emotional and physical well-being of children who are depicted in child pornography. As Weiss (2003) notes, this legislation has been extended to include not just displays of nudity by children but also images that display the genital areas of children in sexually suggestive poses.

The Supreme Court and Child Pornography Investigations

Another recent development that has affected the investigation of virtual child pornography is the recent Supreme Court decision of *Ashcroft v. Free Speech Coalition*, decided in 2002. Under the ruling, law enforcement officers who investigate the crime of child pornography are responsible for providing proof that the images seized are those of actual child pornography. This decision concerns the application of the Child Online Protection Act, which makes the possession or viewing of images containing those perceived to be minors engaged in sexual activity illegal. Plaintiffs successfully argued that such broad legislation had the potential to violate an individual's First Amendment rights because, under the Child Online Protection Act, many big-budget Hollywood films where adults portrayed juveniles engaged in sexual activity could be considered child pornography. By using a string of recent Hollywood films that received critical praise, but contained images of adults playing children and having sex, the Free Speech Coalition was able to successfully argue their claim.

The Court was slightly divided over the issue, with some indicating that there was a difference between the Hollywood films and what is known as "morphed images." A morphed child pornography image being a picture that appears to be a child engaged in sexual activity but upon closer inspection is found to be a false image that involved no child in the production of the materials. Instead, a computer user skilled in the use of digital imaging software has morphed a picture of a child in a harmless picture, such as a child at the mall, with a picture of a young adult engaged in sexual activity. According to the opponents of the statute, the law did little in these cases because there was no harm committed on a child. It should be noted that one of the original arguments was that the statute was designed to protect children from sexual abuse. Proponents of the law argued that the statute was designed not to limit Hollywood, where images of sexual situations were rarely depicted graphically, but to protect children. Further, they argued that the statute did protect children, not because the children were necessarily involved in the manufacturing of child pornography but because the children are harmed through the use of the child pornography. It was their contention that regardless of whether the images on the pornographic pictures depicted children or not, there was still a significant danger to the use of the material— the danger coming from the fact that the images and videos were used to groom children for sexual contact with adults and older children.

As a result of the Court's decision, law enforcement agencies that investigate crimes involving child pornography are now required to prove that videos and images do not contain adults who are attempting to portray children engaged in sexual acts. In other words, when dealing with pictures involving child pornography, investigators are required to prove that the child in the picture is actually a child and not a morphed computer image or an adult actor. While advancements in digital technology have made it possible to generate relatively good fake images that appear to be children, the technology is not so good that images cannot be discerned by law enforcement agencies. There are numerous digital techniques associated with verifying the authenticity and accuracy of photographs and videos. However, in regards to techniques employed by law enforcement agencies there are two potential methods that bear discussion here. These techniques are:

- **Pixel examination.** A pixel refers to a small box containing color. A computer screen is comprised of numerous, potentially hundreds of thousands of, pixels in order to generate pictures on the screen. The use of this technique involves using digital equipment to ensure that the image originally included in the picture has not been modified nor had additional images added. Pixel examination is accomplished by examining enlarged images and comparing the pixels to ensure that there is no blurring or smudging that would indicate doctoring. The problem with this technique is that as technology gets better, it is possible that a superior enhancement program could be developed. If this were to happen, then this technique could be removed from use if better examination programs were not developed.

- **Comparing the image to a database of images collected by the United States Customs Service.** While this method is workable, it is also problematic for at least two reasons. First, while the Customs database is exhaustive, individuals who use child pornography may engage in the manufacture of their own images, thereby rendering the Customs database useless. Second, if every state and local law enforcement agency begins to ask the U.S. Customs Service for assistance, it is only a matter of time before the agency will have to deny help because of a lack of resources.

One technological advancement that is helping with this endeavor is the development of computer forensics software that allows users to compare images they obtain from a digital storage medium with images from the Customs database, or with other state law enforcement agencies' databases. Using mathematical applications, the characters in these files are assigned a hash value. Every file that contains the same data will have the same hash value. However, modifying one portion of the data will drastically modify the hash value. Therefore, the comparing of hash values can provide sufficient evidence that an image is an actual piece of child pornography. Child pornography evidence media is hashed and the hash library from known child pornography images is compared to the evidence media. If the hash values are the same then the image is an actual piece of child pornography. If not, then the law enforcement agency must accept that the image is non-authentic or must attempt to determine if the image is merely one that has not been catalogued into the known child pornography has library. Currently, there are few who have been forced to use these techniques. Many investigators who work with child pornography report that the same images continue to turn up on suspect's computers. Therefore, once an image is determined to be an actual image of child pornography then when it is encountered again it is easily determined to be illegal. However, with the increasingly lower costs of digital cameras it may only be a matter of time before newer images developed by the pedophile become a bigger problem.

Combating Child Pornography

While it is common for individuals to believe that the only method of fighting child pornography lies in the operations of law enforcement agencies, the truth is far from this belief. Law enforcement personnel are already stretched relatively thin as it is; the result of numerous budget cuts and increases in operational duties. Therefore, the question becomes: How do we handle child pornography? Is there a method of completely removing child pornography from existence? Unfortunately there does not appear to be a method of completely abolishing child pornography. Despite the best efforts of law enforcement agencies, it should be remembered that they could not abolish child pornography before the release of the Internet. It is therefore unreasonable to believe that it can be abolished now. Where, then, does the solution to at least controlling the problem come from?

According to the operators of Operation Blue Ridge Thunder, the most effective means of preventing child pornography lies in education—a process they call target hardening. This merely means that potential victims of high-technology crimes (in this particular case potential victims of child pornography) should be provided with proper education to ensure that if they are still victims, they are not easy victims. Educating potential victims may take one of several formats, but the best education comes in the format of training seminars and publications for parents and potential victims. Numerous anti-child pornography agencies provide publications and seminars addressing the dangers of child pornography and unsolicited contact online. Law enforcement agencies should consider working with such agencies to inform the general public about the potential dangers of child pornography and the Internet. This approach is certainly cheaper if the result of these educational presentations is that fewer children are victimized by child pornographers. It is important to remember that federal law enforcement agencies that have traditionally handled the investigations of crimes involving child pornography are now finding that their focus has been shifted to matters of national security. While perhaps the agencies have not completely stopped investigating child pornography claims, they are moving away slowly.

Other individuals have recommended the use of Internet monitoring programs to protect children from predators online (Akdeniz, 1999). The majority of these programs works by denying children access to certain websites or prevent children from accessing certain software on a computer. In essence, the programs prevent users who do not have access to passwords or disabling features from gaining access to known pornography sites; sites containing questionable words (sex, nude, porn, and other more explicit terms) and file transfer programs such as Microsoft Messenger or America Online Instant Messenger. While these programs have their place in the process of target hardening, the previous chapter on hacking should have provided the reader with an understanding of how dangerous it is to rely on computer programs to police human activities. No program is completely secure and there are at least two problems with the use of these child protection programs. First, the listing that these programs rely on for operation cannot keep up with the number of Internet sites that develop over time. Despite the attempts by the software to provide updates, it is not uncommon for websites to open up on one day and then shut down on a second day. The better programs would seem to be those that attempt to ban websites based upon words used on the web pages. However, even these programs are susceptible to deception, as there are ways around the use of this software. For every child protection software package available, there is a website devoted to circumventing the protection. Children today who are using the computer are likely more computer literate than their parents and with the help of these websites can reprogram the protections to allow for unlimited Internet access. Many children are now brought up around computers. It is rare to encounter a child who cannot perform at some level on a computer today. Children are exposed to computers both at home and at school by an early age. Their parents, on the other hand, may not have ever been exposed to computers, as they were not as prominent during their formative years. More adults are learning about computers everyday, and those who have grown up using computers are now parents who are aware, but there are still many whose children surpass their computer abilities. For these individuals, battling over computer software protection may be a waste of time, and education may be more properly applied to the situation.

Conclusion

Child pornography has been used by pedophiles for centuries, beginning in the early 1800s and leading up to today. The materials are merely presented in a new and, some would argue, improved technological format. When child pornography was first released in China, the items were used as a means of satisfying the sexual fantasies of men. Today, images of child pornography still see use as a means of sexual gratification for pedophiles, but there is also a new use for the materials. Images of child pornography are now also used to groom potential child sexual victims for future relationships.

The grooming process is a multi-step process by which the pedophile desensitizes the potential child victim to sexual activities. During the early stages of the grooming process the pedophile will approach the child in order to discuss some aspect of the potential victim's life or interests. Following this phase, the pedophile will begin sending images of soft-core pornography to the child. These materials, while many are not even sexual in nature, are used as a means of convincing the child that it is acceptable for adults and children to interact. Once the pedophile is sufficiently convinced that the child is becoming receptive to the materials, the images will increase in sexual contact. Eventually, the images will contain images of children having sex with each other. Once again, these images are used as a means of convincing children that the activities occurring in the images are considered acceptable. At this point, the pedophile will complete the final phase of the grooming process. The images sent to the child will now normally consist of juveniles engaged in sexual activity with adults; this is of course used to remove any final emotional obstacles the child may have in regards to sexual activities with an adult. It is at this point that the pedophile will almost always attempt to arrange a physical meeting with the child, as a means of engaging in sexual activity. According to many law enforcement agencies, these cases are becoming more and more common and the frequency of their occurring do not appear to be slowing in the near future.

One of the problems with the investigation and prevention of child pornography is the fact that the materials are so easily traded via today's technology. Prior to the release of the Internet in the early 1990s, it was believed that child pornography would be completely under control within a couple of years. The public release of the Internet, however, completely destroyed this belief as child pornography increased to an even greater level within three years of the technology's release. Today, the problem has become exponentially more complicated, as well as rampant, because of increases in digital imaging and high-speed Internet connections. Technology is now at a level where child pornography may be created, copied, and disseminated by almost anyone willing to invest a few hundred dollars. Further, the images can be copied and disseminated for almost no fee.

The courts have ruled repeatedly on legislation concerning the protection of children. Investigators who handle high-technology crime investigations are now required to prove more than just the presence of a criminal act; today, they must prove that the images involved in the criminal act are indeed actual images of child pornography. While the technology has not advanced to a level where this authentication is difficult, the constant improvements are enough to convince many that there is a very strong potential that future imaging software packages will provide pedophiles with superior images.

Review Questions

1. Discuss the history of child pornography. More specifically, how were the materials used in the past and how are they used today?

2. What is the grooming process? What are the steps in the process?

3. Legislators have worked to make the manufacture and distribution of child pornography a crime. Discuss some of this legislation.

4. How have some online organizations handled the problem of child pornography on the Internet? How has law enforcement responded to these activities?

5. What have many researchers begun recommending as a means of reducing or controlling the child pornography problem? Is this an effective technique?

Further Reading

Casanova, M. (2000). "The History of Child Pornography on the Internet." *Journal of Sex Education and Therapy*, 25, 245-252.

Sanders, E. (2001). "Children's Online File Swapping Often Yields Porn, Report Says." *Los Angeles Times*, 07/28/2001.

Online Resources

Condemned.org—organization that provides information on how to handle reports of child pornography on the Internet. Available at www.condemned.org.

Florida Department of Law Enforcement—very comprehensive website that contains information relating to child pornography and the problem of "traveler cases." Available at www.fdle.state.fl.us.

Kidsap Organization—provides information on how pedophiles are using the Internet to solicit sexual acts from minors. Available at www.kidsap.org.

United States House of Representatives Report on Children's Access to pornography Through Internet File-Sharing Programs. Available at www.house.gov/reform/min/pdfs/pdf_inves/pdf_pornog_rep.pdf.

Chapter 5

Financial Fraud and Con Artistry on the Internet

Thanks to the opportunities provided us by the Internet, many businesses are now moving their operations "online," or at least are adding an Internet component to their physical world business. After all, how many large, retail department stores do not maintain an Internet presence of some sort? How many service industry businesses allow consumers to access information via the Internet? There are not many that do not, as these companies have realized the potential the Internet provides for increasing customers. Recently, the Internet has even seen an increase in small, local businesses developing a presence on the World Wide Web. Think back to the last time you typed in a search related to a criminal justice related topic. Were there not many lawyers and small law firms represented? Interestingly enough many of these individuals post information that will be received by individuals who are outside the practicing jurisdiction of the attorney or the law firm.

With these increases in Internet business, there have been many new frauds to develop that employ Internet technology. Two of the more commonly encountered, and interesting, online fraud schemes involve online auction fraud and the purchasing of wives and prostitutes online. Online auction fraud refers to fraudulent sales or purchases from Internet auction sites. The purchasing of wives and prostitutes is one of the newer developments of online fraud, and involves the fraudulent activities of mail-order bride and escort services. Each of these activities will be discussed in the following sections.

Online Auction Fraud

In the past five years there has been another incredible movement in regard to consumer purchasing—the online auction. Online auctions have combined the availability of the Internet with the human nature of consumers to spend as little money as possible. There are several online auctions websites, but two of the more popular sites are Yahoo Auctions, hosted by Yahoo.com and eBay Auctions, which is hosted by eBay.com. Internet auctions in the past have proven that anything can be sold on the Internet because there is always someone willing to purchase odd collectibles and materials. Several of the more ludicrous auctions are:

- The man who offered to sell his family online to the highest bidder. Here, the man promised that the auction bidder would receive a happy family ready to spend holidays and family events with the winner.

- The sale of an island. Apparently, an island located off the coast of the United States was offered for sale. The location of the Island was ideal for the development of a remote casino resort.

- Escort services. Escort services were auctioned for a brief period, with the winner to receive an "unforgettable afternoon" (Lieberman, 2001).

There are of course legitimate auctions conducted daily as well. These auctions work by allowing consumers to select screen names that will grant them access to bidding and auction watch services. Once a screen name is accepted, the consumer is allowed to search through the items available for auction. The larger auction sites will allow users to search either the entire site or to search only the sections believed to contain the most auctions for items you wish to buy. Yahoo Auction and eBay, for example, allow users to search subsections devoted to vehicles, books, movies, or memorabilia. Once a consumer finds the item they are looking for then they are allowed to examine several important pieces of information.

First, the item screen allows the consumer to examine the screen name of the individual who is selling the item. From here, the consumer can also determine how much longer the auction is scheduled to continue. For those who have already engaged in online auction activities, many have discovered that by waiting until the end of the auction, the price can be kept to a minimum. Second, this section contains information on the rating of the seller. Here, the consumer is presented with information on how other auction site consumers and sellers feel about the individual selling the item. This feedback can come in the form of both positive and negative reports, with a number displaying the amount of external comments made about the seller. By selecting the highlighted number next to the seller's name, information related to what others have said about the seller will be displayed. If the consumer merely wants to know the percentage of individuals who have responded positively about the seller, then they must merely examine the section beneath the seller's name, where this information is easily provided. Of course the problem with this system is that eBay itself is not involved in the process, meaning that a user could create various screen names and then just give himself good marks for past service.

After reviewing this information the consumer will determine whether they wish to bid on the item or not. By clicking on the "submit" button, the consumer is taken to a screen where they enter the amount they are willing to pay for an item. The maximum dollar amount a consumer is willing to pay is used so the auction software can act as a proxy bidder. For example, if we are willing to pay $15.00 for an item, and the item is currently selling at $8.00, we will enter that we will pay the $15.00. If no other bids are received for the merchandise then the software bids no more for us, and we win the auction with a bid of $8.00. However, if someone else attempts to bid $10.00, the computer will automatically increase the bid to $11.00 and indicate that we are the high bidder; this is used as a means of convenience so consumers do not have to spend unreasonable amounts of time in front of the computer. The consumer merely enters what they are willing to pay for the item and then checks back throughout the auction period to ensure that no person has made a higher bid.

Once the auction is over the winner is alerted via e-mail and arrangements are made for payment and shipping. There are several companies that provide services to frequent auction bidders. These services allow users to merely indicate who the money is transferred to and what their e-mail address is for confirmation. The buyer's credit card is then charged only for the amount of the purchase (plus shipping and handling, of course). In an ideal situation, the individual will then mail the item off. The truth, however, is that many times the ideal situation is not what is found.

Twenty-five-year-old Robert Beck of O'Fallon, Missouri, sits in front of his computer, on March 19, 2003. Beck ignored his distrust of online auctions and paid $1,900 for a top-of-the-line home-theater speaker system. It never arrived. Detectives say the sellers scammed at least 500 people of more than $100,000. The victims blame eBay's anti-fraud software. (AP)

There are thousands of horror stories related to merchandise ordered but never received by the consumer. Further, there have also been situations where the money was never sent to the seller. The latter version of auction fraud fails to warrant serious consideration in this section because the failure to transfer the money will normally result in the individual in question not mailing the merchandise. Rarely will a seller be convinced to mail the materials before they receive some form of payment. When a consumer fails to pay for the materials they allegedly won, the seller is merely inconvenienced by the need for re-advertising the position. The true problem of auction fraud lies in the former scenario where the consumer has paid for the merchandise but has yet to receive the materials. What is the consumer to do? Do they merely write off the loss?

The larger auction sites are aware of the problem of auction fraud, and many of the companies have begun offering advice and services related to handling instances of fraud. For example, the following discussion will involve the recommendations available from eBay in regard to how to handle cases of fraud:

- Attempt to persuade the seller to send the merchandise or a refund. At this stage, it has been recommended that the buyer contact the seller using his or her e-mail or telephone number. If, within 14 days, there have been no advances toward solving the problem, there are three approaches to employ, with each depending upon the situation. A third-party dispute resolution company can be used as a means of convincing the seller to finish the transaction. This approach may be useless, so there is also the possibility of contacting the buyer's credit card company. Many credit card companies offer special protection for materials purchased via the Internet. Finally, the shipping company can be contacted. While this may seem like an odd solution to the problem, conversations with the shipping company may become important evidence later. Occasionally, fraudulent sellers will attempt to convince the buyer that the materials have been shipped and that there is no need for worry because the items are on their way to the buyer; this is not normally the case.

- Notify eBay. If a seller has paid for the materials and they have not received the item, or if they receive an item that is not what they bid on, then eBay asks to be notified. At this time, the buyer will file a fraud alert that will act as a formal complaint against the seller. This information is provided to others in the future who may consider bidding on items offered by the fraudulent seller. Further, this form is required as a precursor to filing a protection claim for financial reimbursement.

- File a protection claim. Buyers who have already contacted their credit card company and have filed an online fraud alert are eligible to apply for a protection claim that will help to determine how much, if any, financial reimbursement eBay will provide. According to eBay the majority of the items are covered up to a $175 limit. The requirements are stringent in that the buyer's credit card company has to be notified and the protection claim must be requested within 30-90 days of the ending of the auction.

- Notify law enforcement. This is considered the final step and involves notifying either a local law enforcement agency or a report with the United States Postal Inspection Service. There is also the option of reporting the incident to the

National Fraud Information Center. Traditionally, there was little point in reporting the incident to local or state law enforcement agencies, but in recent months more agencies are willing to handle such investigations.

Once law enforcement is notified, the question becomes how to locate the seller and confirm their identity? The larger auction websites require verification, normally through a credit card, before any item is allowed to be sold. However, there may be auction websites that do not provide information that is as thorough. In this case there are several ways of approaching the investigation. The first method involves ensuring that the individual's registration materials are in fact accurate and that the individual accused of failing to provide merchandise is in fact the individual guilty of the criminal act. If it is discovered that the registration materials are, in fact, bogus, then the investigation will turn to the electronic communications between the buyer and seller.

According to eBay's guidelines, by the time a buyer has notified law enforcement, there should have been a number of communications between the buyer and the seller. If the buyer maintained these e-mails, and in many cases this may be a problematic issue, then an investigator can examine those e-mails to determine where the individual messages were sent from. The exact procedure for tracing electronic communications will be discussed in detail in chapter seven, but suffice to say that it is possible to trace a majority of electronic communications back to their source. With this information, the investigator may begin filing the necessary legal paperwork to visit the seller for further evidence of the criminal activity.

Of course, there is one problem associated with preparing and executing the search warrant on the seller's home. Many times the buyer and the seller do not live in the same state, and it is rare indeed outside of larger metropolitan cities that the buyer and seller will be from the same municipality. Therefore, there comes the issue of jurisdiction. While this should not be a major concern, as most law enforcement agencies are willing to help each other, there are some factors that need to be considered. For example, the investigator from the location of the buyer should not expect the burden of preparing the legal materials to fall upon the investigators and personnel in the cooperating agency. These agencies will most certainly disagree with such an attitude, and even worse the agency may have never handled a case involving an Internet fraud case and may not have the personnel to handle such a request.

Assuming that we now have the cooperation of the authorities in the seller's community, what is our next step? What materials do we want to seize? What charges will be brought against the seller? Because the alleged crime involved an Internet auction, it will be important to seize the computer to obtain Internet-related evidence stored on the seller's hard drive. This evidence may consist of pictures of the item taken by the seller and uploaded to the auction site, communications between the buyer and the seller or remnants of the auction web page stored on the seller's hard drive. All of these items are important components of proving that the seller did, in fact, intentionally deceive the buyer. As to the exact charges to file, this will differ from state to state. However, many states have statutes that govern fraudulent selling practices. As such these statutes would normally qualify for use an auction fraud case in much the same manner as if the case had involved a traditional transaction between buyer and seller.

Buying Wives and Prostitutes Online

Both the process of purchasing a wife through a mail-order bride service and the process of soliciting a prostitute have been around for years. In fact, prostitution has been labeled "the world's oldest profession." Neither operation, however, has traditionally been considered a criminal activity involving the Internet. In recent years this has changed, as more mail-order services are maintaining online catalogs and contact information. Prostitutes are also maintaining a presence on the Internet, with the majority of the ladies referring to themselves as escorts and charging an exorbitant fee for their company. The Internet is now plagued by mail-order bride websites, with some placing the number of such sites at well over 30,000. The number of escort websites is unknown, but more than likely these sites equal or surpass the mail-order bride websites. Some may question if there is any difference between a mail-order bride and an escort? Aren't they almost the same?

According to those who use the services of mail-order bride companies, the companies are far from being the same as an escort service. To those who have not used the services of either company they do appear to be similar. Perhaps a brief discussion of how these operations work should be undertaken at this point. Mail-order bride services work by arranging "dates" for women in foreign countries who desire to meet and marry a male citizen of another country (many times the other country is the United States). These weddings are often used as a means of ensuring that the women may stay in the United States and therefore leave a country that may be undesirable. In return for leaving their native land they agree to marry the man in the new country. There are a small number of people who believe that not all of these women are desperate to leave their country and are using the service merely as a means of meeting men. The fact that the majority of these women marry men in the United States, or whatever other country, is perhaps the only justification for distinguishing between mail-order brides and prostitutes.

Prostitutes, on the other hand, use the Internet to arrange dates with men who will, in turn, pay them for their company. While many of these women arrange these dates using titles like that of "escort," the majority of these women do, in fact, meet the definition for prostitute. There is money exchanged and the women provide a service, with the amount and types of services being provided varying from individual to individual and agency to agency. With the power of the Internet many of these women are now moving away from agency-related dating services and are operating as individual entities. In the following section we will discuss each of these acts in more detail.

Mail-Order Bride Services

The concept of a mail-order bride is not new. According to one mail-order bride company, Natasha Club, the procedure began centuries ago when settlers would write back to their homelands for a bride. The concept survived over the years, and in 1980 the industry underwent a massive re-emergence. It was during this time that American men became interested in mail-order brides from areas such as the Philippines, Thailand, Japan, and China. Bridal agencies began to spring up into existence, offering to simplify the process of obtaining a wife from one of these countries. These agencies assembled printed catalogues containing the pictures of women who were available to interested American men. For a small fee, these men could contact these women via information provided by the bridal agency. The business gained notoriety and before long there were mail-order bride agencies springing up across the United States and around the world. With the influx of mail-order brides, the Immigration and Naturalization Service is credited with reapplying the phrase "mail-order brides" to describe the women coming to the United States from around the world.

In the early stages of this resurgence, it was Asian women who were most requested by American men. However, during the 1990s, the Soviet Union collapsed and the market began to shift away from Asia and into Russia. With the fall of the Soviet Union there developed a series of states where women who so desired could leave their homelands. The catch was that, in order to leave permanently, these women would have to marry Americans who would, in turn, bring them to the United States. Many American men began to believe that Russian women were more beautiful than women from Asia and the Pacific areas. Additionally, it was stated that Russian women were more culturally similar to Americans than were Asians, and the language barrier would play less of a role as Russian women could learn English faster than Asian women. This discovery resulted in even more mail-order bride agencies beginning operations, many specializing in the arrangement of marriages for only Russian women.

The development of the Internet revolutionized the way these agencies conducted business. First, there was little need for the use of mail-order catalogues, which were incidentally expensive to print and costly to mail out. Now, interested men could visit a website and thereby gain access to more of the materials and information on international women. While Natasha Club still claims that American men are fascinated with Russian women, there are a number of websites in operation today that involve Asian women, Russian women, African women, and almost any other nationality. Basically, any women who desire to leave their homeland may employ the use of a mail-order bride agency. It is worth noting that there is an abundance of Russian women available on mail-order websites. For example, on one Asian mail-order bride site, there were 300 available women listed. The Russian mail-order bride company, Natasha Club, boasts of more than 2,000 Russian women waiting to meet American or European men.

The term mail-order bride is considered extremely derogatory by those who are engaged in the business, and is especially frowned upon by the women who participate in the program. From the standpoint of these women, the use of the term "mail-order bride service" is quite hurtful. Perhaps these feelings of resentment or anger come from a general lack of understanding how these agencies operate. Generally, a man will log onto one of the mail-order websites and begin looking through the online catalogue of available women. When a suitable young woman is located, the website will offer to provide contact information for that woman. The price for access to this information varies from company to company, but has been seen for as low as $9 per contact number. It is recommended by the majority of these bridal agencies that men select more than one woman, just in case she is already communicating with someone else and is not ready for another relationship.

If the young woman selected is interested in what the man has to say, then she will provide the man with her personal contact information; normally, the only contact information allowed by the agency is that of the mailing address for physical letters and an e-mail address for electronic communications. The initial letter is used as a means of convincing the young woman that there is an interest and that the man is worthy of her attention. What information do many of these women look for in their letters? The majority of the online agencies post brief biographical sketches on the website for men to examine. The bios provide information into what each woman is looking for in a man. Some of the more commonly desired traits are:

- Men who are friendly and outgoing

- Men who love to go to the theater

- A passionate partner and lover

- A man who makes a good living and earns lots of money

- A man from _____ (some women only want to move to America or Europe, etc.)

When the woman responds and expresses interest, the two will begin communicating on a regular basis, and at some point the man may be encouraged to come to Russia and visit his new friend. Many mail-order bride agencies will sponsor entire groups of men going to Russia on "dating parties" or "dating tours" where agency representatives will arrange a series of dates with the women spanning their entire stay in the country. If the men find that the woman they have been conversing with is perfect for them, then they will begin the process of trying to bring the woman back to the United States.

Administrators of mail-order bride agencies claim that misunderstandings concerning how their industry operates impacts people's perceptions of their business. These individuals argue that their service is far from that of a prostitution service. While many individuals are under the impression that one merely selects a woman from the catalog and they are mailed to them within a few weeks, the truth is that many of these agencies merely act as international matchmaking services. Whether this assessment is accurate is questionable, as there is little research concerning mail-order bride services and their operations. If the industry currently operates in this manner, then there has been a change in ideology. The industry is not without its own problems and scandals. Mail-order bride agencies, by the very nature of their work, are ripe with potential scandal and fraud.

Mail-Order Bride Fraud

There are several types of mail-order bride fraud, ranging from scams that involve merely the women themselves defrauding men to scams that involve the mail-order bride agencies scamming money from men. Many times the women will make contact with several men and will begin talking about how much they love their letters and would very much like to meet them in person. The man, in turn will offer to provide the lady with funds for travel if she is coming to visit in the states (or wherever the meeting is scheduled). The money is sent to the young woman so that she can visit her new love, but a problem arises. After the man has sent money, the letters will oftentimes cease and the man will hear no more from the young woman. Even worse than this scenario is the situations where one woman is able to successfully defraud the same man multiple times. Through a combination of activities, the woman will convince the man that she made a mistake and that she really does want to come to his homeland and become his wife. Once again the man may be weak with desire and send more money to the young woman; many men are weak with desire on the basis of the pictures these women submit to the online bride catalogs, with the majority of these images being extremely glamorous, if not erotic.

Occasionally, these scams will also end in another discovery—the woman is actually a man. Here, a man will submit photos to a personal website or an agency website. Using the most provocative and sexually charged photos possible, these scammers will solicit money from unsuspecting men. Often the ruse to gain the money is the same as that used by women—the need for money to come visit their new love. With more than 30,000 mail-order bride agencies in existence, there is a need for better understanding of how to handle these fraud cases, but there is a bigger need yet to understand how to spot these cases.

Elena Petrova (2002), originator of a blacklist of Russian mail-order bride agencies that are notorious for scamming potential men, provided the following information on warning signs that a man may be in the process of being scammed. Petrova provides this service because she believes that less than five percent of women listed with mail-order bride agencies have fraudulent intentions, and therefore men should approach the majority of agencies with confidence. However, should any of the following warning signs become apparent, then the man should immediately cease communications and report the agency to authorities, or to the blacklist. The warning signs are:

- Contact originated from a personals website where anyone can post their ad for free. The description the woman used to describe her ideal man is a standard response indicating that race and age do not matter.

- All contact is electronic in nature and contains a new picture of the woman. These e-mails will arrive almost daily and the pictures sent will be numbered and sent in numerical order.

- Within five letters the woman has already indicated that she is in love with the man, yet she has never asked truly serious questions concerning finances or interests; additionally, the woman will mention honesty and its importance numerous times.

- From the very first communication, the woman will indicate that she is very poor and that her financial situation will not improve in the future. According to Petrova, it is also common for the woman to indicate that she is a student and has no money.

These guidelines work for one simple reason—scam artists do not read the individual communications. Because there is the possibility that one scammer may "work" more than 100 men at a time, there is no way to answer each message personally. Therefore, there are preset messages that will be sent out, and the messages correspond to the aforementioned warning signs. Another warning sign that the woman corresponding is a scammer is the repeated use of the same pictures with a different name. For example, one woman, or even one man, will post the same picture on multiple personal sites with different names.

Mail-Order Bride Agency Fraud

Occasionally, the fraud will not come from the woman the men are corresponding with but will instead come from the agency representing the women. As stated, many of these mail-order bride agencies now use the Internet as a means of more promptly providing their services. The websites list pictures and brief biographies of their women, and for a small fee the agency will sell the contact information to men. The prices for these contacts depends upon the number of contacts purchased Normally, one contact will range from $8 to $15, while purchasing multiple contacts will range in cost from $5 to $10 for each contact. Interested men will then pay for these contacts using their credit cards.

It should already be becoming more apparent to readers what types of fraud are possibly committed by these agencies. The first form of fraud involves fraudulent credit card transactions. Here, men will find that they have paid for contact information using a credit card, and months later they are still being charged for contacts they have not requested. Some agencies now also run a monthly subscription service that uses a credit card number. When a man cancels his subscription he may find that the company will continue to charge his credit card for months.

Another form of credit card fraud involves agencies sending fake contact information out to men. Here, a man may request 15 contacts, pay for 15 contacts and then only receive 10 contacts. Occasionally, the contacts will also contain information that is insufficient for the man to contact the woman. In these cases there are normally no women. These agencies also use the same pictures of women with different names; pictures can be downloaded from any of these websites and then merely renamed.

Legal Issues Involving Mail-Order Brides

Historically, there has been little by way of regulation of the mail-order bride industry. The Immigration and Naturalization Service has maintained the practice of labeling these services as mail-order bride services, and is quite aware that they act as nothing more than means to provide aliens with legal status in the United States through marriage to an American citizen. However, there is little by way of a statute that criminalizes the behavior.

There is a move toward a small level of regulation in the industry, but the legislation is geared toward protecting the women once they arrive in America more than it is designed to protect the American men from the women. The impending legislation aims to require background checks for all men wishing to obtain a mail-order bride. In recent years there has been an increasing number of mail-order brides who have arrived in America expecting to live a life they have dreamed of, only to discover that their husband is abusive drunk. The legislation will require all men who are applying for marriage with citizens from other countries to undergo a background check. Should the man be found to have committed domestic violence in the past, then he will be denied application.

Of course, the fraudulent activities involving credit card payments to mail-order agencies have the same remedies as those of identity theft. If the agency continues to make payments after the owner has discontinued service, there are means of correcting this problem through the credit card's issuer; this process will not be easy and will be extremely time consuming. If a man has sent money to his "potential bride," then the solution is not nearly so easy to consider. Because the fraudulent activity has taken place in another country, law enforcement personnel from that country are charged with either investigating the crime themselves or at least providing assistance. The current lack of international agreements concerning fraudulent financial activities could lead to a situation where an investigation will never take place. Proper care in the first place is the best solution to the problem.

Individuals who have been defrauded through one of the aforementioned mail-order bride scams, do have the option of reporting the fraudulent activity to various online reporting sites. There are Internet fraud sites that allow victims of fraud to report the type and agency responsible for the victimization, and there are specific websites designed for reporting mail-order bride frauds. Neither type of organization, however, can guarantee that reporting a website will result in the reimbursement of lost money. In fact, it is not even possible for these organizations to promise that the website or agency that committed the fraud will be removed from the Internet.

Prostitution Online

Prostitution has long been considered the world's oldest profession, and today it has found a new method of commission. In the past men were able to contact prostitutes via one of several ways. These methods of contact included reference by friends, contact via the streets or interaction through brothels. Interested men were exposed to a variety of fraudulent activities, ranging from paying for women that did not exist to paying for women who would rob them during intercourse. While today these same frauds are in existence, there are many new methods of fraud thanks to the way in which these individuals operate their businesses. The term "individuals" is used because there are now men who operate as prostitutes in much the same manner as women have historically been considered to have operated. However, the majority of prostitution operations, both online and in the physical world appear to still involve females.

Now, there may be some readers who question how prostitution can occur online? Does the author refer to cyber sex prostitution or real world prostitution? When using the term online prostitution, this author is referring to the process of soliciting sexual acts via the Internet. These women, and occasionally men, employ the Internet as a means of contacting potential customers. This does not mean that one can just access the Internet, type "prostitute" into a search engine, and receive a listing of available women. Although this method may work, typing in that particular search term will result in thousands of meaningless search returns. The Internet is used in the facilitation of prostitution in two ways. The first merely involves the use of the Internet as a means of communication between "johns," or those who solicit the services of prostitutes, and therefore warrants only a brief mention. The second use, however, involves the use of electronic communications and websites to facilitate meetings between prostitutes and customers; this use warrants a slightly more extended coverage because it is here that fraudulent activities are encountered.

Use of Internet by Customers

When we think of the Internet, it is common for us to think about the web pages that we visit to check the latest news or to shop for the latest goods and services. There is another popular aspect of the Internet that sees less coverage in the minds of everyday web users—the newsgroup. Newsgroups and message boards, which some websites referred to as online forums, are developed based upon topics and allow users to log into a private area (although there are public message boards) and post messages to each other. All other users then read these messages and responses are provided through multiple posts commonly referred to as discussion threads.

In recent years, a significant number of message boards related to prostitution have been developed. Interestingly enough, the men who are looking to solicit prostitutes design many of these message boards. The United Kingdom has one of the largest and best-known message board services that deal with this issue. In the U.K. individuals who solicit the services of prostitutes are known as "punters," the U.S. equivalent of what we call "johns." There is a website dedicated to punters and their activities, the punternet.

On the punternet website individuals are encouraged to write in and post messages concerning their encounters with prostitutes across the United Kingdom. These messages are known as field reports and contain information relating to the following:

- The date and time. Field reports indicate what time the encounter with the prostitute took place and how long the encounter lasted. The information is used as a means of determining how long a prostitute is known to spend with her customers. Attached to this section is information on the cost of the encounter, which allows other users to see if prices remain constant and to see the costs of extra time.

- The location where the encounter took place. Here, users post information relating to where the prostitute works; some women operate out of special apartments they rent for business purposes, while others operate out of agencies. Along with this information, users provide information related to how easy the place was to find, was the location secure, and was the location away from the streets or other areas with nosy neighbors or passersby.

- Description of the woman. In this section of the field report, users provide general information relating to the body of the prostitute. Common remarks involve breast size, hair color, and whether the woman, or women, was overweight or not.

- Description of the sexual act. Here, users place information relating to the actual sexual activities, including what activities the woman was willing to do and how well she performed. In this section there is an entirely new form of language, or slang, used to convey these ideas.

The punternet contains well over 25,000 field reports that can be broken down by who filed the report, which prostitute was involved in the report, or which agency sanctioned the encounter. Here in the United States there are similar websites, although none appear to be as well known as that of the punternet. These websites allow for users to post similar information, but does not necessarily put the information into such an easy-to-find format. The majority of these message boards, and there are hundreds, provide information on how to find prostitutes, how to protect oneself from being robbed by a prostitute and the average rate for a prostitute's services.

One of these message boards divides postings by country, state, and city. Contents of this message board routinely involve individuals writing in and requesting information on how to find prostitutes in a given area. The following is an example of how these postings operate.

Figure 5.1
Mock Posting

Joker1 2/10/03 14:23 Central Time Zone	I will be in the St. Petersburg, Florida area in the coming days and would like to know the best place to locate SW. I would like affordable but clean. No druggies.
MysticPie 2/10/03 16:23 Pacific Time Zone	I recommend you stay on the main streets of Washington and Lacordia. Many of the women are not as attractive, somewhere between 4 to 7, but they are generally clean and cheap. Hope you have a good time.

While the above message is not real, it is representative of many postings. Notice how the first individual (Joker1) asked for the locations of SW; this is one of the slang terms that refers to street walkers. Interestingly enough, despite the difference in cultures many of the slang terms used on the punternet are also used on the U.S message boards. The second user (MysticPie) responds by telling Joker1 where the best place in town is to meet these affordable street walkers. He or she even goes one step farther, informing him that the attractiveness of the street walkers ranges from around 4 to 7 on a scale of 1-10. Other postings have discussed the price of various AMP (Asian massage Parlors) and escort services, along with what activities the women can be expected to participate in with customers. Individuals who have never interacted with prostitutes are even provided with information on how to approach street walkers and how to ask for which service. Some postings even detail how law enforcement sting operations work and where they are more prominent in the city.

These message boards can provide a wealth of intelligence for law enforcement agencies. Currently, there are few, if any agencies that check such boards for information relating to trends in prostitution activities occurring in their jurisdictions. Many of the services are free and can be located with a little time and patience using key search terms on almost any of the Internet search engines.

The Internet and Prostitution

The exact origins of prostitution are unknown, although it is generally accepted that the act has been around since before the third century B.C. According to some historical accounts, there lived love priestesses and priests in temples, and sexual intercourse between they and believers resulted in a more intense relationship with God. During the Middle Ages, the prostitution industry changed. The Restoration resulted in prostitution houses being banned, and prostitutes being charged with criminal activities. Sexually transmitted diseases combined with the Church's regulation of the activities of prostitutes to begin changing the way society viewed the industry. Unfortunately, prostitution will more than likely continue for centuries to come, as there will always be men willing to pay for sex and women willing to sell sex.

Historically, prostitutes worked either in brothels or via the act of "street walking," which required the women to walk up and down busy avenues in the hopes of meeting men who were looking for companionship. When law enforcement began to crack down on openly operated brothels, many of these agencies attempted a new strategy; these agencies changed their operations from brothels to escort services. The difference between the two being that an escort, unlike a prostitute, was not required to have sexual intercourse with a client. These escort agencies then began advertising in telephone books and through classified ads. During the early 1990s, many law enforcement agencies were able to slow down the advertising for these agencies by convincing advertisers that the agencies were fronts for prostitution. Incidentally, there are many escort agencies that are still listed in phone books. All one has to do is merely pick up a phone book and search through the "E" section of the yellow pages. The efforts of these law enforcement agencies were undone, however, by the public release of the Internet. By the mid 1990s, more and more of these escort agencies were advertising on the Internet and maintaining their own websites discussing their activities.

These escort websites normally consist of information relating to how to contact the agency and how much the services cost. The websites will also list the various women who are working for the agency and which services each offer. For example, some women may not feel comfortable with extra women being present and others may not offer the "full service," which is a term generally used to describe complete sexual activity. One of the most commonly cited benefits to online advertising is the easy worldwide access. An individual preparing to visit New York may search the Internet for escort agencies available in the area in which they will be staying.

Escort agencies are still extremely popular; once again anyone doubting this should sign into any search engine and conduct a search. However, the development of the Internet has changed the way prostitution operations engage in business. Today, more and more women are striking out on their own and abandoning the use of escort agencies. The rationale behind this is financial; without an agency to interfere with business, an escort can keep all of the funds from their activities and do not have to pay out as much as 40 to 50 percent of their earnings to an agency.

Many of these new independent escorts maintain their own themed web pages, such as Kandie, a young woman who operates out of the Tampa, Florida area. Kandie claims that men who purchase her services are guaranteed an out-of-this-world experience that will more than justify her expenses. In regard to expenses, the majority of these women operate in much the same manner. Interested men will use either a phone number or an e-mail placed upon their website as a means of arranging a "date" with the escort. Upon arriving at the arranged meeting place, the woman's pay will be safely deposited in either a sealed greeting card or a sealed envelope. Many of the women are also under the impression that if they refuse to talk about sex then they are not guilty of prostitution; many of the websites specifically instruct interested men to not talk about sex at any time during the encounter (Kunerth & Gutierrez, 2002).

What kinds of women advertise themselves on these websites? Are we talking about traditional street walkers? Generally, women that would be considered street walkers are not the women who are placing advertisements on the Internet. The women who are placing advertisements are normally former playmates, penthouse pets, pornography stars and other similar women who are out to make good money. On average these women escorts make anywhere from $200 to $2000 for an hour of entertainment. Escorts make anywhere from 4 to 40 times that of streetwalkers for similar services. Further, the women who sell their services believe that the men who will solicit their services from the Internet will be more educated, financially secure, and respectful of their bodies. While this is generally true, there are situations where high-priced escorts are still raped, robbed, or physically assaulted. There are countless stories told by escorts of weekends with computer company executives at $20,000 a weekend. However, for every good story there is more than likely a horror story dictating a woman's abuse and suffering (Roane, 1998).

There are some former street walkers who have made the transition from street-level prostitute to high-dollar escort. These women have even gone so far as to band together and form Internet dating services, where men can go and select one of the women. The websites operate in much the same manner as escort agency websites, but the women are still free to select their own customers and they maintain all of their own earnings. Many of these women cite similar reasons for wanting to leave the streets: education and the financial situation of clients. For many women, the most important consideration is that a pimp is no longer necessary when the Internet is used to advertise services. Pimps are historically known to be physically and sexually abusive, and frequently they take large percentages of the women's earnings. This should not be construed as meaning that all pimps have moved out of the picture. There are some escort agencies that are nothing more than fronts for pimps that had the foresight to implement advertising on the Internet.

A couple of years ago there developed a new twist to the online prostitution industry. In referring back to the first portion of this chapter, the reader should remember that there was a discussion concerning auction frauds and some of the more oddly encountered items for sale on auction websites. In 1991, it was discovered that somewhere between 10 and 20 dozen escorts were selling their services through online auctions. The highest bidder was awarded "a night to remember." Along with auction websites there was also the use of Priceline as a means of peddling their services. Priceline allows users to specify how much they are willing to pay for a service (generally the service is something like a flight or a hotel) and then companies working with the website will compete to provide the lowest price for the service (Lieberman, 2001). Recent attempts by this author to locate these services on auction sites today have proven unsuccessful, but there is still the chance they exist and have merely modified their search terminology.

Unfortunately, not all encounters with these women are free from problems. Many of these online escorts actually require a deposit before they finalize a meeting arrangement, and the preferred method of payment is that of a credit card. Just as in the other frauds discussed in this chapter, there are several websites that will merely take the credit card numbers and never provide any return of service. These women merely make their living off of scheduling dates they have no intention of keeping; this activity appears to be popular with streetwalkers who have moved their operations to the Internet.

Another problem associated with online prostitution is that regardless of how much more professional the women appear to be on their websites, the majority are quite the opposite of what they hold themselves out to be on the Internet. Men who solicit the services of these women have found that they have been robbed when they return from the shower and their wallets or car keys are missing. One individual on a message board actually discussed the anger and embarrassment he suffered when the woman stole his wallet and his clothes so that he could not come after her. Reporting the crime was delayed because he had to find clothing and then explain how this woman, whose real name he did not know, had gotten into his bedroom at the hotel.

Finally, there is a form of fraud that is less financially or physically threatening, yet still maintains a cost to the victim. Occasionally, an individual may schedule a date with one of these women on the basis of their website, only to discover when the woman arrives that she is not who she appeared to be on the Internet. Some women will use "flattering" photographs or photographs of other women as a means of attracting men to their service. However, when the time for the date arrives, these other women will show up claiming that the original girl got sick and that she is there to fill in and show the man a good time. Rarely is there a price difference and these men are then forced to pay for the services of a woman they were not interested in the first place.

Law enforcement agencies in larger metropolitan cities have begun investigating claims of Internet prostitution, but unfortunately the investigations are only small-scale operations when compared with traditional prostitution stings. Part of the problem with this is perhaps the requirement of understanding how to contact prostitutes who advertise on the Internet, and the other part of the problem may lie in the fact that few individuals are trained to handled investigations that occur on the Internet. In Chapter 7, the reader will be introduced to online sting operations and the difficulties associated with conducting such an operation. Another reason for such a small number of investigations could be that prostitution is a vice crime that is rarely investigated unless there is a complaint about the activity. How many individuals are going to complain to law enforcement that they found an online prostitution website? Probably very few.

Many of the investigations involve having officers go online and make "dates" with the escorts. Investigators converse via e-mail and if the women live within their jurisdiction they will arrange a date with the woman. Occasionally, an escort may be operating from outside the jurisdiction of an agency. When this occurs the agency has two options. One is to contact a law enforcement agency within the jurisdiction of the escort's operation. The second option is to inquire as to whether the escort is a "circuit girl." The term circuit girl refers to an escort who travels around the country and takes appointments at each stop. Generally, these women will follow large-scale sporting events or national events. The calendar of events is listed on the escort's website, along with contact information for gentlemen who are interested in arranging a date during her stay in the city.

The limited success of law enforcement efforts to curb online prostitution has led some to question whether efforts to stop the activity would be better spent on more productive endeavors like preventing child pornography and violent crime. Legislation concerning prostitution will always be an issue, as there are long running debates concerning the need for legislating sexual activity. Whether one agrees with the selling of sexual favors or not, there is no doubt that prostitution will continue to spread and the Internet is constantly finding greater use in the industry. Any agency that maintains operations to prevent prostitution will soon be forced to recognize the presence of Internet prostitutes and begin formulating response plans to investigate these crimes. Perhaps the answer to preventing Internet prostitution fraud lies in target hardening as well, making potential victims more aware of the danger. However, when it comes to sex it seems that rational thinking is sometimes neglected in favor of pure lust. Prostitutes know this and they work that angle when preparing to defraud a victim.

Conclusion

Fraud is far from a new activity; it has merely seen extensive modification as technology has continuously developed. Today, fraud still occurs using traditionally physical world activities, but there is also a new electronic twist to the activities. Thanks to the Internet and the World Wide Web, it is now possible for individuals desiring to commit these crimes to reach a far wider target audience. The increasing reliance on the Internet as a means of conducting business has been instrumental in the development of this mindset. The numbers of businesses that operate online are staggering, and there are new operations developing every day. Three of the more rapidly developing businesses involve Internet auctions, mail-order bride services and escort and prostitution services; each enterprise offering a wealth of goods and services along with a wealth of potential for fraud.

Internet auctions have steadily risen in popularity over the past few years, where today there are auctions for almost any type of good or service. Some auction websites specialize in items like books or computer accessories, while other websites are far more general in nature. One of the best known, if not the best known, U.S. auction website is that eBay, where consumers can bid on almost anything item imagined. In fact, it is often said that anything can be sold on eBay, and recent auctions have proven this to be an accurate assessment. In the past four years the eBay auction service has been used in attempts to sell everything from families to one individual's attempt to sell their soul.

The merchandise may be legitimate, but there are many who attempt to defraud consumers by failing to provide the merchandise at the close of an auction or will send merchandise that was not bid upon. As the frequency of these fraudulent incidences increase, there is a need for consumers and law enforcement to become more aware of how fraud schemes operate through auction websites. Consumers who are victimized have several avenues of recourse ranging from reporting the incident to the credit card issuer or reporting the incident to their local law enforcement agency. Within the last few years more law enforcement agencies have begun investigating these activities with an increased level of vigilance, but the question remains as to whether the crimes are controllable.

The mail-order bride industry also offers another opportunity for consumers to become victims of fraudulent activity. In the past there has been little in the way of regulation of this industry, and by all accounts there will not be any regulation in the near future. Legislation being discussed today refers to regulating which men are allowed to file for marriage with the women from these other countries. There is no discussion of how to prevent the fraudulent activities associated with women who solicit finances from the men they meet on chat forums and mail-order bride message boards. Further, there is the issue of how to handle international credit card fraud, which is common on some mail-order bride websites. Individuals may subscribe to a mail-order bride website and then after unsubscribing they are still billed for membership. While not physically threatening, these crimes are extremely expensive for victims when they attempt to repair the damage done to their financial accounts and their credit.

Finally, there is the crime of online prostitution and the fraudulent activities associated with encountering these women (and occasionally men). Prostitution is rapidly becoming more prominent on the Internet, with many websites acting as classified services and information directories for women who desire to sell their services at rates ranging from $200 to $2,000 per hour. Many prostitutes now prefer the Internet because of the type of customer they will encounter, with many online escorts claiming that their customers are more educated and considerate if they solicit their company via a website. The ease in which one gains access to the Internet has allowed many women to move from working for escort agencies to working as independent escorts. The fact that many of these operations involve clients purchasing an engagement with an escort via a credit card has led to a new method of fraud. Further, not all escorts are as high class as their fees may lead one to believe. There are still many escorts who will rob their clients during the course of "playing." While larger law enforcement agencies have begun investigating claims of online prostitution, there are still many agencies that have not considered the issue. These smaller agencies may be the more important agencies to consider these operations because of the potential for the operations to run out of small, rural areas.

Like many other fraudulent activities, the answer to controlling these activities may lie more in education than in enforcement. The Internet provides too many opportunities for fraudulent activities for law enforcement to investigate. The dollars spent investigating these crimes may be better spent in educating potential victims in a process known as target hardening. Prostitution and fraud has been around for centuries and law enforcement has been unable to eradicate the problems. Once again we are at a point where perhaps education must be considered over enforcement. Neither will eradicate the problem, but perhaps one has a better chance of controlling the situation.

Review Questions

1. In responding to auction fraud, what are the proper steps for handling cases of fraud?

2. What is mail-order fraud? How is the crime committed?

3. What are some warning signs associated with mail-order bride fraud?

4. Discuss the various means by which prostitution can be committed via the Internet.

5. What are some strategies employed by law enforcement agencies investigating online prostitution?

Online Resources

eBay—website that hosts auctions for a variety of materials. Very in-depth coverage of auction fraud and the steps to initiate a complaint against a seller or a buyer. Available at www.eBay.com.

TechTv—website associated with the TechTV television station. Has a variety of articles related to online prostitution, mail-order fraud, and auction fraud. Available at www.techtv.com.

Chapter 6

Emerging Crimes on the Internet

Crimes like those discussed in previous chapters: hacking, child pornography, and identity theft are crimes that have already become established on the Internet. There are several crimes that have not yet established themselves, but are rapidly becoming more commonplace in the realm of high-technology crime. It is important to note that when it is stated that the crimes are established, it means that these are crimes that everyone realizes are illegal and there are statutes that criminalize the behaviors. In this chapter we will discuss some of the crimes that are only just beginning to see increased recognition. The crimes are cyberstalking and Internet piracy.

Cyberstalking refers to the harassment and psychologically threatening remarks that lead a victim to fear for their life because of actions by others on the Internet. Individuals who are victims of this form of crime often discover that someone has become upset with them because of something they may have done online. As a result, individuals on the Internet will blast the victim with threatening e-mails, instant messages, and any other form of electronic communication. Internet piracy is an extremely new term and is used to refer to the theft of copyrighted movies, music, and software through the use of the Internet and file sharing software programs. Internet pirates are today considered to be one of the greatest threats to the music industry and a growing nuisance for the movie industry. Each of these crimes will be discussed in more detail in the following sections.

Cyberstalking

The term cyberstalking is a relatively new term, but this should not come as too great of a surprise. The term stalking, which refers to the harassment or physical threatening of a victim, has only been in use since the early 1990s. Prior to the early part of the 1990s, victims of stalking were routinely informed that there was nothing that could be done until a suspect made a physical attempt on a victim's safety or well-being. After a series of high-profile incidents concerning stalkers, California became the first state to criminalize the behavior. The original statutes, however, failed to consider a situation that could involve technology or cyberspace.

Cyberstalking refers to the stalking or harassment of a victim through electronic or digital means. Perhaps the best example of how cyberstalking occurs is the case of Jane Hitchcock, as discussed in her book, *Net Crimes and Misdemeanors*. Hitchcock was victimized by a literary agency that employed a mail bomb attack on her and her husband's e-mail account. A mail bomb is an attack where the victim is flooded with copies of the same e-mail; e-mails are generally large in file size and designed to overload the e-mail server of the victim. Victims of cyberstalkers are selected for a variety of reasons. In the case of Hitchcock, she was targeted because of a negative comment she posted on a message board concerning a literary agency. Initial attacks involved only the e-mail bombs. However, after Hitchcock changed her e-mail address the harasser continued his activities, eventually posting Hitchcock's personal information on a website where she was listed as a sexual deviant desiring to act out rape fantasies with strangers. After being alerted to the presence of these postings Hitchcock went out and learned to fire a handgun, citing a fear for her life.

Where many could have given up under the frustration of being turned down for help by law enforcement agencies, Hitchcock used her situation as a means of launching a campaign to increase awareness and support legislation concerning electronic harassment. Through a series of presentations to state legislatures and conferences, Hitchcock was instrumental in Maryland's and California's passage of legislation criminalizing cyberstalking. Following in the footsteps of these states, many others have also criminalized the activities associated with electronic harassment and cyberstalking. As of today, there are very few states that have not criminalized electronic harassment.

How Cyberstalkers Operate

Cyberstalking was originally considered harmless because there was little physical danger to the victim. The electronic nature of the attack led many to believe that the act was more akin to a nuisance than a threat. Unfortunately, this belief was neither true then, nor is it true today. It is believed that many physical stalkers may begin their activities through electronic means, only to continue their activities into the physical world (Casey, 2000). The tie between the physical world and the electronic world should not be hard to accept, as victims can be selected in many of the same ways. Former co-workers, classmates, and neighbors are common targets of cyberstalkers. Society's acceptance of and reliance on electronic communications have made such activities easier in the sense that a vast majority of people maintain some form of presence on the Internet, even if it is only an e-mail address.

Individuals interested in locating someone's information may not have to search very hard to locate data. Business cards that are handed out almost always contain an electronic contact address, and students of universities have their e-mail addresses listed on the university's website. If a stalker is, in fact, a business acquaintance or co-worker, then the business card will not be hard to obtain. Likewise, a classmate attending the same university will have no problem locating the web page containing the e-mail address of the intended victim. A stalker interested in a victim that does not fall into either category may still locate electronic contact information via the Internet. If a victim maintains a web presence there is almost always a copy of the e-mail address somewhere in cyberspace. A simple search utilizing Google or Yahoo may be all that is necessary.

Once the electronic contact information is obtained, then the stalker may take one of many actions in harassing the victim. Three of the more commonly employed tactics involve e-mail bombs, forgery of messages, and the posting of harassing messages online. The e-mail bomb and the forgery of messages were illustrated in the Hitchcock case, but the final method of attack, while less discussed, can be a serious incident. When a stalker attacks a victim with an e-mail bomb the threat or attack is easily discerned, in that the victim receives so many e-mails that they are unable to check their e-mail without effort. However, when someone posts a forged message or posts a harassing message on a message board, there is an additional consideration—whether the individual meant what was written.

When someone posts a harassing message on the Internet, it is easy for those who read the message to merely dismiss the contents and move forward. However, to the individual the message is addressed to, the situation is many times taken very seriously. The problem is that for cyberstalking or electronic harassment to be proven many statutes require the victim be capable of proving that they are in fear for their safety. With this in mind, how can a victim prove a concept such as fear that does not have a physical boundary? Some individuals may respond that if an individual is scared for their life then they are in fear; however, in the eyes of the court this level of fear may not meet scrutiny. A few years ago there was a law enforcement officer who discovered a message posted on the Internet in which individuals asked others to kill the officer. The officer contacted authorities in the area where the website was maintained, but the court found that the website was such that a reasonably prudent person was not capable of fearing anything posted.

Was the judge correct? If not, then how can it be proven that a victim was truly in fear of their life? One method of determining whether a threat is only perceived or is in fact legitimate may involve examining the frequency and content of the message. Take the previous example of the law enforcement officer. Was the message posted on the Internet so general in its content, that the message only mentioned a desire for the officer to die? In the case at hand, a well-trained and experienced defense attorney could plant doubt into the minds of the court as to whether the message was legitimate. However, should the message have contained dialogue concerning a desire for the officer to die, and then also contained the officers name, address, telephone number and schedule of activities, then the same attorney may find it more difficult to discount the officer's fear. Similarly, if there is one message posted concerning the wish that the officer die, then it is easy to discount. If there are 20 to 100 messages, all repeating the same request for the officer to die, then discounting the message would be much more difficult.

Cyberstalkers, once they have chosen their victims and have established their method of assault, will normally take advantage of one of the Internet's greatest benefits—anonymity. While complete anonymity is almost impossible given the nature of computers and networks, there are many methods of delaying identification on the Internet. E-mails and message board postings can all be easily faked, thereby initially leading blame away from the actual suspect. E-mail forgery takes only a slight amount of computer skill, or a program obtainable via the Internet. If properly done, the message will appear to come from a forged site, and any attempts to send e-mails to the stalker or harasser will result in the forged e-mail site receiving the messages.

As stated, however, it is hard to remain completely anonymous. Through analyzing the header information of an electronic communication it is possible for law enforcement agencies to locate the source of forged e-mails. Message boards work in a manner similar to e-mails, but can many times be forged with even less effort. Many message boards require users supply information relating to an e-mail address, but there is no confirmation that the address is correct. A stalker could easily insert someone else's information into the registration form and any contacts sent in response to a message would be directed to an unknowing user.

Another development in electronic communication that warrants discussion in this section is the use of anonymous remailers to send out harassing electronic communications. As electronic communication has become more accepted, there are many privacy advocates who have argued that the tagging of messages with information in the headers violates a user's right to privacy. Anonymous remailers have developed in response to these concerns. These services work by allowing messages to be routed through their computers. During this process of routing, the headers containing information that could be used to identify the original sender are stripped from the message. Individuals who use these services present a new problem for investigators because the effort required to locate an individual utilizing such a service is considerably greater than the efforts necessary to locate an unskilled individual. However, this does not mean that individuals cannot be located if they use these services, only that locating the suspects takes more time. The remailer service must keep a log of activity, and with the proper legal process the information can be obtained by an investigator. Because of privacy concerns, these services will not normally work with a law enforcement agency without a search warrant or court order, but if prompted they are required to provide the information.

The Law Enforcement Response to Cyberstalking

In the past, reports of cyberstalking were handled in much the same manner as were reports of identity theft. In other words, victims were either turned away from law enforcement agencies or informed there was nothing that could be done. Victims were routinely told to stay off the Internet if someone was harassing them via the computer. Recent statutory changes have brought forth a realization that cyberstalking is a dangerous crime and warrants serious consideration by law enforcement officials. Following Maryland and California, many states have either added statutes related to cyberstalking or have modified pre-existing statutes to cover harassment through electronic or digital means. Today a majority of states now have statutes relating to the crime, but there remains an obstacle—awareness. Some personnel in law enforcement agencies still maintain the view that electronic harassment is not a problem serious enough for concern. Increasing concern and understanding among law enforcement personnel will be instrumental in combating this form of high-technology crime.

For investigators who elect to investigate these crimes, then it is important to remember that cyberstalking is not so different from stalking in the physical world. An investigation involving a case of cyberstalking should begin with an examination of the victim's neighbors, classmates, and co-workers. It should be kept in mind that,

Tennis star Anna Kournikova listens to her attorneys Brian James, center, and Steven Chaykin, left, February 23, 2005, in Miami-Dade County Circuit Court in Miami. William Lepeska, who was accused of stalking Kournikova in person, by mail, and on the Internet, was ordered Wednesday to permanently stay at least 1,000 feet away from her if he gets out of jail. Lepeska was detained in a psychiatric unit on $250,000 bond. (AP)

unlike physical stalking, there is one benefit to investigating a case of cyberstalking—the digital evidence trail. The digital evidence trail refers to digital evidence that is left behind during the commission of an electronic crime. In the case of cyberstalking, the stalker has left behind a trail leading back to the computer where the messages were originally sent. Examining how the cyberstalker has operated will assist the investigator in tracking the suspect.

If the victim has been receiving e-mails and only e-mails, then it is possible that you are dealing with a stalker of limited skill. This means that the investigation may be no more complex than locating the cyberstalker's Internet service provider through the utilization of tracing techniques discussed in later chapters. However, if the victim has received e-mails, instant messages, and had forged messages posted to message boards, then it is likely that a more advanced stalker is operating. Individuals who are capable of forging messages to bulletin boards, while not necessarily considered technical experts, are more likely to understand that e-mails can be traced and will therefore likely employ the use of a remailer service.

While the use of a remailer does not completely prevent location of a suspect, there are questions remaining as to how long remailers will continue to provide necessary information. As the debate over legislation of cyberstalking has heated up, so too have the arguments concerning the criminalization and removal of free speech that comes with regulating threatening or harassing speech. One of the more interesting arguments to develop from these debates is the belief that cyberstalking is leading to a form of censorship for women. The reasoning behind this belief appears to stem from the belief that women are the most sought out victims. While it is true that women are targeted at a high rate, it is worth noting that men can just as easily be victims of cyberstalking. If women are being censored, then so are men. However, the truth is that censorship is not a result of these actions, but rather increased awareness is a result. With increased awareness, it is possible that some may feel they are being censored as it is recommended that individuals limit the amount of information that is placed on the Internet. The maxim concerning hacking rings true in regard to many other high-technology crimes as well—no computer and no information is safe when it is placed on the Internet. Despite the best efforts of professionals, the Internet was not designed to be secure; it was designed to be a communication and research tool. The only way to secure personal information 100 percent is to not put the information in cyberspace.

Internet Piracy

Over the past several years, the music and video industries have undergone dramatic changes. Like many other areas of life that have undergone change in response to advances in technology, purchasing movies and music has moved to the Internet. No longer are consumers required to wait in long lines for hours or even days while attempting to obtain the latest releases. Today, one merely has to connect to the Internet and begin downloading their favorite forms of electronic media—all of which can be accomplished without leaving the warm confines of their homes.

It is now believed that as many as 3 million users are online at any given time, swapping music at a rate of 2.6 billion songs per month and movies at a rate of 12 to 18 million per month. As a result of such wide-scale digital piracy it has been stated that songwriters are now losing $240 million a month to Internet piracy. However, if the problem continues on unchecked, it is believed that by 2005 this figure could approach $3.1 billion a year (Gillen & Garrity, 2002).

There are constantly raging debates concerning whether others are being harmed by the frequency of online file sharing. For example, Hollywood insiders fear that online sharing of movies will result in a sharp decline in box office sales. However, those who support file sharing programs have countered this argument and claim that file sharing will impact only the sales of videos and digital versatile discs (DVD) in the near future. According to these supporters, there will be no decline in box office sales because people will always enjoy taking in a movie in the theater. The downloading of sharing of digital movies is of course cheaper than the purchase of tickets to the box office; however, the fact is that people will always enjoy the face-to-face contact with peers that can only come from seeing a movie in a theater.

Within the past three years the discussion of file sharing through the use of software known as peer-to-peer networking, or P2P as the software is commonly referred to in trade literature. The vast majority of the coverage, however, has contained discussion of theories generated by those in the music and movie industry, and have therefore been considered by many to be one-sided and lacking in the presence of true empirical research. Many of the articles written in the past year have criticized universities for security policies and usage policies that have been described as "weak" or "lacking." There appears to be a belief that universities have become breeding grounds for Internet piracy. While there is little in the way of support for this argument, it is probable that this belief comes from the fact that universities are notorious for having open access to high-speed Internet connections, a fact that has in the past resulted in making universities attractive targets for hackers and other technologically savvy attackers. However, in the case of file sharing there is considerably less need for hiding one's identity, which is one of the draws to the university computer's open access, and with each passing day the university's high-speed Internet connection provides less attraction as similar high-speed connections are made available to individuals by Internet Service Providers. In an attempt to better facilitate an understanding of how the Internet is used in the commission of piracy, and how the criminal justice field can counter the growing problem, it is first necessary to briefly examine the development of the software and technology that contributes to these activities.

History of Peer-to-Peer Networking

The concept of peer-to-peer networking is not foreign to those involved in the fields of computer science and networking. The networking protocols that make up the Internet were designed to allow for the sharing of files and resources among computers. In fact, it was the need to share resources that led researchers at the Massachusetts Institute of Technology (MIT) to develop the early forerunner of the Internet, the ARPANET-Advanced Research Projects Agency Network.

Having read the previous sections, it is important to note that there are several legitimate uses for peer-to-peer networking programs. The problem is that few people employ the software for legitimate business-related reasons. With the recent media frenzy concerning the illegal use of the software, there is little doubt why peer-to-peer software has become synonymous with the violation of copyright law. Today, there are probably few people who are even aware of the software's origins, as there is a general belief that the technology was developed as a means of transferring music, movies, software, pornography and other digital forms of information. Perhaps one reason for this association with the term and the criminal use of the software is that of the Napster software, which is regarded as the originator of file sharing. Napster was developed by a college dropout and released in the late 1990s. The software's developer was 19 years old at the time he wrote the software, and he wrote the software as a means of swapping music files that were stored on his computer. Napster was the first file sharing program to take advantage of the fact that audio files, and more specifically music files, could now be stored in a manageable file format, the new MP3 format. The greater compression of audio files accomplished by the MP3 algorithm also allowed for faster file transfers via telephone lines.

The abbreviation, MP3, denotes motion pictures group audio layer 3, and is a compression algorithm that allows for compression of audio files at a rate of 10:1 or 12:1. The MP3 algorithm works by stripping away portions of an audio file that is inaudible to the human ear, in a process known as perceptual audio coding. The value of MP3 compression became immediately apparent with the release of the first version of the Napster software. Prior to employing the MP3 compression algorithm, a music file stored on a computer could be as large as 40 to 45 megabytes in size, and would take around one and one-half hours to transfer over a phone line connection that was limited to a speed of 28.8 to 56.6 kilobytes a second. After using the MP3 algorithm, the same music file would be around 3 to 5 MB and would take around 8 to 15 minutes to transfer.

Users of the Napster software were required to download a program from the company's official website that would allow for access to the Napster music servers, which was a collection of central computers administered by the Napster company. Once users logged onto the Napster network they were asked which files they desired to share from their computer's hard drive. When a user established their shared folder, they were allowed to begin uploading and downloading music files. The one limitation to the file sharing allowed under the Napster software was that it only allowed for the sharing of audio files that were compressed with the MP3 algorithm.

Napster became incredibly popular in a short time. With the increased awareness of the software's existence, hundreds of thousands of individuals began using the technology to transmit audio files that were copyright protected. At Napster's highest volume of file sharing, it has been estimated that 87 percent of the files on the network were believed to be in violation of copyright law (Berger, 2001). As more people began to use the software, and more individuals in the computing industry took notice, the Recording Industry Association of America (RIAA), along with several high profile musical groups like the heavy metal band Metallica, began to take legal action. In 2000, the RIAA and Metallica filed suit against the Napster Company. According to the RIAA, the lawsuit was the result of Napster's failure to acknowledge numerous written requests to have copyrighted songs removed from their servers. Napster immediately attempted to counter the lawsuit by arguing that their situation was analogous to that of Sony in the case of *Sony Corp. of America v. Universal City Studios, Inc.* The court, however, disagreed with Napster, finding that the situation was considerably different from that of Sony in that users of Sony products were using the videocassette recorder technology as a means of viewing non-commercial programming at a later date. Napster, however, was being used as a means of circumventing copyright protections and was costing artists considerable amounts of money as fewer people were purchasing commercial music products after using the Napster software (Greene, 2001).

After Napster began to accept that they were more than likely going to lose their legal fight, they began a series of creative arguments designed to stall their eventual demise. One of the more creative arguments involved Napster alleging the record industry had failed to provide sufficient proof of which copyrights they owned that were allegedly being violated through the use of the Napster software. The argument was creative in that it was later discovered that Napster knew the recording industry did not maintain these particular records in digital format. Therefore, the RIAA would have to invest time and money to transfer the information into an acceptable digital format to meet Napster's request (Pitta, 2001).

The stall tactics were unsuccessful in saving the company, but the attempts did allow for other peer-to-peer software manufacturers to begin developing new and improved versions of the file sharing software. As Napster was being brought down by the RIAA, programs like Morpheus, Bearshare, Limewire and Kazaa were beginning to aggressively gain popularity among file sharers. Because these software manufacturers had witnessed the attack on Napster, the newer file sharing programs differed from their predecessor in two primary ways. First, these programs do not operate through a central server; this means that each user is in essence running its own miniature server, which removes the software manufacturer from liability. Second, these newer file sharing programs allow users to share a wider variety of files. Utilizing the newer programs, users can now, in addition to music files, trade movies, software applications, pictures and document files. Due in part to these changes, subsequent legal maneuvers against the software manufacturers have resulted in little progress. However, should the legal maneuvers ever begin to catch up again with the peer-to-peer file programs, there are some who speculate that advances in technology may once again modify the procedure to the point where better pirating techniques will once again circumvent the legal restrictions.

The Current State of Debate

The original benefit of using the MP3 algorithm was the speed associated with downloading files compressed with the technology. Today, it could be questioned whether compression is even important to peer-to-peer file sharers, as high speed Internet access is more commonly available. Cable modems and Digital Subscriber Lines (DSLs), which are referred to as broadband Internet connections, allow for transfers of data at speeds greater than 50 times that of traditional phone modems. Both forms of broadband Internet access are becoming more commonplace in residential establishments and allow for such rapid data transfers that the time saved by using MP3 compressed audio files is becoming minimal. With this change in Internet availability, there is a debate as to whether or not the traditional target of choice for the RIAA-the university-is still even an acceptable target. Historically, universities provided an attractive source of Internet use for file sharers because they provided high-speed Internet connections. Today, however, this is not necessarily true. The RIAA does not agree that universities are no longer primary sources of Internet piracy.

In response to this criticism, several universities have begun implementing better policies concerning the use of university Internet access. Despite efforts such as these to curtail those who would misuse university computing services, the RIAA has attempted to force universities to ban the use of peer-to-peer software on university campuses. Over the past few years several larger universities have received letters indicating that they will be named as defendants in future lawsuits if they do not remove access to peer-to-peer file sharing programs. As a result of these letters, at least one university has responded by seizing computers used by university students to share copyrighted materials. The RIAA insists that they have no desire for universities to seize computers. Instead, it is their desire for universities to block access to peer-to-peer programs. In fact, the majority of universities has not begun seizing computers and has ignored the RIAA, citing that regulation of peer-to-peer programs would result in the university becoming a "spy" for the recording industry (Ostrom, 2002).

The constantly raging debates have led some to question where the answer to curving the problem lies. The issue of ethics education has recently begun receiving extensive consideration. Researchers who have studied the frequencies of file sharing have found that a majority of users do not perceive the sharing of files via the Internet to be an ethical problem (Levy, Brown et al., 2000). One of the more commonly cited reasons for not viewing such activity as unethical is the ease in which the software is available via the Internet. Few, if any, of the software applications require users to pay any type of fee for downloading or using the services. With all of the materials being free, it is easy to see how some individuals could employ this reasoning.

Recently, the issue of pay services for music and movie downloads has become a common source of discussion. Many experts in the music industry claim that the solution to preventing the problem of Internet piracy lies in instituting pay services for the copyrighted materials. Users of the file sharing software have yet to fully embrace the idea, citing that the use of the free software frequently leads to their purchase of the CDs and movies they have been downloading. Some, however, have claimed that paying a small service fee would be acceptable because the result would be file sharing in compliance with all state and federal laws. Research would seem to dispute the argument that file sharing leads to increased levels of consumer purchasing, as studies have shown that very few individuals who use P2P file sharing programs to obtain music will actually purchase music CDs.

Responses to the Problem

With increasing pressure from the RIAA, legislators have begun drafting legislation that deals specifically with the issue of copyright protection on the Internet. One such piece of legislation is that of the Digital Millennium Copyright Act (DMCA), which deals with copyrights of materials that are digital in nature. While the DMCA has received some coverage because of its mention in several high-profile copyright infringement cases, it has only been raised in a limited capacity when discussing the issue of peer-to-peer networking.

Instead, the recording industry, while arguing for better legislation, has turned to creative means of responding to the problem of peer-to-peer file sharing. For example, the RIAA has applied the use of "spoofed" files, which are files that appear to be a popular song or movie but when opened contain no content (Snider, 2002). The use of these files does little to punish those who share files, but it does result in frustration for users who devote the necessary time to download the file, only to subsequently discover that the file is a fake. Other techniques involve the use of NetPD software that allows users to trace a copyright protected file that is being traded online. The creators of the software claim that the software is even capable of tracing the file back to the original individual that posted the file, but the software has received little attention in recent months and this feature has never been verified (Masson, 2000).

Many now believe that attempts by the RIAA and programmers to develop copyright protections will be unsuccessful. Citing research conducted by Forrester Research, some researchers have claimed that the solution lies in accepting MP3 technology and developing better awareness campaigns. Because of the large number of users who share files, a situation has been created where the criminal justice system cannot handle the problem with any true level of success. The belief that enforcement by the criminal justice system is impossible has led some to argue that the solution lies in empowering the copyright holders to protect their materials. One bill introduced in the past (H.R. 5122) by Congressman Berman would allow copyright owners to remove copyright protected materials from the computers of individuals who are sharing the files online and via peer-to-peer networks. Bill H.R. 5122, which is commonly referred to as "Berman's Bill" would allow for copyright owners to interdict, redirect and spoof users who are sharing files; the problem with this aspect of the bill is that many believe the bill would allow for copyright owners to launch denial of services attacks against individual users.

Other opponents of the Berman Bill claim that passage of the bill would create a scenario analogous to that of the Wild West, where the user with the greatest technological "guns" will win. The Berman Bill may be too broad and would allow for copyright owners to hack into the computers of personal users who are found to be sharing copyrighted materials, thereby creating a dichotomy in that hacking is still criminalized under the United States Criminal Code. So, can one piece of legislation legalize such attacks against users and then in turn penalize these users when they respond to the attacks. Currently, the Berman Bill is still in Congress being debated and will likely never be passed as it currently stands.

Conclusion

In this section two emerging high-technology crimes have been discussed. While at first glance the two activities are drastically different: cyberstalking is an act that leads to fear for safety and occasional physical harm, while Internet piracy is more of a financial crime that impacts the pocketbooks of copyright owners. On the other hand, both of these acts share one similarity. Neither activity has traditionally been considered a problem worthy of concern for the criminal justice system.

Cyberstalking, while not a physically dangerous crime in and of itself, does routinely lead to the physical stalking or endangerment of a victim. As electronic communications have advanced, the problem of cyberstalking has increased accordingly. Over the last five years the criminal justice system has begun to accept that the crime is a dangerous activity and one that warrants coverage in our legal system. All but less than ten states have passed legislation regulating cyberstalking via electronic or digital means. The problem is that awareness of professionals in the criminal justice system has yet to catch up with the advances. It is increasingly important for law enforcement officers to understand the potential harm that can come from cyberstalking. Only from this understanding can more professionals undergo training to increase awareness of the problem and techniques to investigate the crime.

Internet piracy, unlike cyberstalking, is more of a financially destructive crime. However, the problem of Internet piracy is rapidly becoming the most highly debated high-technology crime of the decade. It almost appears that identity theft, the fastest growing of the high-technology crimes, is being replaced as the crime of discussion. The efforts of the RIAA have led to a situation where every day provides a new group of individuals who are ready to debate the pros and cons of trading music and movie files via the Internet. It should be noted, however, that while it is music and movies that are most often discussed in these debates, the trading of software has also become a serious problem. Legislation concerning the trading of movies and music has been slow to develop, as traditional copyright protection statutes govern the trading of such files. There has been a move for increased levels of legislation providing for the rights of copyright holders who have been victimized by file-sharers. The problem with the passage of such legislation is the declaration of open war that would come from such a law. A high-technology battle over copyrighted materials serves the best interests of no participants involved.

Based on the information available on both acts, it is possible that the best solution to combating these emerging crimes is education. Increasing awareness of how the criminal acts are committed, how victims are selected, and why victims are selected is important to developing awareness programs. Each of these crimes may be mitigated, although not completely prevented, by the victims. Of course, no matter how hard someone tries to maintain control over his or her Internet presence, there remains the possibility of becoming a victim of a cyberstalker. The fact that victims run an equal chance of being selected from the physical or virtual world assures this fact. However, education and understanding of the problems associated with sharing too much information via the Internet can reduce the likelihood of a victim being selected on the basis of their presence on the Internet alone. Similarly, education and understanding of who is impacted by file sharing via the Internet is quite possibly the only solution to slowing the increase in frequency of this crime.

Review Questions

1. What is cyberstalking?

2. Discuss the methods employed by cyberstalkers to harass their victims.

3. How has law enforcement's focus on cyberstalking shifted in recent years? Why was this shift necessary?

4. Briefly discuss the history of peer-to-peer file sharing. Was the technology ever used for legitimate purposes?

5. How has the legal system responded to the problem of peer-to-peer file sharing?

Further Reading

Golangelo, A. (2002). "Copyright Infringement in the Internet Era: The Challenge of MP3s." *Alberta Law Review*, 39 ALBERT L. REV. 891-913.

Ginsburg, J. (2000). "Copyright Use and Excuse on the Internet." *Columbia VLA Journal of Law & the Arts*, 24 COLUM.—VLA J.L. & ARTS 1-45.

Blackowicz, J. (2001). "RIAA v. Napster, Defining Copyright for the 21st Century?" *Boston University Journal of Science and Technology*, 7 B.U.J. SCI. & TECH. L. 182-193.

Online Resources

Working to Halt Online Abuse—website dedicated to informing users about harassment on the Internet; contains links to statistics concerning cyberstalking, as well as links to more information on how to respond if you are a victim of cyberstalking. Available at http://www.haltabuse.org/.

National Center for Victims of Crime—website dedicated to providing information on helping victims of stalking; contains links to information on how to respond to a stalking incident, as well as links to information on how to sue a stalker for financial recovery. Available at http://www.ncvc.org/src/.

Investigating the Internet: Examining Online Investigations and Sting Operations

Many of the crimes discussed in earlier chapters are investigated in much the same manner as any other crime. Normally someone is victimized, this person reports their victimization, and law enforcement personnel respond by attempting to locate the person who has committed the criminal act. However, some technology-assisted crimes require little, if any, physical contact with the victim. In these cases victimization occurs via the Internet. Therefore, locating and tracking an offender can sometimes be extremely difficult. Take, for example, the crime of child luring. A victim may be located in the same city, a different state, or even a different country (although this last option is the least likely, as the perpetrator generally desires to make physical contact with their victim at some time and living out of country would present an expensive opportunity). How does law enforcement go about beginning its search? After all, if there is little physical evidence, then the question becomes where to begin the search? The answer is, of course, on the Internet. Despite the common misconception that individuals are anonymous when they are surfing the World Wide Web, there are several methods of locating a suspect through their digital footprints.

Tracing a Suspect on the Internet

To understand how a suspect can be traced on the Internet, it is important to first understand how one accesses the Internet. When an individual connects to the Internet, they are not actually connecting directly into the Internet, nor are they connecting directly into the World Wide Web. Instead, they are connecting into their Internet service provider, which is often referred to as an ISP. The ISP is the company that provides Internet and e-mail services for a monthly fee. Perhaps the best known ISPs are America Online and Earthlink. When a customer dials into the system, in the case of narrow band connections like a 56.6 modem, or connects to the system, in the case of broad band connections like a Cable Internet connection or a Digital Subscriber Link (DSL), then the ISP provides the customer access to the Internet and the World Wide Web.

In order to confirm that the customer does not exceed their allotted monthly usage, and to maintain records for billing purposes, each customer is assigned a temporary internet address. This address is referred to as an Internet Protocol (IP) address, and allows the ISP to locate the customer while they are online. Each customer is assigned a unique IP address when they are accessing the Internet, thus providing each person an identifiable tag. To further simplify this concept consider the following: the World Wide Web has been defined as the Information Superhighway, and ISPs have been referred to as access ramps onto the superhighway; the IP address is then equivalent to a person's license plate when they are cruising the information superhighway. Everyone has to have a license plate, and this license number can be used to track down the vehicle's (computer's) owner.

Before continuing on it is important to delve deeper into IP addresses and how they work, as the IP address is the principle mean by which later discussions on tracking a suspect will focus. The first thing that must be acknowledged is that multiple persons can use the same IP address. While it was stated earlier that each person is provided a unique IP address by their ISP, this does not mean that the customer keeps that IP address throughout their contract with the provider. There are only a limited number of IP addresses available for use, and each address must be registered by the owner. Therefore, an ISP may have hundreds of thousands of IP addresses but have millions of customers. When a customer connects to their ISP, they are assigned an IP address that may or may not be one they have used in the past. This process of constantly reassigning IP addresses upon each connection by the customer is known as dynamic IP addressing. However, each time the IP address is assigned to a customer, the ISP's computers monitor which customer has been granted the IP address, how long they maintain the address and from where they have accessed the ISP's service. Once again, these records are used for billing purposes, as well as to provide evidence should a customer claim their Internet account has been fraudulently accessed. If the ISP has the customer's account name, the IP address, and the location where the connection was made from, then they can verify that the customer has been defrauded or that the customer is attempting to defraud the ISP. For law enforcement investigators these same records can be used to locate a subject.

Not all IP addresses are dynamic in nature. Some companies and universities have purchased blocks of IP addresses that they use on a regular basis. These companies may be using a combination of Intranet networking, which refers to the connection of computers within the same organization, and Internet networking, which refers to the connection of computers from around the world. Many of the computers on the network may keep the same IP address to simplify networking throughout the company or university. IP addresses that do not change each time they are accessed are referred to as static IP addresses. In the past, there was a belief that cable Internet users and DSL users were statically assigned IP addresses. However, this is not true for the same reason that ISPs cannot afford to allow customers their own IP address—there are simply too many persons utilizing these services today. Today, businesses and larger universities that were quick to purchase blocks of IP addresses are the most likely organizations to maintain static IP addresses.

Now that we have an understanding of what IP addresses are and how they are assigned to customers, the question is what does an IP address look like? And how do we find out who "owns" a given IP address at a given time? First, the IP address appears in the following format: ###.##.##.##. For example, a valid IP address would appear as 142.54.35.32. Depending upon the operating system that a person is using, a computer's IP address can be located using a series of keystrokes, or by clicking on an icon associated with the computer's network settings. Even if an investigator does not have direct access to a machine that has been used in a criminal act, it is still possible to locate a computer's IP address. For example, consider the crime of hacking. If a computer is hacked into, and data has been damaged or stolen, then it may be possible to recover the IP address of the suspect's computer if the individual did not erase this information from the target's computer. Once again, the type of operating system will dictate how this information is displayed.

Once the IP address is located, then the next task is to determine who owns the IP address. To prevent two separate companies from attempting to license out the same IP address, each IP address that is in use must be registered by a company or individual. There are several international registration agencies and the database detailing available addresses is linked together. This means that if a person registers an IP address in China, then that IP address is not available for a company that tries to register in America. Internet Protocol registries operate these databases. Companies that wish to register their IP addresses in North America will utilize the American Registry of Internet Numbers (ARIN). This organization maintains information on who registers an IP address, who to contact if information regarding the IP address is needed and when the IP address was registered. It must be noted, however, that these organizations do not contain records related to which customer is assigned an IP address at any given time. Records of use are maintained by the company or individual that owns the IP address. However, the use of an Internet registry is necessary to determine who owns an IP address so that the actual user can be identified through the owner's computer records.

There are several ways of accessing an Internet registry, but two of the more common methods involve the use of websites. The American Registry of Internet Numbers maintains a website where queries can be made at www.arin.net/whois. A user merely has to access the website, query the IP address involved in the incident, and click the search button. After a few seconds, a complete record of who owns the IP address will be provided. This information can then be used to contact the company that owns the rights to the IP address.

Another method of obtaining information on the owner of an IP address involves the use of the Sam Spade website, located on the World Wide Web at www.samspade.org. The Sam Spade website contains not only an IP address query, but also a series of other query options that are beyond the scope of this writing. Perhaps the best reason to utilize the Sam Spade query tool in place of the ARIN tool is the fact that Sam Spade queries multiple databases while ARIN only queries the United States database. This feature becomes important if your suspect is not operating from within the United States. Reflecting back to earlier chapters, many of the crimes discussed are so problematic because they can be committed from anywhere in the world. If our hacking suspect is operating out of China, and our IP query only considers registries for the United States, then there will be no information available on the IP address. These two services are not the only ones available, as there are several other services such as www.network-tools.com. The two discussed above, however, have been used regularly by this author and have rarely presented any problems.

Locating Information from E-Mails

Several high-technology crimes involve the use of electronic communications, with one of the most commonly encountered means of communication being that of electronic mail, or e-mail. The process of identifying an e-mail's owner is similar to that of identifying a user on the Internet; one must locate the sender's IP address and then conduct a query. So, how does one locate the IP address within an e-mail? Answering this requires a brief introduction to how e-mails travel along the Internet.

When a person addresses an e-mail, the recipient's e-mail address is inserted into the "to" line on the form. This address normally takes the form of "screename@ISP.com," the user's screen name (normally not their real name as there are too many people using e-mail today) followed by their ISP's name (e.g., America Online, MSN, Yahoo, or Google). When the sender clicks the send button, the e-mail message is routed to the ISP designated after the "@" sign. However, the message does not move directly to the intended recipient's ISP. Because the Internet is a vast network and there are so many people attempting to access information on this network, the message is delivered to multiple computers on its way to the intended recipient. Further, each computer that receives a copy of the message retains a copy of the e-mail. This is done as a means of ensuring that the message will reach its intended recipient. If, for some reason, the original message is lost during transmission, then the last computer to handle the e-mail will communicate with the next computer and resend the e-mail message if necessary. This process continues until the message reaches the server of the recipient's ISP.

While this process may seem confusing at first, it is sometimes easier to understand when translated into an example involving physical deliveries of messages. Consider if you wanted to send a handwritten message to one of your classmates who sits four rows over and three seats toward the front of the class. After composing your message you would have to find some way of getting the message to your friend. Because you are in class and the distance is too great to simply throw the message, you will be forced to pass the message along to another classmate, who in turn will continue to pass the message along. However, what if your classmate drops the message and it floats through a vent in the floor of the classroom? You have, in essence, lost your message. If each time the message was passed to another classmate, that classmate made a copy of the message, then should the message be lost it would only be a matter of the next person asking for the copy.

This is how e-mail is delivered from computer to computer along the network. While this process is of obvious benefit in preventing lost messages, it is also of benefit in tracing electronic communications. If for some reason the final computer in the chain of custody does not have a copy of the message, or if the identity of the final computer is undeterminable, then an investigator can reverse track the message through the other computers.

Now, let us return to the issue of tracing an electronic message. Every e-mail message has a header section that contains information relating to the path in which the e-mail took on its route to the intended recipient. In the early days of e-mail, early being in the mid to late 1990s, this header information was included in the text portion of e-mails. Perhaps you remember receiving an e-mail during this time and having to forward through a bunch of letters and numbers that did not relate to your actual message. Because few people actually understood the value of the header, subsequent e-mail programs have removed the header information from the text of the e-mail. This has cleaned up the text of an e-mail message but created a slight problem in investigating e-mail-related crimes. With the header no longer prominently displayed in the text it is not uncommon for a victim to bring in a copy of a harassing e-mail without this header information. As a result, the investigator asked to handle the case may find that his investigation is over before it begins if there is no more evidence.

The aforementioned discussion should not be construed to mean that there is no method of obtaining the header information. The header is removed by default, but can normally be easily revealed to a user. For example, when a user of America Online receives an e-mail there are four lines to the message. Line one is the "To" line, indicating who the message is intended for. This line should be examined because it is not uncommon for an AOL user to receive an e-mail that was intended for someone with a similar screen name. The second line contains the "From" line, which indicates who the message is originating from. Individuals asked to investigate a crime involving an e-mail should not assume that the address is the "From" line is authentic. As will be discussed later in this chapter, it is possible to forge the information contained in this line. The third line is the "Date" line and contains the date and time information related to the message. The fourth line is the "Subject" line, indicating what the message is about. Beneath this fourth line is a hyperlink, which is a word (or words in some cases) that when clicked will take you to another web page or another portion of the web page a user is currently on. In the case of the AOL message, the hyperlink is the word "Details," and this link will open a separate box that contains the header information for the e-mail.

Outlook Express, a popular e-mail utility included with many Microsoft software suites, is slightly more complicated but can be located with practice. A listing of e-mail messages is provided in the top pane of the outlook window, while the text of the e-mail is contained in the bottom pane. By selecting an e-mail message from the top pane, and then right clicking and selecting "Options," the header information can be displayed in Outlook. Other programs are similar in their operations, meaning that individuals involved in investigating criminal activity involving electronic messages should practice locating the header information in several different e-mail utilities. Many times the parents, if a child is involved, or even the victim may not be aware of how to locate this information. Merely telling the victim to bring in a copy of the electronic message in question may result in the victim returning a copy of the text message, which is almost useless for any information relating to tracking a suspect.

Examining an E-mail Header

Now, let us actually examine an e-mail header and briefly discuss each part of the header information. Located below is an example of an e-mail header sent to a victim of cyberstalking. Notice that the "from line" appears to indicate that the message is from John Smith at First National Bank.

When some people first examine an e-mail header they lose hope because it appears to be a collection of computer gibberish meant to only be read by a computer. The truth is that this is a fairly accurate interpretation. However, if you break the header down into three sections, interpretation becomes much easier. For our purposes we will refer to the three sections as Section A—Return Path Information, Section B—Routing Information and Section C—Identification Information. This examination will begin with Section A—Return Path Information. Information presented on this line is who the e-mail was originally sent from, or at least who

Figure 7.1
Sample E-mail Header

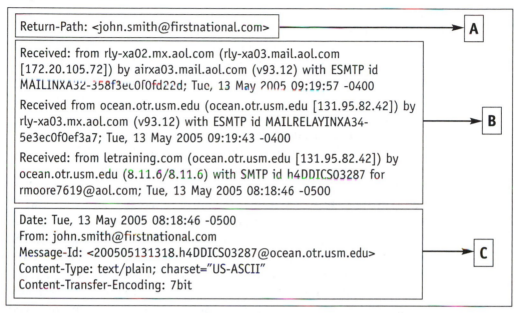

Return-Path: <john.smith@firstnational.com> ————————————————————→ **A**

Received: from rly-xa02.mx.aol.com (rly-xa03.mail.aol.com
[172.20.105.72]) by airxa03.mail.aol.com (v93.12) with ESMTP id
MAILINXA32-358f3ec0f0fd22d; Tue, 13 May 2005 09:19:57 -0400

Received from ocean.otr.usm.edu (ocean.otr.usm.edu [131.95.82.42]) by
rly-xa03.mx.aol.com (v93.12) with ESMTP id MAILRELAYINXA34-
5e3ec0f0ef3a7; Tue, 13 May 2005 09:19:43 -0400   → **B**

Received: from letraining.com (ocean.otr.usm.edu [131.95.82.42]) by
ocean.otr.usm.edu (8.11.6/8.11.6) with SMTP id h4DDICS03287 for
rmoore7619@aol.com; Tue, 13 May 2005 08:18:46 -0500

Date: Tue, 13 May 2005 08:18:46 -0500
From: john.smith@firstnational.com
Message-Id: <200505131318.h4DDICS03287@ocean.otr.usm.edu>   → **C**
Content-Type: text/plain; charset="US-ASCII"
Content-Transfer-Encoding: 7bit

the e-mail server thought the e-mail was from. The phrase "thought the e-mail was from" is used because it is extremely easy to fool the computer into believing that someone else sent the message. In the current example the e-mail was in fact sent by the author and not John Smith at First National Bank. However, the computer only knows what it is provided by the user, and the user told the computer that John Smith was sending this e-mail. It is important to examine this information and make note of the address, so that later in the examination you can compare e-mail addresses.

Section B—Routing Information is perhaps the most important section for determining who actually sent the e-mail. This section contains a listing of every computer that the e-mail message has passed through on its way to its intended recipient. Remember, an e-mail must makes its way through several computers and each computer will keep a temporary copy of the e-mail in case the message does not reach the next computer. Examining this information tells the investigator where the message has been. It should be noted that this information stacks in reverse order, meaning that the first received from message is not who the e-mail originated from, but rather the last received from message is where the e-mail originated from. In the current example the last "received from" statement indicates that the message was received by ocean.otr.usm.edu from ocean.otr.usm.edu [131.95.82.42]. The IP address provided here is the IP address of the computer that actually sent the message. Some e-mail clients have even begun making this tracking process easier by including a section labeled "X originating IP" and then providing the IP address of the computer that sent the message. Unfortunately, not all e-mail clients have become as investigator friendly.

Once the IP address is obtained, then the investigator can begin the process of applying for a subpoena, a court order, or a search warrant to obtain information on the user who sent the message. As discussed earlier in this chapter, once an IP address is obtained, then one of several registration services are used to determine what Internet service provider maintains the IP address. Once the Internet service provider is identified then the company can be contacted to provide more precise information on the customer using the IP address. The process of contacting the Internet service provider and determining what level of legal service is necessary will be discussed in detail in the next chapter.

Section C—The identification information provided in this section is important for identifying the date and time the message was sent from the suspect computer. When the Internet service provider is contacted, then the network administrator will need to know what day and time the IP address was being used by a customer. If the IP address is dynamic, then the time and date must be provided in order to determine who was using the address at that particular time. This section also contains the message ID. This is the identification information generated by the mail server when the message is sent. As the message moves from computer to computer the message ID is used to ensure that the proper message is both sent and received at both ends.

Online Investigations: Proactive Versus Reactive

In recent years there has been a growing amount of news coverage devoted to the issue of online narcotics and alcohol sales—the most popular being coverage of date rape drugs purchased in portions and mixed by rapists. However, the level of narcotics distribution via the Internet is relatively small when compared to crimes such as identity theft, digital child pornography, and cyberstalking. Each of these crimes occurs with greater frequency on the Internet and therefore involves greater levels of electronic communications. The question facing law enforcement has been whether to handle these crimes in a reactive or proactive manner. Cyberstalking and identity theft are almost always viewed in a reactive manner because a victim's compliant is necessary in order to begin an investigation. However, digital child pornography has become such a widespread problem that many agencies have begun employing proactive investigations in attempts to control the problems that develop from this activity.

Because digital child pornography is the most likely crime to be proactively investigated, a brief explanation of these investigations may be beneficial to readers. Law enforcement agencies may attempt to locate individuals collecting and distributing child pornography by spending time on the Internet under the guise of being a small child or potential victim for the groomer. Federal law enforcement agencies have been employing this tactic for years with the Federal Bureau of Investigation's Operation Innocent Images, but today several smaller municipal and state law enforcement agencies are also assembling teams to handle these investigations. Officers who work with these teams often spend either one-half or one-quarter of their work week online visiting various child-related chat rooms. A screen profile is generated for the officer that indicates he or she is a child of anywhere from six to fourteen years of age. The officer will then spend time chatting and interacting with others in the chat room in hopes of luring out a potential groomer. Groomers often employ similar techniques in creating their own screen names in such a manner that the name and profile appeals to young children within their target age.

The officer will continuously chat with various other chat room members until the groomer initializes contact. The officer will then continue talking with the groomer until a case has been established against the individual. Often this means that the undercover officer will allow the groomer to transmit images of child pornography and/or attempt to arrange a meeting. Once sufficient evidence has been collected then an arrest warrant is issued for the groomer. The groomer's ID may be discovered in one of several ways. First, during conversations the groomer's name may be revealed to the undercover officer once the individual feels they can trust the child. This may occur during the later stages of the grooming process when the individual is attempting to establish enough of a relationship for a face-to-face meeting. Unfortunately, this method of identification is rare because individuals who solicit children are often not willing to reveal their true identities to anyone out of fear of being caught. After all, these individuals are now aware that law enforcement agencies perform these types of investigations and therefore are not willing to risk being discovered so easily.

The second method of identifying the groomer involves an actual face-to-face meeting between groomer and undercover officer (who the groomer believes to be a child). The groomer will transmit a meeting time and physical description for the child/officer and the two will meet in public. When the individual arrives at the meeting point he or she is arrested and charged with soliciting a minor for sex, distribution of child pornography, or any other crimes committed by the groomer during the course of the investigation. This method is commonly employed by agencies and requires the least amount of technological skill. However, building a relationship where the groomer trusts the child, and vice-versa the child is perceived to trust the groomer, may take a considerable amount of time. Also, if at anytime the individual suspects he or she may be talking to an undercover law enforcement officer they may break contact and never be heard from again. This leads to the final means of identifying a groomer—tracking an IP address.

As discussed earlier, if an individual is connected to the Internet then there has to be a record somewhere of their activities. Law enforcement officers who work undercover and exchange e-mails and instant messages may use these communications to locate a suspect's IP address, leading to

New Jersey Attorney General Peter Harvey, left, and State Police Superintendent Col. Rick Fuentes, second from left, announce the arrest of 39 people on child pornography charges, at the State Police Computer Forensic Laboratory in Hamilton, NJ, on January 27, 2005. Charges resulted from an investigation, "Operation Guardian," in which detectives used new technology to detect child pornography files shared over the Internet. (AP)

identification of the groomer and an eventual arrest. E-mails are the preferred method of tracking an offender because the e-mail header records the information from each computer—the sender and the receiver. Instant messages, on the other hand, involve direct connections between computers. Once the message is sent then the connection is dissolved and the record of the IP address is often harder to locate. Regardless, once the IP address is located then the individual can be located utilizing the techniques discussed earlier in this chapter. This method of identification is the most technologically challenging but is also often used in cases where the groomer suspects something is wrong and breaks off contact. As long as there have been e-mails transmitted between suspect and victim then the identity of the groomer can often be determined.

While currently child pornography is the most commonly encountered crime that is proactively investigated, the widespread growth of identity theft is certain to soon result in proactive investigations of this crime. The investigations will have to be modified in accordance with the crime and it will be interesting to see how officers investigate identity theft. Of course there are already several problems associated with carrying out these investigations when considering child pornography investigations. First, there is the issue of training and technological skill. Many officers, especially in smaller law enforcement agencies, may not enjoy the computer or the Internet. This means that someone may have to be trained to handle online investigations. Part of this training involves the technological side of conducting online investigations, including such issues as: how to connect to the Internet, how to establish a screen name and profile, and how to exchange files via the various chat software programs. However, there is also the consideration of training to address the cultural side of the online world. The language and mannerisms of those who "surf the World Wide Web" are different from that of those who do not interact in the virtual world. Officers who do not understand the language and mannerisms will quickly find that they have trouble developing any level of relationship with others in the chat rooms. Because words are the only means of communication between virtual citizens it is important that officers who are going to conduct online investigations be more than vaguely familiar with a few of the words and acronyms (acronyms being used on a regular basis by frequent chat room members).

A second issue of concern involves the legal issues associated with conducting an online undercover investigation. Here the major issue is that of avoiding a scenario in which a suspect could argue that he or she was entrapped by the investigating officer. Once again, because words are the only means of communication, it is important for an officer to ensure that he or she is capable of wording their interactions in such a manner that there is no doubt about who instigated the relationship. The United States Supreme Court, in the decision *Sorrells v. United States* (1932), established that for entrapment to be claimed there must proof that the law enforcement officer encouraged the individual to commit the crime and that absent the officer's urgings the defendant would not have been predisposed to commit the crime. In other words, if the officer had not come looking for the groomer or the identity thief, then would they have found someone else to whom they would transmit illegal images? Often this issue is avoided by ensuring that the investigating officer is not the one who makes first contact with a suspect and then ensuring that the suspect is the first to mention or transmit illegal images or other illegal data.

The issue of online sting operations has been discussed by at least one appeals court in the decision *United States v. Poehlman* (2000). Here, the defendant claimed that he was entrapped after he was arrested for meeting with an undercover officer with the intent to engage in sexual activity with minor children. Poehlman claimed that he had recently suffered a nasty divorce and that he was looking for a friend who would support his lifestyle as a preoperative transsexual. Upon meeting Poehlman in a chat room, the officer began discussing how she was looking for someone to train her daughters in the ways of the world. Poehlman claimed that he was not interested in that type of relationship and the officer indicated that if he could not help her daughters they were through interacting. Desperate to maintain the relationship Poehlman claimed he began chatting with the undercover officer about how he would train the daughters. Poehlman was arrested when the undercover officer asked him to come to her home town to train her daughters.

Poehlman admitted that he had crossed state lines after promising to train the girls. However, he stated he had not intention of sleeping with the girls. In reality, he claimed he was coming to meet the women he had been chatting with in hopes of establishing a relationship with someone who understood and accepted his lifestyle. It was the court's opinion that when the undercover officer indicated she would move on to someone else if Poehlman would not train her daughters, the idea for the crime was planted with Poehlman. Therefore, it could not be proven that he was predisposed to engage in sex with children, and the guilty verdict was overturned because of entrapment.

Thankfully there are software programs today that can help an agency that desires to record their online investigation activity. One such program is Camtasia, which allows users to digitally record the images on the screen of their computer and convert these files to mpeg movie formats. This means that an officer could activate the Camtasia program and if there is later a claim that an inappropriate comment was made, then the officer could admit the recordings into evidence and disprove this claim. Likewise, training programs that address the technological issues involved with online investigations should also include a section on legal considerations and the proper methods of preserving evidence associated with online sting operations.

Conclusion

Online criminal activity almost requires law enforcement to conduct online investigations. Thankfully, there are still methods of verifying the identity of many online criminals. Through the use of the Internet protocol address (IP address), an online suspect may be identified and located. These tracking techniques are especially important to investigations that involve the crime of digital child pornography. Because online pedophiles use e-mail as a means of transmitting the images and grooming the children for future sexual behavior, understanding how to read an e-mail header and use that information to locate a subject is of immeasurable benefit.

Law enforcement agencies have also been forced to begin implementing sting operations in an attempt to locate child pornographers and groomers before they have the opportunity to make contact with their child victims. These operations are still in their infancy and are not employed by many agencies. However, over the next 10 years these operations are certain to play a greater role in the control of child pornography and identity theft. As more agencies begin to implement these programs the procedural and legal issues will become more commonplace. Agencies must ensure that officers who are going to handle online investigations and online sting operations are familiar with several aspects of handling such investigations. First, it is important that officers be familiar with the cultural issues associated with interacting with their target population. Officers who appear to be from outside the social circle may find themselves cast out and unable to make any connections. Second, it is important that officers be familiar with the technological side of online investigations. Online investigations will require that the officer be familiar with a variety of chatting software programs, as well as various screen capture programs to capture evidence of the communications between officer and suspect. Finally, the officer must be familiar with basic legal issues in order to prevent a suspect from successfully claiming he or she was the victim of entrapment. Training for online investigators could address this issue in a minimal amount of time by providing tips associated with how to handle initial contacts with a potential suspect, as well as how long a relationship should be allowed to develop and what types of communications are considered acceptable.

Review Questions

1. What is an IP address and how does it relate to an online investigation?

2. Discuss briefly how e-mails are handled by the various servers en route to their intended destination.

3. Why do you believe so few state and municipal law enforcement agencies have attempted to establish online investigative teams? Why may this change in the future?

4. What are the three primary methods of locating a suspect encountered during an online investigation? What are the advantages and disadvantages of each method?

5. What are three training issues that will benefit law enforcement officers who desire to conduct online investigations? Is there any one that is more important than the others?

Online Resources

Operation Innocent Images Information Site—web page devoted to press releases and information relating to the FBI's Operation Innocent Images; contains information on how the initiative began, as well as how successful the operation has been. Available at http://www.fbi.gov/pressrel/candyman/iini.htm.

Operation Blue Ridge Thunder—website dedicated to providing information about Operation Blue Ridge Thunder and its mission; also contains information for parents and children regarding how to stay safe when surfing the Internet. Available at http://www.blueridgethunder.com.

Chapter 8

Seizure of Digital Evidence

The concepts of computers and the Internet were not even fathomed when the Constitution to the United States was drafted. The founding fathers could not have imagined that one day Americans would conduct personal business, professional business, and entertainment activities from the comfort of their own homes. However, it is amazing that the founding fathers had enough foresight to ensure that the Constitution could be adapted to handle any advance possible, even if there is the potential for some confusion or misunderstanding in the early stages of this adaptation. Today, the Fourth Amendment to the United States Constitution is the bedrock for courts when it comes to determining the admissibility of technological evidence.

The Search Warrant Requirement

It is from the Fourth Amendment that such activities as unreasonable searches and seizures are forbidden; thereby protecting citizens from aggressive, overreaching, and inappropriate seizures of information from their personal computers and Internet service providers. This is not to say there are not problems with relying on the Fourth Amendment when it comes to determining what information may be seized. After all, a pivotal word in the Amendment is "unreasonable." What is unreasonable when it comes to the search and seizure of digital evidence? What about unreasonable, in light of non-technological evidence? There really is little by way of a universally agreed upon definition for "unreasonable." According to Orin Kerr (2001) of the Computer Crime Intellectual Property Section of the United States Justice Department, the best definition of "unreasonable" requires that for a search to be reasonable you need one thing—a properly drafted search warrant that satisfies the requirements of particularity and scope pertaining to the items to be seized. Over the past decades there have

141

been numerous court decisions to discuss the particularity and scope issues when it comes to evidence that is not digital in nature. Unfortunately there have been few decisions to address the issue when it comes to digital evidence. Even more problematic is the fact that the few court decisions that have been provided are from the various lower courts and not the Supreme Court. What this means is that by region the seizure of digital evidence may be handled differently in various circumstances. Law enforcement agencies that operate within one of the judicial districts that have addressed the issues may have some form of guidance, while those agencies operating outside of such a judicial district may have little information regarding how the courts could rule in a case of first impression.

With this information in mind, it is recommended that any search warrant involving the seizure of digital evidence be as thorough as possible. The particularity requirement of the Fourth Amendment has generally been interpreted to require that a search warrant contain a complete analysis and description of the place (or places) to be searched by law enforcement officials. Once again, when discussing the issue of computer technology it is important to understand how rapidly technology evolves. In recent years technology has advanced to the point where data storage requires smaller physical devices capable of storing massive amounts of data. Take for example the CD-ROM disk. One CD-ROM can store 500 times the amount of data that a traditional floppy disk could store. Further, one flash drive, which is sometimes referred to as a thumb drive because of the device's small thumb size physical casing, can store as much as four to five times that of a CD-ROM. If an individual is using a computer in the commission of a criminal activity, then there is the possibility that any or all of these devices may be employed in the criminal activity. Thus, a very important question develops: What information should a law enforcement officer include?

In at least one court decision, the court found that an officer's failure to specifically list all digital evidence that could be encountered at a crime scene resulted in a search warrant that was overly broad and allowed for officers to engage in what is often referred to as a "fishing expedition," wherein officers broadly write the warrant and seize as much as possible in hopes of finding incriminating evidence (*United States v. Hunter*, 1998). Many manuals or training materials relating to the handling of digital evidence recommend that the proper means of avoiding this problem is to include as many items as possible as well as the following phrase: "including but not limited to." It is believed that this wording will allow officers to show that they are looking for specific evidence but that there is the potential for the suspect to have additional evidence that may not have been accounted for in the search warrant. The problem is that at least one court has ruled against the use of this phrasing.

In *Matter of Search Warrant for K-Sports Imports, Inc.* (1995), the court ruled that use of the phrase "including but not limited to" resulted in the search warrant's violating the particularity requirement of the Fourth

Amendment. Of specific question in this case was whether business records could be viewed by law enforcement officers during the search. It was the government's contention that law enforcement had no intention of viewing the company's business records. Regardless, the court felt that potential for entry into a private place was present and therefore the search warrant was overly broad and in violation of the Fourth Amendment.

It should be noted, however, that other courts have upheld search warrants that did not specifically list all potential computer-related evidence. For example, in *United States v. Upham* (1999), the court held that a search warrant calling for the seizure of all computer-related devices was sufficient because such a search would be necessary to ensure that all evidence was properly collected. The court appeared to acknowledge that digital evidence may be located in a variety of locations and listing all locations may be impossible regardless of preplanning for the search.

After considering the aforementioned areas, it is possible that one might believe the only solution would be for law enforcement officers to provide a thorough list of every item that could potentially contain digital evidence. This is not necessarily the situation. Some legal scholars have argued that courts are sure to interpret the Fourth Amendment liberally in future criminal cases. Unfortunately, there are others who are not so certain that awaiting liberal decisions is the best idea. After all, the key phrase in awaiting such a decision is "future." Today, it is perhaps best for law enforcement officers to list all possible known targets of digital evidence and then include a statement concerning how digital evidence may take many forms and there is the potential that the suspect may have additional pieces of technology that was not included. This explanation could then be later used if the government is accused of attempting to secure a broad warrant for purposes of "fishing" for evidence. Hopefully such thorough and careful planning would prevent evidence from being excluded in a judicial district that has yet to fully address this issue.

Amendment IV

The right of the people to be secure in their persons, houses, papers, and effects, against unreasonable searches and seizures, shall not be violated, and no Warrants shall issue, but upon probable cause, supported by Oath or affirmation, and particularly describing the place to be searched, and the persons or things to be seized.

One final issue that must be considered when examining the search warrant requirement is the judge's level of understanding. Here, the issue is whether the judge issuing the search warrant understands exactly what he or she is agreeing to allow to be searched. This concern is partly attributable to the fact that new advances and terminology are being used every day in the field of computer science. It is important that law enforcement officers who request a search warrant ensure that the signing judge understands what is being seized. Authors, and investigators, Clark and Diliberto (1996) recommend that all officers who request search warrants involving digital evidence and computers carry a pocket dictionary of computer terms. The judge may then be provided with these easy-to-understand definitions, should there be any doubt as to what the search warrant is calling for in terms of seizures. Of course, officers who encounter this problem may also find salvation through the good faith clause of the exclusionary rule. The good faith clause would require that officers prove that they acted upon what they thought to be a valid warrant, and proving this may require extra effort that could be avoided through use of the dictionary and planning on the front end of the search.

Preplanning Associated with the Search Warrant

There are numerous questions associated with the preplanning of a search warrant, due to the fact there are numerous types of digital evidence that could be desirable for evidence, and each may require separate seizure techniques. In the past few years, computer technology has seen advances that allow for incredible storage capacity on a smaller storage area. For example, in 1994 the average computer hard drive was 500 MB or less. Today's computers come standard with a 30 to 40 GB hard drive capacity. This means that in eight years, the storage capacities of computers have increased 80 times. Hard drives are not the only storage medium that has seen increased size capacity in recent years, as technology has now been developed that allows computer users to store up to 1GB of information on a disk the size of an individual's thumb. This storage device connects to a plug on most all computers manufactured today and allows users to transport files between computers.

Another consideration is the number of computers located at the site upon which the search warrant is to be executed. Ideally, law enforcement personnel would only be asked to seize one computer at a time, and this would allow for the officer to devote their entire concentration on the acquisition of that one device. The reality, however, is far from this scenario. In actuality, many times more than one computer will be seized at a time and because each computer on the scene will be running and occupied by a user, law enforcement personnel must take into consideration several additional factors that govern the seizure of these devices. If there is no plan in place for this scenario, then evidence could be destroyed by personnel onsite before the computer could be seized. Pursuant to the search warrant, personnel must ensure they only seize computers that are covered by their search warrant.

Situations that involve the presence of multiple computers will normally be those that involve businesses or similar operations. In these situations, an additional consideration will be whether there are computer-use policies in place. Many times this may be difficult to discover, and the only source for verifying the existence of this information is to contact the company's system administrator. Of course this is not an option if it is the system administrator that is believed to be committing the criminal act under investigation. The presence of an acceptable use policy may be beneficial if during the execution of a search warrant an additional computer that was not covered in the warrant is discovered. An acceptable use policy informs company personnel that they have no privacy interest in the computers on which they perform their job tasks. A computer such as one discussed could then be seized without a warrant and searched after a second search warrant is obtained at a later time.

The issue of operating systems in use by the computers is an important consideration, and is one that will be discussed in detail in later sections. For now, suffice to say that the determination of which operating systems the computers are running will guide the investigator's decisions in regards to powering down the computer before disassembly.

Another consideration for investigators is whether the actions of their search warrant will affect any federal legislation. For example, if the computer-related evidence to be seized is used in the transmission of e-mails or other electronic communications there is the possibility that the Electronics Communication Privacy Act of 1986 (short-titled ECPA) may govern the actions of government agents. A more detailed examination of the ECPA and the limits placed on investigators will be discussed later in this chapter. Suffice to say that the ECPA regulates the amount of information that law enforcement officers may obtain with certain levels of service. Currently, an officer needs the following level of service to obtain information about a potential suspect under the ECPA:

1. Subpoena—basic subscriber information

2. Court order—transactional information

3. Search warrant—the actual content of e-mail messages.

If investigators fail to consider the provisions of the ECPA they may find their evidence is inadmissible.

Another piece of federal legislation that must be considered by investigators is that of the Privacy Protection Act (PPA). This legislation appears to have been originally drafted to protect those who publish books, magazines, etc. from having their materials confiscated and released by law enforcement officers before they are made available to the public. Of course the main consideration here is that the materials they are protecting may not be illegal materials. If the materials are in fact legal, then law enforcement officers are under a duty to return any publishing materials back to the owner as soon as possible so as to not unduly delay or disturb the business of the computer's owner. One of the original purposes for this laid in the fact that a business should not be made accountable for the actions of an employee they may not have been aware was committing a crime. Today, it is believed by some that the provisions of the Privacy Protection Act may be interpreted to include individuals who write web pages or conduct other web page design work. Put simply, this means that a company involved in the design of web pages and other web design work must be afforded the same protection and promptness of service that a book or magazine publisher would be afforded.

Finally, investigators must consider whether there is the presence of a computer network in the building in which they are executing the search warrant. In today's business world it would be a rare case where a business with multiple computers did not run a network. With this in mind, investigators should once again attempt to contact the business's network administrator, unless of course this is the individual suspected of committing the criminal act. The presence of a computer network invokes an additional consideration as to where the data is actually being stored. Unlike computers not connected on a network that are required to store their files on hard drives within the computer, networked computers may store their files on another computer that is generally considered a server. The server is many times a computer locked away from other computers that may not have a monitor and is used for nothing more than storing files and applications. The presence of servers can be both a positive and a negative event in the investigation of a computer-related crime. They are good because many times there are daily, weekly, or monthly backups created for files stored on the servers. This means that even if the original evidence was destroyed, there exists a copy somewhere on the company's premises. The negatives to the use of network servers are the facts that the server:

1. may not be included in the warrant and
2. the server may be located off-site.

A search warrant for computer-related evidence may not include the server in its description of evidence allowed to be seized if investigators are not aware of the presence of an off-site server. If this situation occurs, then investigators will be forced to obtain a new search warrant before seizing the server. Even more disturbing is the recent development of technology that has provided a means for storing servers at locations far away from the business. It has been argued by some that the use of these servers have gained widespread acceptance following the terror attacks of September 11, 2001, as more businesses are finding value in the storage of information off-site or maybe even overseas.

Planning for the Seizure of Electronic Communications

Preparing for the seizure of electronic communications such as e-mails requires a separate level of preparation. As mentioned earlier, the ECPA regulates the information about an electronic message's owner, as well as information relating to the actual electronic communication. The ECPA was developed in response to the rapidly changing technological environment involving communications. The provisions or the ECPA are designed to protect communications that are sent via electronic methods. While the current text deals specifically with the issue of e-mails, the ECPA has also been used to regulate the interception of other electronic communications including wireless telephones and similar devices.

The ECPA provides for three levels of service: (1) subpoena, (2) court order, and (3) search warrant. The first level of service is the subpoena. The subpoena can be used to obtain basic subscriber information. Historically, most of this information related to the name and owner of a particular electronic communication. However, following the terrorist attacks of September 11, 2001, the amount of information available from a subpoena has increased. Today, investigators who employ this level of service may obtain each of the following: name, address, local and long distance telephone connection records, session times and duration, length of service, types of services used, telephone number or IP address, sources of payment (to include bank account or credit card information), and the content of e-mails that are older than 180 days and have been previously opened by the owner.

Consider that a suspect informs an investigator that he/she has been victimized by a particular person online each night for the past two weeks. The individual does not have an actual name but does have a screen name that indicates the user is an AOL customer. Using a subpoena drafted with this online identity, the investigator could get the name, address, and billing information for the person who registered that screen name with AOL. The issue of being able to open e-mails that are greater than 180 days old and has been opened is one of interest. It appears that the initial thought behind this section is that e-mails that have been opened and left on the Internet service provider's web server are less protected by privacy interests. The question then is why 180 days? Why is 180 days considered acceptable, and why not 90 days?

The second level of service is that of the court order. Sometimes the court order is referred to as a 2703d court order, named after the section of the code that details the requirements for obtaining the order and what information may be provided through the court order. The court order is also sometimes referred to as an articulable facts order, receiving its name from the fact that applicants have to present articulable facts that the information is necessary and should be seized through the use of a court order. Currently, the information obtainable through the use of a 2703d court order includes past audit trail information, as well as addresses of past e-mail correspondents. The audit trail information is not as useful today as it was prior to the changes brought forth by the USA PATRIOT Act. Under the old code, the court order was necessary for billing information and information relating to how much use the individual got out of his/her service provider. This information is now available with a subpoena. The addresses of past e-mail correspondents is of benefit to investigators, especially investigators who are handling the investigation involving child pornography or identity fraud. The list of past e-mail correspondents will allow investigators to determine how many individuals in the public could have been exposed to the individual's behavior.

The third and highest level of service is the search warrant. The search warrant is what is needed to seize e-mails that are less than 180 days old and are stored on the Internet service provider's web server. It should also be noted that each level of process supercedes the lower level, meaning that a court order will not only allow for the collection of information requiring a court order but also information that would be obtainable through a subpoena. The use of a search warrant will then allow for examination of e-mail contents, as well as audit logs, addresses, and billing information. The search warrant, while allowing for the most collection of evidence is also the hardest level of service to obtain. To obtain a search warrant it is necessary for the investigator to complete a statement of underlying facts supporting the issuance of a search warrant. In this statement the investigator must show that a crime has been committed, that the individual who owns the account is linked to the crime and that the electronic account contains information relevant to the investigation of the case.

When any of the aforementioned documents are requested, the investigator must decide whether he/she wishes to allow the suspect to be notified of the investigation. If the suspect is not to be notified then the Internet service provider should be alerted to the need for secrecy. Prior to submitting the subpoena, court order or search warrant, it is customary for investigators to submit a request for the preservation of evidence. This document merely informs the Internet service provider that one of their customers is under investigation and that all materials relating to the account should be preserved until a reasonable effort can be made to obtain one of the three levels of legal service.

The preservation request is important because many Internet providers maintain a large customer base with a limited amount of technological storage capacity. If the company has no indication that the materials need to be preserved then many times the company will erase old records to make room for new records. Consider once again the customer base of America Online. With millions of customers, the chances of the company maintaining information relating to what IP address is linked to what screen name for more than a few weeks are very slim. Therefore, the letter of preservation lets AOL know that the records are important and every effort should be made to protect the materials until the investigator can obtain the proper documentation. The letter of preservation is also where investigators may request the

Internet provider to not alert the suspect for a period of 90 days. If for some reason there is a problem that prevents the documentation from being received within that 90-day period, the ECPA allows for a one-time extension of the delayed notice for another 90 days. The requirement is that the requesting investigator must request this secrecy and indicate that failure to maintain secrecy could be damaging to the investigation.

There remains some debate as to how electronic messages that are unopened should be handled. After all, if the message has not been opened by the recipient then is the message still in transit despite the fact that it is stored on the server? There is a general consensus that there are wiretap statutes that would allow for the interception of e-mails, but is a wiretap order required to read unread e-mails? Currently, the answer is no. As of this time the use of a search warrant is all that is necessary to obtain the content of unopened e-mails that are less than 180 days old. Direct interceptions of electronic communications through the use of sniffer programs require the use of a wiretap order that requires a high burden of proof. For this reason the use of such orders are limited to extreme circumstances where time is of the utmost importance to a person's safety.

The Assembly of an Adequate Search Warrant Team

As technology assisted crimes continue to increase in frequency, some law enforcement agencies may opt to form a special unit to handle the execution of search warrants involving digital evidence. The need for such a unit is debatable, but one should never fear opting on the side of caution and preparation. Operating in much the same manner as a high-risk warrant execution team, a search warrant team trained for the execution of search warrants involving digital evidence ensures quick and accurate seizure of evidence from computers and other technological devices. Perhaps the best argument against the use of search warrant teams is the cost of assembling a team of individuals capable of handling digital crime scenes, and then balancing this cost with the number of technology-assisted crimes the agency will investigate. Agencies that operate in small communities might well find themselves unable to justify the formation of such a team. However, agencies in larger cities should seriously consider forming search warrant teams, as the near future is sure to hold more technology crime investigations for state and local law enforcement agencies.

The formation of a search warrant team is important if for no other reason than the potential for mishandling of digital evidence. With few technology-assisted crimes leaving physical evidence, the mishandling of digital evidence could result in the forfeiture of a case. Law enforcement agencies that do decide to institute a search warrant team are encouraged to follow the guidelines developed by Clark and Diliberto (1996). The team is made up as follows: case supervisor, interview team, sketch and photo team, physical search team, security and arrest team, and a technical evidence seizure and logging team. The hiring of new officers is not necessary, as law enforcement officers outside of the actual high-technology crime unit can staff some portions of the team.

The case supervisor is the chief administrative officer of the team and responsible for overseeing the day-to-day operations of the investigative team. Along with being responsible for assembling the team and providing reports to higher administration, the case supervisor is also responsible for annual budgeting, scheduling, and the conducting of the execution of a search warrant; in essence this individual coordinates the execution of the search warrant (Clark & Diliberto, 1996). Case supervisors do not necessarily have to have extensive training in the area of computer forensics, but they should be experienced in the execution of search warrants.

The interview team normally consists of a minimum of one person who is skilled in interrogations, and is responsible for assembling witnesses and or suspects at the scene of the search warrant's execution. Once assembled, this group of team members will conduct interviews with witnesses or suspects. Much like the case supervisor, there is little need for members of the interview team to have extensive training in the area of computer forensics. However, such training could assist the team in formulating the types of questions to be asked of the witnesses and suspects (Clark & Diliberto, 1996). The members of this team, though, must have extensive training in statement analysis and interrogation techniques in order to ensure that those at the scene of the search warrant's execution obtain the most accurate information.

The sketch and photo team is responsible for recording on video, or logging by photograph, the area of the crime scene both before and after a search warrant is served. This team is important because the pictures and video may be necessary if the case goes to court and the suspect argues that evidence was planted at the scene of the search warrant by investigators on the scene (Clark & Diliberto, 1996).

The physical search team is responsible for identifying and marking all evidence discovered at the crime scene. It is recommended that color-coded sticky dots be used during the marking phase for two reasons. First, coding assists investigators in identifying evidence that does not contribute to the case. Second, computerized equipment can be more easily reassembled if the wires are color-coded. The members of the physical search team need only enough training to assure a thorough search of computer evidence conforming to search and seizure law, and the team can be staffed by personnel drawn from other units (Clark & Diliberto, 1996).

The members of the security and arrest team are normally made up of uniformed police officers. The primary responsibility of this team is to provide security of the area surrounding the crime scene in which the warrant is served, and its members assist in the arrest of suspects at the scene. Such duties require no specialized training in computers because these individuals are normally uniformed officers. Therefore, team members can be any uniformed officers who are trained security and arrest techniques (Clark & Diliberto, 1996).

The members of the technical evidence seizure and logging team are the most highly trained within the search warrant team. This team, which Clark and Diliberto (1996) recommend maintain at least two or more individuals, is responsible for the safe seizure of the suspect's computer or any other relevant digital evidence. The ideal make-up of this team is a minimum of one computer investigator, who provides information on the proper procedures to follow, and one computer professional, who provides information on the proper methods of disassembling the computer.

At first glance the size of the search warrant team recommended by Clark and Diliberto (1996) appears quite large. However, the majority of the team can be drawn from other units. In fact, the only necessary full-time positions are those that require special training and technical certification: the case supervisor and the two members of the technical evidence seizure and tagging team. Hence, a search warrant team can be staffed at relatively small costs.

Warrantless Search Doctrines and Technological Evidence

The best method of obtaining digital evidence remains the use of well drafted search warrant. After all the use of search warrants aid law enforcement in ensuring that the search is viewed as reasonable, thereby ensuring that the evidence will be admitted into trial should such a need develop. Should law enforcement personnel determine that the option of using a search warrant is not available, then it is up to the government to prove that the circumstances justified not using a search warrant in the situation. The United States Supreme Court has recognized relatively few exceptions to the search warrant requirement, and those that have been addressed have not been interpreted in light in of technology. The section below addresses some of the more commonly encountered warrantless search doctrines and how the various lower courts have attempted to merge the traditional doctrine with technology. When examining these warrantless search doctrines it should be noted that the majority have allowed the seizure of digital evidence but have not directly addressed whether an in-depth examination is warranted absent a subsequently obtained search warrant.

The United States Supreme Court has generally held that a person maintains a reasonable Fourth Amendment expectation of privacy in closed containers. This belief was espoused in the case of *United States v. Ross* (1982), and has been relied upon by some as an indication that computers should be treated as a briefcase or a filing cabinet. Orin Kerr of the Computer Crime and Intellectual Property Section of the Department of Justice makes this assertion in the CCIPS's guidelines for searching and seizing digital evidence. Kerr's assertion has also been supported by several court decisions, some of which have directly made the comparison of a hard drive to a filing cabinet (*United States v. Barth*, 1998). The decision in *United*

States v. Blas (1990) actually extended this level of protection beyond computer hard drives when the court held that a pager or any similar electronic device should be treated in a manner comparable to that of a closed container. These statements are introduced in order that the reader understand that despite the discussion to follow, the use of a well-drafted search warrant should always be the first choice when conducting the seizure of digital evidence.

The Expectation of Privacy

The expectation of privacy is central in the acceptance of Fourth Amendment protection. The question then becomes one of whether it is possible for one to lose their expectation of privacy in digital evidence? The answer is, of course, yes, there are certain situations in which an individual's expectation of privacy may diminish or completely disappear. For example, should a person provide a copy of digital evidence to a third part, the original owner may lose their original expectation of privacy. This scenario could also develop if an individual ships his or her computer, which contains evidence of the owner's narcotics dealings, to a friend in another city. The person who receives the computer may install the device, open several files, and then realize that the materials are illegal. If this person chooses to alert law enforcement, then the original owner would have trouble arguing that he maintained an expectation of privacy in materials that he willingly turned over to a person outside of his control.

This loss of control becomes an even more interesting issue when one considers the idea of online web postings and chat room sessions. If someone posts information in a chat room, then is it possible to argue that the owner maintains an expectation of privacy in the materials? According to the case of *United States v. Charbonneau* (1997) the answer to this would be *no*. In this case the court ruled that an individual did not maintain his right to privacy in information that was posted to an America Online chat room. The primary consideration by the court was whether a person could maintain an expectation of privacy when there is little or no means of ensuring that the person on the other end of the computer is in fact who they claim to be. This very concept is central to the conducting of online sting operation, and the ability of an individual to maintain privacy in electronic communications posted to chat rooms would in essence prevent such operations.

In 1997, two researchers posed an interesting question and one that is closely related to this issue of privacy online. Seeger and Visconte questioned whether the Internet is public or private, and coined the term "privlic," because of their perception that the Internet is a combination of both public and private. The Internet is private because one may access the network from the privacy of their home, where incidentally a reasonable expectation of privacy does exist, but the materials are projected out for anyone on the Internet to see. While Seeger and Visconte's term is amusing and does pose an interesting hypothetical question, in practical terms the Internet and postings could not maintain a semblance of private communication for each of the aforementioned reasons—everyone can gain access to the materials and therefore the owner has no knowledge of who is actually receiving the information. If a third party has a right to report any information they deem important, then individuals in a chat room who read a chat session and discover information they deem necessary to report to law enforcement officers should be well within their rights.

Warrantless Consent Searches

The courts have long held to the belief that a search warrant is not necessary if the owner of property agrees to allow that property to be searched or seized. This idea can then easily be transferred to the discussion of computer-related evidence. There are, however, several factors to consider when attempting to seize a computer or search a hard drive on the basis of consent. First, does the individual granting the consent have a legitimate right to consent to the search? The issue of third party privacy expectations returns to this discussion. In *United States v. Smith* (1998) the court found that a search of a suspect's computer was valid despite the fact that consent was granted not by the suspect but by the suspect's girlfriend. It was the opinion of the court that there was evidence that the two individuals shared a common living space and therefore an expectation of privacy in the computer could be overruled by consent from either party. Also considered by the court was the fact that the computer files obtained were not password protected, a fact that led to the belief that the files were accessible by anyone in the house.

Other courts have taken a more direct stance in regards to live in partners and family. In *United States v. Durham* (1998) the court found that a mother could not grant consent to law enforcement officers for a search of her son's computer. This ruling came despite the fact that the mother owned portions of the computer equipment and the materials were located within her home. The court relied on two issues in coming to its conclusion. The primary issue being that the young man had taken steps to ensure that neither his mother nor anyone else in the house could access the files on the computer. The secondary issue was that the son paid a small fee to the mother for living with her, which in the eyes of the court allowed for an expectation of privacy to develop in regards to the child's room in which the computer was located. The mother may have owned the computer, but the zone of privacy in the room coupled with the fact that the mother had lost the ability to access the computer resulted in the inability of the mother to grant consent.

It would then appear that the key component of consent is whether the individual granting consent has access to the computer and/or technological device. So long as the individual lives in the residence, has access to the room in which the computer or technological device is located and has access to the computer then the consent search should be lawful. However, the courts have yet to address a scenario in which the computer files are password protected but the password is stored in such a place that access to the password possible for the third party. At first glance it would appear that the individual's placing a password on the files would indicate a privacy interest. But the question is whether that privacy interest could be upheld when the access to the files is easily obtained by a live-in partner? It is likely that the issue would be ruled upon in the same manner as the case above involving the mother and her son. The question would turn around whether the live-in partner had access to the computer, an issue that could easily be resolved by determining whether the third party had ever accessed the computer before consent was requested and obtained.

A second factor to consider is whether the consent to search and seize has been given by one who is both free from duress and aware of what he or she is consenting to allow searched. The Supreme Court first required this understanding and freedom from duress in the case of *Boyd v. United States* (1886), and then later extended the use of consent with the decision of *Schneckloth v. Bustamonte* (1973). In *Schneckloth*, the court determined that law enforcement officers did not have to inform a suspect of a right to refuse to grant consent. The officers do have to ensure that the person granting consent is both mature in age and mental capability, as well as ensuring that the individual understands what their consent covers. In an attempt to provide clearer guidance on this issue, several states have actually implemented requirements that all individuals who grant consent to a search be provided with a form that indicates the person understands what is to be searched and how the search could affect them. This form is signed by the individual granting consent and then maintained, should the case go to trial, and should the individual claim that there was no consent given.

The Supreme Court of the United States has never required this level of certainty, but many states continue to apply the practice in some form or another, possibly in an attempt to ensure that there is a meeting of the minds in regards to what is to be searched. If the individual granting consent and the seizing officer do not have the same idea in regards to what is to be searched or seized, there is the potential for the evidence to be excluded. In the case of *United States v. Blas* (1990), the court determined that an officer's request to examine a pager, and the owner's subsequent consent to do so, did not grant the officer the right to search the pager for names or phone numbers. According to the court, the officer's intentions could have been misconstrued as not being a search but rather being a request to examine what the officer could have felt to be a potential weapon. In *United States v. Carey* (1999) the court found that an investigating officer overstepped the bounds of his search when he took a computer off property before he searched the device. The computer was seized under a consent agreement that allowed for the search of any property within the individual's house.

States that do use an informed consent document should ensure that their documents thoroughly address the following components of the search: (1) the area to be searched, (2) what the investigator is intending to search for, (3) the investigator's desire to search within any computer or technological device found within the area, and (4) the potential need to make a duplicate copy of the hard drive (either onsite or offsite). Such a well drafted consent form takes into consideration almost all possible scenarios and may assist an investigator who faces a claim by an individual that he did not consent to a search.

Of course it is the recommendation of this author that no computer be forensically examined on the basis of a consent agreement. Instead, upon obtaining consent to seize the computer a well drafted search warrant should be obtained. Absent a search warrant there is the potential for the individual to revoke their consent, or even worse wait until trial and then claim that they attempted to revoke consent in the middle of an examination. Even a written consent form does not prohibit an individual from revoking consent to a search should the individual change his mind. There have been a variety of court decisions to discuss revoking consent, but the following court decisions from the state of Florida perhaps illustrate this concept best. Consent may be withdrawn by any of the following: (1) the individual may revoke consent verbally (*State v. Hammonds*, 1990), (2) the individual may revoke consent through an intentional act such as grabbing the investigator's hand in order to stop the search of a particular area (*Jimenez v. State*, 1994), or (3) the individual may revoke consent to a search by fleeing from the search (*Davis v. State*, 1986). Having a search warrant to search the contents of the computer will prevent a suspect from claiming any of these actions were attempted during the search of the computer.

Searches Based on Exigent Circumstances

Law enforcement personnel have long been granted the use of an exigent circumstances claim to justify the warrantless seizure of evidence. However, in order to prove that there were exigent circumstances surrounding a seizure, it is necessary for the government to show: (1) that a reasonable person would believe that entry was necessary to prevent physical harm to law enforcement personnel or others in the surrounding area, (2) that the warrantless seizure was necessary to prevent the destruction of valuable evidence, (3) that the warrantless seizure was necessary to prevent the escape of a suspect, or (4) that the warrantless search was necessary to prevent any further consequences that could delay legitimate law enforcement efforts (*United States v. Alfonso*, 1985).

In the case of *United States v. Reed* (1991) the requirements for satisfying the need for seizure under the claim of exigent circumstances. The requirements are: (1) degree of urgency must be shown, (2) the amount of time it would take to obtain a properly drafted search warrant could prevent the furtherance of justice, (3) is the evidence about to be destroyed or moved beyond the reach of law enforcement, (4) is there danger to the officers, or to the evidence, at the crime scene, (5) does the suspect have information that alerts him or her to law enforcement's intent to seize the evidence, and (6) how easily could the evidence be destroyed by the suspect.

Based on the aforementioned considerations, it is possible that the warrantless seizures of digital evidence under exigent circumstances could play a significant role in the future of high-technology crime investigations. The pure ease with which data can be moved, hidden, and ultimately deleted satisfies the majority of these considerations. Consider the example of *United States v. David* (1991). In *David*, law enforcement officers obtained a suspect's electronic date book without a search warrant. The officer noticed that the suspect, who had previously agreed to assist law enforcement, appeared to be deleting information from the date book. The officer then seized the device and conducted a search of the names and addresses located within. The court agreed with the actions of the officer, finding that in that situation there was sufficient proof that the suspect knew law enforcement personnel were after evidence within the device and in an attempt to prevent the information from being obtained the suspect was deleting the evidence.

It is worth noting, however, that the court also agreed that the exigency ended the moment the date book was seized and there was no further danger to the integrity of the evidence. One of the main issues presented to the courts when addressing exigent circumstances and the seizure of digital evidence appears to be the likelihood that the evidence could be destroyed while a warrant is obtained. In *David* the court felt that after the date book was seized there was no longer an exigent circumstance that would justify searching the date book. Contrarily, in the case of *United States v. Ortiz* (1996) the court found that the warrantless seizure, as well as the subsequent search, was acceptable when phone numbers were retrieved following the arrest of suspect. It was the court's opinion that the exigent circumstances doctrine would apply to the retrieval of phone numbers from a pager because of the potential for loss of the evidence. This line of reasoning was based on the belief that pagers and the data located within are extremely susceptible to deletion and/or damage should the batteries be removed or should the batteries die.

The primary issue in the above cases was whether the evidence would be destroyed should the power be disrupted to the storage device. Of course, the officers in the *David* case did not argue that the batteries were in danger of dying, nor was their any indication that the obtaining of a search warrant would have resulted in the loss of power to the date book. If it can be shown that the removal of power or batteries will not affect the information stored within a device, then at least one court has ruled that there is no justification for searching the device. In *United States v. Romero-Garcia* (1997) the court found that a law enforcement officer exceeded his authority when a search was conducted on a battery operated computer. The officer attempted to argue that should the batteries have died the evidence would have disappeared, but the court disagreed and found that when dealing with computers there is little chance of losing evidence should the batteries die.

Law enforcement officers should consider the seizure of a technological device without a warrant to be a possibility, but the search of the same device should be conducted under the provisions of a valid search warrant. There are some possible exceptions. The older model personal data assistants (PDAs) were notorious for losing saved data after the batteries died. Newer models have attempted to improve upon this as the PDAs have given way to what could be described as miniature computers. These newer devices save data to the internal memory and there is significantly less chance of data loss. Law enforcement personnel who do seize one of these small devices should consider obtaining the search warrant as soon as possible, especially if they are dealing with an unknown type of date book or PDA device.

Searches Incident to a Lawful Arrest

The United States Supreme Court, with their decision in *United States v. Robinson* (1973) established that subsequent to a lawful arrest it is allowable for law enforcement personnel to conduct a search of the immediate area surrounding the scene of the arrest. The rationale of the court was that such a search is in the best interest of ensuring that law enforcement officers, as well as any nearby citizens, are safe. Subsequent decisions have reinforced this concept, while noting that in order to argue a valid seizure of evidence following an arrest, the arrest must be valid and the search must be contemporaneous to the arrest. This means that an officer may not merely arrest an individual with the intent of conducting a warrantless search. Likewise, an officer may not make an arrest and then later in the day attempt to search the surrounding area.

The case of *United States v. Tank* (2000) was one of the first cases to argue for a valid search and seizure of a computer disk following the arrest of a suspect. Officers in the instant case seized a zip disk that was located in the immediate area of the suspect during his arrest. The court allowed not only the seizure, but also upheld the search of the disk's contents. Relying on *Illinois v. Lafayette* (1983), a case in which the court ruled that any article or container in an individual's possession during booking is searchable without a warrant, the Ninth Circuit ruled that the search of the disk was valid because it was in the subject's immediate area during the arrest.

There are at least two potential problems with this ruling, and as such it is not necessarily advisable to rely on this precedent. First, the court appears to have neglected to consider the original intention of the search incident to arrest doctrine: protection. The doctrine was originally designed with officer and citizen safety in mind, and as such was intended to be used to seizing any weapons a suspect may have located on their person or within their reach. Considering this original intent, is it possible that digital evidence could provide a physical threat to law enforcement officers? The answer is probably not. Even if the disk belonged to the world's most dangerous hacker, the government would be hard-pressed to prove that the seizure was necessary for safety reasons.

The second problem with the court's decision involves the length of time between the disk being seized, immediately following the suspect's arrest, and the search of its contents, after the suspect had already been booked. A second requirement of the search incident to arrest doctrine is that the search be conducted along with the arrest. There have been numerous appellate court decision to determine that time has a way of dissipating any exigency that would exist immediately following an arrest. Even if the state could show that the suspect's possession of the disk was dangerous to officer safety, the subsequent search was not in response to danger as the suspect was already taken away. Also, the *Lafayette* decision that was the basis for the court in *Tank* was handed down when there was little or no consideration of technology. In reading the court's decision in *Lafayette*, it appears the intent was to provide means of allowing law enforcement officers to search through an arrestee's wallet, pockets, briefcases, etc. in an attempt to ensure that there were no weapons available to the suspect. As already discussed, even if a suspect was carrying some form of electronic storage medium there is little justification for searching through the storage device unless there is the potential for the loss of evidence because of a possible loss of power.

The *Tank* decision also brings up an interesting question. How long following an arrest is there still an opportunity to conduct a search under the search incident to arrest doctrine? When the search involves technology, the court in *United States v. Reyes* (1996) found that seizures within the first 20 minutes of an arrest would be considered contemporaneous with the arrest. Such a swift search is almost impossible when dealing with digital evidence such as a computer disk. Even a 1.4 MB floppy disk, which contains the equivalent of 500 pages of text, or 25 to 30 image files, could not be searched in this amount of time. It appears that in much the same manner as the exigent circumstances doctrine has been applied, law enforcement personnel are much safer in using the warrantless search doctrine to seize the disk and then obtaining a properly drafted search warrant to complete the search.

Plain View Seizures

In regard to physical realm searches, the plain view doctrine has been interpreted to allow the warrantless seizure of evidence that comes to the officer's attention without assistance from the officer and while the officer is in a place he or she has a legal right to be. Plain view could be encountered in two different types of scenarios involving technology. The first scenario involves searches in the physical realm. For example, suppose an officer is in the process of executing a search warrant for evidence of narcotics trafficking, and during the course of this search child pornography is encountered. Could the officer argue that the evidence came into his view during the course of a lawful search? As long as the search warrant was valid, or there was a good faith belief that the warrant was valid, then the answer is probably *yes*. The officer could in fact seize the child pornography as long as it was immediately apparent that the materials were of an illegal nature. One of the requirements would be that the officer would have to know that the materials were illegal, and if the plain view seizure involves computer disks then there would have to be some markings on the labels that would alert a properly trained officer to the presence of an illegal item. Otherwise how could the officer justify that he knew the materials were illegal?

The second scenario in which plain view may be encountered belongs more in the computer forensics analysis than in the physical search realm. Suppose a forensic analyst is examining a computer hard disk for the presence of more narcotics trafficking. During the course of this search, should child pornography come into the officer's view then could the officer seize the evidence without a search warrant? The answer to this question is still debated and while there may not be a die hard answer, and remember there rarely is when technology is concerned, there have been court decisions to provide some guidance. For example, in the case of *United States v. Carey* (1999) the court determined that an officer was allowed to seize the initial images of child pornography that were discovered during a search of a computer hard disk for narcotics records. The court did, however, limit the seizure to the first images located. All subsequent images were dismissed on the belief that the officer had no longer inadvertently discovered additional images of child pornography. It was the belief of the court that once the officer discovered the presence of child pornography he then abandoned his original search for narcotics records and began a new, unlawful, search for child pornography.

In *United States v. Gray* (1999) the court ruled in opposition to the *Carey* court. In *Gray*, a federal law enforcement agent conducted a file by file analysis of a computer while creating backups of the evidence files to CD-ROM. During this search, the agent encountered evidence of child pornography. The agent made note of the child pornography and then immediately went and obtained a second search warrant for evidence of child pornography. The court applauded the agent's actions, such as stopping and obtaining a new warrant; however, the court also agreed that had the officer not obtained a new warrant then the evidence may still have been admitted. The court claimed that had the agent merely continued to search the disk in the same systematic manner in which he discovered the first image of child pornography, then all subsequent images would have been acceptable as well. The key to the court's opinion was that the agent, by continuing on the same manner, would have discovered these images as they appeared in plain view during a lawful search.

One question that is commonly posed when considering the issue of plain view seizures of digital evidence is whether the opening of a file would even allow for the use of the plain view argument. After all, if the agent has to click the file to open the file, then has the image come into plain view during a lawful search, or as a result of the agent's actions. In *United States v. Maxwell* (1996), a military court determined that the plain view doctrine could not be viewed because the files were manually opened by an investigator. The investigator in question was searching through files for one online screen name when he discovered that there was a second screen name that had not been included on the warrant. The court denied the use of the plain view doctrine, relying on the case of *United States v. Villarreal* (1992), in which the court found that there could be no use of the plain view doctrine in cases where law enforcement officers opened a closed container.

There has been debate in the literature concerning whether there is any situation that would allow an officer to open every file on a computer during a search for a specific type of file. For example, these debates question whether evidence of a graphical nature should be opened if the search warrant is issued for records in the form of documents. While at first glance it is possible to see how this could be of concern. It would seem that to allow such widespread examination would exceed any search warrant. The truth is that such widespread searches are necessary when dealing with digital evidence. Historically, such a separation between evidence that takes the form of images and evidence that comes in document form. Today, however, these file types may be hidden by a variety of techniques. One of the easiest is through the mere changing of a file's extension. A picture file normally ends with .jpeg or .gif extensions. A document ends in .doc or .wpd. However, if you were to take a document file and change the extension to .jpeg, then the operating system would be fooled into believing that the file was an image file and not a document file. If a forensic examiner is conducting a thorough analysis then it may be necessary to open every file to ensure that the evidence listed in the search warrant is not hidden through such deception. This requirement for such a thorough search is what results in lengthy time requirements when conducting a forensic analysis of a computer.

So, while at present there is no clear guidance on this issue, it would appear that the majority of courts support at least the opening of the first image that is not covered under the original search warrant. Subsequent images may require an additional search warrant, but the question is whether obtaining a new search warrant would even result in the loss of evidence. After all, if you are conducting an examination of a forensic duplicate, of which more will be discussed in later chapters, then the evidence is not going to leave the agency's facility. There appears to be little harm in stopping the analysis and obtaining an additional search warrant.

Warrantless Searches by a Private Party

Each of the previous cases and warrantless search doctrines has addressed the behavior by government agents. What if the warrantless search is conducted by someone who is not affiliated with law enforcement? The Supreme Court has recognized that the Fourth Amendment does not regulate the activities of private citizens when it comes to the search and seizure of property. The lower courts have been asked to examine this issue in several cases. In *United States v. Hall* (1998) the court was asked to determine whether a violation of the Fourth Amendment had occurred when a computer repairman notified law enforcement about potential child pornography stored on a computer under his repair. During a routine repair of the computer, the repairman discovered images that he believed to be child pornography. He then immediately alerted his local law enforcement agency. At trial, and on appeal, the computer's owner argued that the repairman was an agent of the government. The court refused to accept this argument and found that the repairman was not acting under color of state law and therefore the Fourth Amendment did not apply in the case.

In *United States v. Barth* (1998) a similar situation was encountered. The issue at stake was whether an accountant's privacy was invaded after images of child pornography were seized during the course of a computer repair. A computer repairman was repairing Barth's computer when images of child pornography were discovered. The repairman was an occasional informant, so he notified his law enforcement contact. Then the repairman returned to continue his search for additional images of child pornography without a search warrant. The court determined that the repairman's search was illegal because he was technically acting under the color of state law from the time the first report was made. After the first image was discovered, there was sufficient evidence for law enforcement personnel to use the one image as justification for a search warrant. When the repairman returned to the computer he was acting in conjunction with the state and therefore the Fourth Amendment was applicable to his actions. The court made mention of the fact that the repairman was an informant, and therefore because of his previous interactions with law enforcement he should have known that he was acting inappropriately when he continued the search. In reading the court's opinion it would appear that law enforcement officers who receive such tips have an obligation to inform their tipsters that they are not allowed to continue searching for additional evidence.

Miscellaneous Warrantless Search Doctrines

There are a variety of warrantless search doctrines remaining. Three of these warrantless doctrines warrant cursory coverage. The first area to be addressed is the seizure of evidence by an employer, and whether there is a difference between the rights of public and private employers. The Supreme Court, in the decision of *O'Connor v. Ortega* (1987), addressed the issue of workplace seizures. Based on this decision, it is generally held that while it is not impossible to maintain an expectation of privacy at work, there is a greatly diminished expectation in the workplace. Each situation will involve its own consideration of all facts surrounding the case. If the individual maintains an office that is locked away from other employees then it could be determined that the individual maintained an expectation of privacy in the materials located within that office, including the computer and other storage media. Consider the example of a government worker who is provided with their own private office. Each night when the person leaves, the office is locked and no one in the office has a key except security and the worker's direct supervisor. Does this person maintain a right to privacy in the items stored within?

Generally, it could be said that this person does have a right to privacy. However, there are additional considerations. One is the consideration of whether the search is being conducted in furtherance of an investigation related to a violation of an organization policy or rule. If the answer is yes, then the individual's expectation of privacy will not prohibit the search. If the search does not involve an investigation of the organization's policies or procedures, then there is still one other consideration that may allow for a warrantless search or seizure. This consideration is whether or not the organization has a policy informing its personnel about their limited privacy expectations in the workplace. Published company policies, or even published governmental policies, directly addressing the expectations of privacy in work-related areas can go a long way toward preventing an employee from claiming a Fourth Amendment protection. In discussing computers and the use of an employer's network, some companies have attempted the use of banners. A banner is a message that appears to a user when the system is turned on or the computer attempts to connect to an employer's network. This banner will normally inform the user that the computer is not to be used for any purposes beyond the employee's assigned task. The banner will also address the fact that employees should be aware that they should expect a limited amount of privacy when using the employer's computers.

A second area of warrantless search that could see elevated levels of debate, especially with the increasing number of youthful technology crime offenders, is the area of school searches. In *New Jersey v. T.L.O.* (1985), the United States Supreme Court found that warrantless searches of students on school grounds may be acceptable under certain circumstances. The school's principal is required to show that there was proof that the student in question was either currently, or recently, involved in the commission of a criminal act or an act that was in violation of the school's rules.

There have been few, if any, cases to directly discuss the seizure of computer-related evidence from a student. However, there have been several decisions to further expand, as well as regulate, seizures of materials from students. For example, in *West Virginia v. Joseph T.* (1985) a school official conducted a search of a student's locker for alcohol. Another student had reported to the school official that he had drunk alcohol at the other boy's home the previous night. It was the administrator's belief that he had a right to search the locker because there was sufficient proof that a student who had drunk alcohol the night before might attempt to bring the alcohol to school the next day and hide the drinks. The court agreed with the administrator, basically ruling that a warrantless search on school grounds requires a level of proof so small that reasonable suspicion is sufficient justification for the search.

There have also been decisions to limit the application of warrantless school searches. For example, in *Cales v. Howell* (1985) the court determined that the warrantless search of a female student's body, by means of a strip search, was excessive. The court felt that such an extreme response to a student's skipping class could not be tolerated. For a search to be considered acceptable, the level of the search must be within reason when considering the particular crime or rule violation that resulted in the need for the warrantless search. In the above case the student was merely skipping class, and while that type of behavior is inappropriate, there should be little doubt that stripping searching a student for skipping class in excessive.

How could the realm of school searches and high-technology crime intersect? Well, the advent of PDAs and laptops has resulted in more school age citizens obtaining these devices for use at school. While personal data assistants may not store a large amount of data, many of the current devices do allow for Internet connectivity and could be used in the commission of a computer-related crime. Laptops are certainly capable of being used in criminal activity. So, while it would be possible to argue that computer technology from a school is being used in the commission of a crime, there are currently few scenarios where such a search involving a computer would be warranted. Several of the aforementioned areas of warrantless search could be utilized in conjunction with the diminished privacy expectations in school and allow for a possible search and seizure.

Conclusion

When attempting to seize a technological device during the course of a criminal investigation, the preferred method should always be through the use of a well drafted search warrant that satisfies the requirements of particularity and specificity. In accordance with this policy, the search warrant should contain as thorough a description of the various technological devices expected to be encountered at the scene of the search. Recognizing that there may be scenarios in which it is impossible to think of every possible type of technology that could be encountered, the courts have allowed some jurisdictions to utilize the phrase "including but not limited to." If the use of a warrant using such terminology is challenged, then the investigator who drafted the warrant could argue that their attempt to list every known technological device that is commonly encountered during an investigation of such a crime should prevent the appearance of a fishing expedition.

Smaller law enforcement agencies, recognizing the increasing use of computer technology in criminal activities but not having the resources to fund an entire unit, may find the development of a search warrant execution team to be of benefit. These teams are composed primarily of officers from other units that are trained on how to handle the very specific process of collecting technological and digital evidence from a crime scene. The use of these teams will help prevent the unintentional destruction of valuable evidence, as well as prevent illegal or inappropriate seizures of additional evidence. These teams can be trained to perform each of their functions while also being trained on the law of search and seizure in regards to technological advances.

Of course there may be certain situations in which an investigator may be unable to take the necessary time to draft a valid search warrant. Should such a situation arise, there has been precedent established that would allow for the warrantless search and/or seizure of technological and digital evidence. The rules are not, however, firmly established and while the general consensus among the lower courts is that an officer may seize such evidence, there is still some question as to whether evidence such as computer disks may be searched absent a search warrant. Currently, the best rule to follow in situations that involve a warrantless seizure is to use one of the established warrantless search doctrines to conduct a seizure of the evidence, and then immediately seek out and obtain a well drafted search warrant to search the internal portions of the evidence.

Review Questions

1. What is meant when the term "well drafted search warrant" is mentioned? How can investigators ensure that there search warrants meet these criteria when technology is involved?

2. Discuss the various levels of legal process required to obtain information relating to electronic communications.

3. What are some considerations for investigators when preplanning for a search warrant involving evidence of a high-technology crime?

4. What was the original purpose of the search incident to arrest doctrine that allows for the warrantless seizure of evidence? How has this doctrine been applied to computer-related evidence?

5. Do you agree or disagree that the search incident to an arrest doctrine has been misapplied when allowing for the seizure of evidence from a disk without a search warrant? Why or why not?

6. Why is the use of consent searches dangerous when evidence relating to a high-technology crime is involved?

7. The exigent circumstances doctrine is one of the most commonly cited warrantless search doctrines in regards to digital evidence. What must an officer show in order to argue this doctrine? What must an officer show to argue the use of this doctrine in relation to digital evidence?

8. What are the components of the high-technology crime search and seizure team, as recommended by Clark and Diliberto?

Further Reading

Department of Justice. (2002). "Searching and Seizing Computers and Obtaining Electronic Evidence in Criminal Investigations." Washington, DC. Electronic version available at http://www.usdoj.gov/criminal/cybercrime/s&smanual2002.pdf.

Clark, F. & Diliberto, K. (1996). *Investigating Computer Crime*. New York: CRC Press

Online Resources

Federal Judicial Center—website providing information relating to the search and seizure of computers; contains links to sample search warrants, as well as information relating to wording of subpoenas and court orders for electronic communications. Available at http://www.fjc.gov/public/home.nsf/pages/334.

Chapter 9

Executing a Search Warrant for Digital Evidence

Once the search warrant is prepared and the pre-planning phase is over, it is time to begin the seizure. An investigator should never be concerned about asking for the assistance of a professional computer expert. The worst possible scenario for an investigator would be for a case to be irreparably damaged because of technical mistakes made by officers seizing the computer or digital evidence. Properly shutting down the computer and packaging the various components is as important to the case as any other stage of the investigation. The presence of a computer professional will allow for someone with experience with various computer operating systems and hardware to diagnose the potential for damage to a system. It is always better to spend the additional time necessary to obtain qualified personnel than it is to allow the evidence to be damaged or destroyed. The following sections provide a step-by-step guide for individuals asked to seize a computer or other technological device. These guidelines are based upon a combination of recommendations made by the United States Department of Justice, various authors on computer technology, and the author's personal experiences in dealing with computers.

The Steps of Executing a Search Warrant for Digital Evidence

Step One: Removing the Suspect from the Computer

An officer's first responsibility when executing a search warrant for a computer or other technological device is to move the suspect away from the computer. The removal of the suspect from controlling potential evidence is an important consideration in any search, but it is of extreme importance when the evidence being obtained is digital in nature and stored on a computer-related device. If the computer is powered on when officers arrive at the scene, then this requirement becomes even more important because there is the potential for the presence of quick-delete programs that allow for the deletion of data with the touch of a single key or quick combination of keys. These programs can be set to delete certain files or to format an entire hard drive, thereby making evidence recovery difficult. Of course deletion and formatting do not necessarily make the evidence unrecoverable, but it may certainly make the recovery of the evidence more costly because of the need for advanced recovery equipment.

These deletion programs are normally configured to allow users to designate a "hot key" that will launch the erase program when a certain combination of keys has been pressed. If an individual is in the process of executing a search warrant for computer-related evidence, and the suspect can get to the computer, then there is a chance that the evidence could be damaged or altered. It is worth noting that few individuals are considered "power-users," the type of individuals that may be using such programs. Just because the investigation does not revolve around a very technical computer-related crime such as hacking, the investigator should not disregard these programs. By always responding as if there is the possible presence of such programs, standard operating procedures can be developed that handle situations involving deletion programs as capably as situations that do not involve such programs.

The possible presence of deletion programs has led to the development of the "no-knock search warrant" question. The question revolves around whether search warrants for computer-related evidence justify the use of no-knock search warrants. While the exigency of digital evidence might satisfy the requirement for a no-knock warrant in the near future, there is little or no judicial support for the issuance of this type of warrant at this time. Generally, there are two accepted methods of removing a suspect from a computer:

1. Through the use of physical force. This method may become necessary but should be reserved for a last option because of the potential for liability.

2. By asking the individual to shake your hand. If the suspect shakes your hand then they can be prevented from returning to the computer. If force then becomes necessary it can be better controlled.

Regardless of how one chooses to remove the suspect from the computer, it is very important that, once they are removed, they not be allowed to return to the computer for any reason. Inform the suspect that their computer will be properly handled and that they do not need to worry about shutting off the machine, as everything will be carefully handled from this point on by professional investigators.

Step Two: Securing the Scene

From the moment the individual is moved away from the computer, the focus of the investigator, or pre-designated replacement, should be on photographing the crime scene. With advances in photography technology, it is recommended that a digital camera be used by the search warrant team. At a minimum there are two benefits to the use of this form of camera:

1. Non-reusable film is not a factor, because film is not used. Once the warrant is executed, the investigator can take the camera back to the office and upload the images to a secure file on their computer. Images can then be viewed from the computer or printed by a film company.

2. Perhaps the biggest advantage to the use of a digital camera is the fact that photographs can be taken and then immediately viewed at the scene. This prevents situations in which the picture is taken, only for it to later be discovered that the shot was insufficient for proving what was in question.

Another alternative available today, should the department have the necessary funds (and someone willing to run the device) is the use of a video camera. Use of a video camera would allow investigators to better protect themselves from the infamous "the evidence was planted there by the police" charge. Of course, the use of a video camera may not completely remove the argument, but it can provide assistance in arguing that there is no truth to the claim. Digital video cameras are now much easier to use, as well as much more affordable. Much like digital cameras, video cameras today can be used to record the entire search, and then the video can be transferred to an electronic storage medium (computer hard drive, DVD-ROM or CD-ROM).

When investigators take pictures of the scene, special attention should be placed upon providing photographs of the screen if the computer is running and photographs of the blank screen if the computer is off. This allows investigators to show what programs were running on the suspect's computer when the search team arrived. Obvious uses for this include preventing the suspect from using the argument that they were not engaged in the criminal act in question. Another important item that should be photographed or video-recorded is the computer system's clock. This is information that will be beneficial to the computer forensic analysts when they conduct their examination, and may even become necessary to place the suspect at the computer when the crime in question was committed. In examining the system clock, it is important to determine if: (1) the clock is accurate and (2) if the clock is not accurate, then the investigator can note the difference between the actual time and the time displayed on the screen. Some computer forensic examination programs have now taken the issue of time into consideration. Whenever a hard drive or other storage media is imaged (a copy is made for examination) the time of the recording is listed on the imaging and acquisition report. However, not all programs have this feature, and so the old fashioned method of verifying time is still considered the best alternative.

Once the photographing or videoing of the search begins, the remainder of the search should be videoed or photographed. Of course anytime an investigator comes across new evidence, the evidence should be photographed exactly as it is found. Even if the evidence does not appear at first glance to be of use, later discoveries may make the evidence useful. Also, with digital cameras the cost of film is removed from the equation and should the picture prove useless at a later date then the image can be deleted rather easily.

Step Three: Disconnect any Outside Control Possibilities

As one investigator is filming the scene, another should immediately pull the phone line or the network cable from the back of the computer. Just as quick action was necessary to prevent the suspect from damaging any evidence on the computer, the presence of an outside connection opens the door for the remote destruction of digital evidence. If the suspect's computer is connected to the Internet via a phone line then there is the possibility that the evidence could be removed by someone outside of the crime scene. The same phone line connections that connect telephones to wall outlets, also allows computers to connect to the Internet. Internet connectivity that is provided by traditional phone line is known as narrow band Internet service because the data transfer is limited to around 56.6k bps. It is recommended that the phone lines be pulled from the back of the computer because there remains the possibility that the suspect could have the phone line running to a different wall outlet, thereby only giving the appearance of having the phone plugged into the outlet nearest the computer. Some professionals that handle computer-related investigations have begun recommending that an extra phone be brought along during the execution of a search warrant to verify that the phone lines are active where the computer is attached.

While 56.6k bps modems are still used with great frequency, the advent of high-speed Internet connectivity commonly referred to as broadband Internet connectivity has led to the presence of additional Internet connection devices. The two most common home versions of high-speed Internet services are DSL and cable modems. DSL, which stands for digital subscriber line, is similar in looks to a traditional phone line but is connected to a device that separates information traveling through the computer into two sections: (1) voice and (2) data. The DSL device splits transmissions so that voice information can still be carried across the phone line, regardless of whether the Internet account is activated or not. The data portion of the phone line is then used to transmit data while not interfering with voice communications that occur while the user is connected to the Internet. Put simply, the use of DSL lines allows users to surf the Internet while speaking on the telephone line at the same time.

It was this splitting of information into two formats that made DSL popular when it was first released. The connection speeds are advertised at 50 times greater than dial-up, but realistically one can expect about 20 times faster connection. To disconnect a DSL modem, one must still remove the device from the back of the computer. The traditional phone line runs from the outlet to the DSL device, and from the DSL device there is another cord that many times will appear similar to a regular phone cord and runs to the computer. It would be easy for a suspect to run multiple lines around the home, thereby giving the impression that the device was connected to the outlet closest to the computer, when in fact it may be connected to an outlet in another room.

The other common high-speed Internet connection device that is seeing increased use in the home is that of the cable modem. These devices are different from the 56.6k modems and the DSL modems. Cable modems are connected via the coaxial cable that feeds a home its cable TV service (hence the name cable modem). Like the DSL line, the use of this modem allows users to remain talking on the telephone, while they are downloading data or "surfing the web." This device can be identified by following a coaxial cable somewhere around the computer to the modem. From there, the cable modem device will have a cord running to the back of the computer. Once again, the cord should be removed from the back of the computer just to ensure the potential flow of data is immediately interrupted.

Occasionally, one may encounter an Internet set-up where the suspect is running a home network. In recent years, the cost of networking equipment has steadily decreased in an effort to make them more affordable for home users. Normally, however, network connections are used in businesses and university settings. Network cables look like phone line cables, but are slightly thicker and have a larger end connector where the line plugs into the computer. Many DSL and cable modem connections now allow users to connect the devices to the computer through the use of a network cable. Networks have little to do with connection to the Internet, as anyone who uses a network must still have some form of outside Internet service. The use of networking equipment merely allows users of multiple computers to share data and applications. One of the more common uses of a network is to allow users to save data on a computer that is not close to them. In universities, networked computers allow administrators to dedicate a network drive for students to store their work on, and when the drive is full, or at random times, the drive is cleaned of all remaining data. This prevents students from filling up the hard drives of computers in the lab with useless programs and data.

After the terrorist attacks of September 11, 2001, it is believed that more companies are moving toward the use of computer networks to store their company's work. The reasoning behind this is that if there is another disaster, whether natural or man-made, and the building that houses the company is destroyed, then the data are safely stored elsewhere. With the current level of technology, it is possible to store data at a building across the street, or at a building in another country. Investigators should remove the network connection just as they would remove the connection of the 56.6k modem or the DSL and cable modems—from the back of the computer. Investigators should not worry about losing the information that is stored on the network server, as the computer that is seized should still maintain a record of having a network drive. With the assistance of the network administrator, whether willing or unwilling, the network server can be located and the data can be obtained. Of course, once the suspect is notified there is the chance the individual could begin deleting the data. Special care should be taken to ensure that the network administrator does not contact someone who could begin deleting the data if it is believed that the company is responsible for the criminal activity in question. The best solution would be to ensure that there is not such a network drive prior to beginning the execution of the search warrant.

There is one final consideration when encountering a computer currently connected to the Internet. Before the computer is shut down, the investigator may make the decision to photograph the screen of the computer and include photographs of programs or files that are being downloaded. Download utilities may be running and may be minimized at the bottom of the screen (if the computer is running a Windows operating system or a Windows clone). An investigator may elect to maximize the download screen if they have probable cause to believe that the downloading in progress may be related to the criminal act under investigation. If an investigator elects to attempt this, they must ensure their actions are recorded in the search log, and if possible the entire process should be videotaped, so as to prevent the suspect from arguing that they were not downloading what they were accused of downloading. This decision should be left to the lead investigator, and should be decided on a case-by-case basis.

Step Four: Powering Down the Computer

Once the possibility of outside influence has been removed, the next step is to begin the process of powering down the suspect's computer. The type of operating system the user is running will control the investigator's decision to shut down the machine using proper shut down procedures, or merely pulling the plug from the back of the computer. Pulling the plug is many times considered the proper course of action for an investigator because there is the possibility the suspect could install a data deletion program on the computer. If the computer is not shut down in the proper order, then a software program will launch and begin deleting data from the hard drive. Some of these programs will delete data before the investigator becomes aware of the software's presence. As stated earlier, deleting data may not make evidence unrecoverable but it can impede the recovery process and result in the need for a longer (and occasionally more expensive) investigation. It should also be noted that, just as in the case of deletion programs being launched by a suspect when the search begins, there are relatively few suspects who will devote this level of time to protecting their computer. However, preparing standard procedures for seizing the computer will prevent any problems should such programs be involved.

Before an investigator powers down the computer, there are a few considerations to be made. First, if the suspect is currently running programs on the computer, then there is the possibility that one of the programs may contain evidence of the crime in question. Therefore, before the computer is shut down a decision should be made as to whether the potential evidence is important enough to attempt saving the evidence before pulling the plug. Currently, there are two schools of thought on this issue, with some professionals arguing that pulling the plug will not matter, as upon a loss of power the program that is running will save the data in a temporary folder on the hard drive. Temporary folders are where work that has not been saved is stored, but these copies of data are only stored at set intervals. If the evidence was not automatically saved into the temporary folder before the computer was shut down, then the evidence may be lost. The contents of the temporary folder are deleted when the operating system shuts down the computer via normal shut down procedures, so subscribing to this line of reason could certainly impact one's decision to properly shut down the computer or pull the plug.

The second consideration is whether investigators should become familiar enough with computer operating systems that should the need arise for the investigator to work with the operating system he or she can feel comfortable. Of importance in this consideration is the ability to determine what, if any, files are open and stored in the computer's Random Access Memory (RAM). Data is stored in RAM memory while the computer is powered on, and upon turning off the power to the computer the RAM data is removed. Because the data may not have written to the hard drive or other storage media, files stored in RAM that are lost are not normally recoverable. If an investigator is familiar with the basics of operating systems then a quick glance at the screen will generally allow for searching for files in RAM. If any files are found that could relate to the case-at-hand, then they can be saved to an external storage media provided by the investigator.

The Window's operating system, which is reportedly the most commonly encountered operating system for law enforcement officials, makes the locating of files running in RAM easier. In looking at the bottom portion of a computer screen, there are small boxes containing text. If the box contains the words "untitled," then it is likely that the files have not been saved and are stored in RAM. An investigator may enlarge these files by clicking on the text box, a process that allows the file window to then take up either the entire screen or a portion of the screen. An investigator may then choose to save the files with a name that they can easily be identified as one created during the investigation. Consider an example where an investigator encounters a list of narcotics buyers found open on a suspect's computer. The file is determined to be vital evidence and the investigator determines to save the contents to an external floppy disk. Perhaps the file name selected for the file would be something similar to "investigate1.doc," or some other filename related to the case number. The filename is then entered into a search log containing all information relating to the execution of the search warrant. This way, should the integrity of the file be challenged at a later date, there are written reports supporting the investigator's statements. It is important to reiterate that the file be saved to an external storage medium, as even saving a small file to the hard drive may corrupt evidence stored on the suspect's hard drive.

If the suspect is running a version of Linux, then there are two methods of determining whether there are files running in RAM. The first, is used when the Linux operating system is running in the Windows X mode; this mode was recently added to Linux operating systems in an apparent attempt to appeal to users of the Microsoft operating system. The controls and operability of the Windows X program are very similar to Microsoft's Windows operating system, yet still retains enough individuality to differentiate between the two systems. When examining a computer running Windows X, the files that are active in RAM will be displayed at the bottom of the screen in a small window. Once again, files can be enlarged and saved to an external storage device using a name familiar to the investigator. If, however, the suspect is running the Linux operating system in Command prompt mode, then locating files in RAM is considerably different. From the command line prompt, an investigator must type "ps" to get a list of programs running in RAM. From there, the files of importance would need to be saved before shutting down the computer. Saving files via command line interface can be complex, and as such it is recommended that the individual on scene merely shut the computer down if they cannot obtain assistance from someone trained in the use of Linux.

Once all files running in RAM have been handled, the next step is to shut the computer down. A determination of the operating system version that the suspect is running will control the decision of whether to pull the plug or to properly shut the computer down using the shut down features of the operating system. In the following section, several operating systems are discussed with the intent of providing recommendations on handling the powering down of computers running each operating system.

Microsoft Operating System

This operating system is licensed by Microsoft Corporation, and has numerous versions on the market. Fortunately, as newer versions are released the older versions generally begin to see less use as people update to newer versions. The majority of Windows operating systems are best shut down by pulling the plug from the back of the computer. The plug should be removed from the back of the computer because there are devices that provide power to a computer after the plug has been pulled from the wall. Some of these devices can even be programmed to deliver a high voltage discharge to the computer's motherboard if the power is cut off from the wall outlet. The use of these devices is incredibly rare, but the mere existence of these programs warrants their discussion and consideration. The recommended shutdown procedures for each of the following Microsoft operating systems are as follows:

> ***Windows Version 3.11***—The plug should be pulled from the back of the computer. This version of Microsoft Windows should only rarely be encountered as this version has been outdated since 1995. The structure of the operating system, however, allows for users to lose power abruptly without damaging data.

> ***Windows 95***—The plug should be pulled from the back of the computer. This version replaced Windows 3.11 and like its predecessor allows for loss of power without loss of data. However, there is still a minimal possibility of data damage.

> ***Windows 98***—The plug should be pulled from the back of the computer. Like Windows 95 and 3.11 this version can recover from a sudden loss of power.

> ***Windows 2000***—The plug should be pulled from the back of the computer.

> ***Windows 2000 Server***—The computer should be shut down using proper shut down features built into the operating system. The server version of the operating system is designed for security and for maintaining high volume Internet traffic. As such, the immediate loss of power to the system could provide a greater chance for damage to data. Computers running Windows 2000 Server should be shut down using the internal power-down features included within the operating system.

> ***Windows ME***—The plug should be pulled from the back of the computer. This relatively short-lived replacement for Windows 2000 can survive the immediate loss of power that comes from pulling the plug from the back.

> ***Windows XP***—The plug should be pulled from the back of the computer. This is Window's latest operating system, and is capable of recovering after having the power immediately shut off.

Identifying which of the operating system is running can be straightforward. At the bottom left side of the screen, computers running Windows 95 and later contain an icon (some would call it a button) that contains the word "Start." Clicking on the start icon with the left button of the computer's mouse will result in a listing of programs and options appearing. On the left side of this pop up screen, is the operating system version written vertically. This being said, it is possible to customize the Windows operating system so that the identifying information may not be listed after clicking on the start icon. Should a situation arise where the operating system is unfamiliar to the investigator, and initial attempts to identify the operating system are unsuccessful, then the plug can be pulled. Because the majority of Windows operating systems allow for this form of powering down, an investigator who cannot determine the type of operating system runs a minimal chance of damaging evidence. The investigator may also stop and obtain a computer science professional's assistance in identifying the operating system.

Computers that cannot be powered down by pulling the plug and require the investigator to power down using the internal features of the software, can generally be shut down using the following procedures. The majority of Microsoft Windows operating systems allow for users to shut down the computer by clicking on the start icon. One of the options that will appear will be "Shut Down." Selecting the shut down option will lead to the computer powering down.

Macintosh Operating System

This is the operating system designed by Apple computers, and currently used in the Macintosh computers that bear the Apple logo. This operating system is perhaps most unique because of the fact that hardware and software configurations have traditionally made interoperability between Macintosh computers and other computers that followed the original design of International Business Machines (IBM) almost impossible. In recent years, there has been rumor in the industry that the newer Mac computers can better recover from immediate losses of power. Older versions of the Macintosh computer, however, required the computer to be shut down. Failure to follow proper shut down procedures could result in the data on the computer's hard drive becoming inaccessible. Once again, the investigator must make a judgment call as to whether they wish to attempt proper shut down procedures, or if they wish to merely pull the plug. The Macintosh computer is seeing increased use thanks to: (1) better interoperability and (2) advertising. In fact, many hard core digital video editors claim that Macintosh is the only computer worth using in the production of high quality digital videos. Given the nature of crimes like child pornography there is the possibility that this computer will see a greater increase in use as more people become familiar with the software. As of today, however, the Mac is used rarely, but warrants consideration in any discussion dealing with computer operating systems. The popularity of home production of digital video has led more users to begin working on Macintosh computers, because of the Macintosh's superior programs in this area. Unlike the computers running the Windows operating system, files stored in the RAM must be found using the "Finder" key at the top right hand side of the computer screen. This command will provide an investigator with information on which programs are running in the background of the computer. Once the files are located, then the investigator can decide whether to save the files or shut the computer down without saving the information. Once files have been properly saved, the computer can be shut down by selecting the "Special" option from the top menu bar of the screen. From here, the option "Shut Down" is selected and the Macintosh operating system will begin shutting down the computer.

Unix/Linux Operating System

UNIX has been around for decades, and is a very popular operating system for Internet servers. True computer users, those individuals who could be considered true hackers, love the power and the reliability of the Unix operating system. It was this same desire for use that led a foreign computer programmer to develop the Linux operating system. Linux contains many of the same features as that of UNIX. An investigator who encounters a computer running the Linux operating system must take care in shutting down the computer. The design of the UNIX and Linux operating systems does not allow for sudden losses of power to the computer. Pulling the plug from the back of a Linux or UNIX computer can cause damage to the operating system's kernel.

The purpose behind pulling the plug on an operating system is to prevent the suspect from using a program that deletes data from the hard drive if the computer is not shut down in a specific pattern. The potential for damage to the Linux/Unix kernel is so great, that investigators are better off to risk the possibility of damage by shutting the computer down. Linux computers are shut down by typing the command "shutdown h now" at the command prompt. The command "now" is used because Linux allows users to establish times in the future when the computer is to be shut down. It is important to remember that some newer versions of Linux allow for programs to be run in a Windows-like environment. With the Linux Windows X program, when a user shuts down the Windows-like program the computer is not powered down. Instead, the program returns the operating system to the command prompt. It should be noted that when dealing with a Linux or Unix operating system that an immediate loss of power when the computer is at the command prompt is just as damaging to evidence (and the system) as cutting the power when the computer is still in the windows environment.

Another important reason for properly powering down the Linux operating system lies in the manner with which Linux handles past commands. The last 100 commands that a user types into the command prompt are stored in the Linux memory when the computer is properly shut down. While the presence of history commands may not be of great assistance in cases involving child pornography or identity theft, they may be of invaluable assistance during the investigation of crimes involving computer intrusion and hacking attacks.

The similarity to UNIX has made Linux a very popular alternative operating system by those who consider themselves hackers, whether they are true hackers or whether they are, in fact, script kiddies. There are many hacking utility programs that are written exclusively for use on the Linux operating system. It is the enthusiast's obsession with Linux that makes this operating system more prone to software booby traps than that of Windows and Macintosh operating systems, and it is for this reason that special care should be taken when dealing with computers that are found to be running the Linux operating system.

Laptop Computers

The previous sections have dealt with powering down computers running the various operating systems. The problem, however, is that each of these sections discussed the handling of desktops. The question now becomes how to power down a computer that relies on a dual source of power. Remember that the solution for certain operating systems was to merely pull the plug from the back of the computer, thereby rendering the computer without power. These computers that rely on dual sources of power, most notably laptops, cannot be handled in the same manner. Pulling the power cord on a laptop will only result in the internal battery generating power.

When dealing with a laptop, the same holds true for each of the aforementioned operating systems. If the operating system would require the computer be shut down if the suspect was running a desktop computer, then the computer would have to be shut down if the operating system was running on a laptop. The problem with pulling the plug on a laptop is the presence of the internal battery. Whenever the AC power cord is removed, the computer merely switches over to the reserve battery, which keeps the computer running until all of the power in the battery is drained. If an investigator encounters a laptop being used in the commission of a criminal act, then the solution is to remove the battery from the laptop. The majority of laptop batteries are easily removable with the sliding of a lever on the bottom of the computer, or at most the removal of a few screws. The battery should be pulled, labeled and packed with the laptop, in case the computer needs to be powered back up at the lab or in court.

Step Five: Disassembling the Computer

Once the computer is powered down, then the next step is for the investigator to begin disassembling the computer and preparing it for transportation. If there is only one computer, the potential for problems at this level is significantly less. Occasionally, however, a seizure may result in the acquisition of more than one computer. When this happens, it is important that personnel ensure the computers are disassembled in such a manner that the investigator can later reassemble any or all of the computers either back in the lab or in court. To prevent confusion and to provide stability, it is recommended that the same procedures be followed regardless of whether the seizure involves one computer or multiple computers.

Individuals who are familiar with computers may have no problem reassembling a suspect's computer, but there is the possibility that the suspect (or their attorney) may attempt to argue that a certain device was not connected to the computer and therefore they could not have committed the crime in question. To prevent this, or at a minimum to reduce the risk associated with this argument, it is recommended that each cord or device be labeled as it is being unplugged from the back of the suspect's computer. One label should be applied to the wire or device, and another label should be applied to the back of the computer at the port where the device was unplugged. Should an investigator encounter a computer that has ports that are not in use, then the port should be taped and labeled as not in use.

Some investigators have found that the use of masking tape is fine for labeling seized computers. Others have found that the use of colored labels is better suited for the task. The true difference between the two labeling methods is only appearance. With masking tape, all of the ports have tape placed below them and the type of device that was unplugged is written on the tape. With the use of colored labels, each port is color coded and the device that is removed is affixed with the same colored label. The investigator still marks which device was unplugged from the port, but the use of color labels allows for quicker discovery of the device and the port. Also, ports that are not in use can be assigned their own color. The true benefit in using color coded labels is in the seizure of multiple computers. In place of color coding each port, each computer would be color coded and all of the ports would be marked as each device is unplugged. The benefit here is obvious; all red coded wires would connect to the red computer and all orange coded wires would connect to the orange computer. The use of this coding scheme could be used to reassemble an entire network relatively easily if called upon.

Once the computer is disassembled then investigators need to begin examining the area for additional hardware that could be potential evidence. Many times these external devices may contain more evidence than could be expected. For example, child pornographers who are manufacturing their own videos may have a digital video camera attached to or placed near the computer. Even if the evidence has not been transferred to the computer, there is the possibility that evidence may be stored on the digital camera in the form of a video tape or video CD. Perhaps a more commonly encountered example is the suspect who uses their scanner to scan illegal images into a digital format. Because some people leave the last image scanned into the computer on the bed of the scanner, it is important that the bed always be checked for potential evidence. Other people leave all forms of documents and papers on the scanner bed. It is not uncommon for an individual to store their passwords on a piece of paper and then store the paper on the bed of the scanner so the information if easily accessible. If the scanner is not examined prior to leaving the scene then it is likely that the evidence will be gone forever. Likewise, if the bed of the scanner is not examined before the device is packaged for seizure then the evidence may not be rediscovered until the device is reconnected; if the device is ever reconnected.

The decision as to how much of the peripheral equipment is to be seized is a question to be answered by (1) the investigator's determination based upon facts of the case and (2) the search warrant authorizing the seizure. If the search warrant authorizes the seizure of the additional peripherals and the agency has the storage space then there is truly no harm in seizing all of the evidence. One of the benefits of seizing everything is that when the computer forensic examiner begins his or her examination, it may become necessary to have the original parts available to reconnect the computer. There have been situations in which this author has been asked to examine a computer, only to find that not all of the cables were seized with the computer. The computer in question was so old that no monitors in the police department would work with the computer. The entire imaging process had to be completed out of memory, without the benefit of onscreen direction. Was it impossible to image the drive? Obviously not. Was it extremely inconvenient? Yes, it was. Another benefit of taking the approach of seizing all peripherals connected to the computer is that if the investigator is asked to reassemble the computer at a later date (for example, in court), then all of the devices can be located and reassembled using the color coding system used during the disassembling process.

Step Six: Securing Additional Evidence from the Scene

While the computer may be the primary piece of evidence listed on the search warrant, it is important to remember the need to seize additional evidence that may be surrounding the computer. Of course a primary concern when discussing this issue is whether the additional evidence was included in the application for the search warrant or its whether the collection of such items falls within one of the carefully predefined justifications for a warrantless seizure. Ultimately, the preferred method of seizure would involve having the materials on the search warrant. Remembering the need to include items such as floppy disks, manuals, etc, in the search warrant can save time and effort during the execution of the search warrant.

Floppy disks are normally located in the area immediately surrounding the computer. This does not, however, mean that the disks will only be found in that area. Some of the reasons people may move floppy disks around are so that they are:

1.   not seized during a search like that being currently discussed;

2.   not damaged in an emergency such as a fire or other natural disaster;

3.   not easily discovered or obtained by friends or relatives.

As the floppy disks are seized, they should be taken to a central individual who has been pre-selected to catalog the evidence obtained at the scene. This individual will ensure that the floppy disks are write-protected, which means no data can be added to the disk or deleted from the disk, and that disks are labeled with the following information:

1.   the room and location in which the floppy disk was found

2.   the officer who located the floppy disk

3.   any identifying information that the investigator deems necessary

The write-protecting of the floppy disk is meant as a means of assisting the computer forensic analyst. When the analyst attempts to image the floppy disk contents in order to begin searching them for evidence, he or she will have to adjust the write protection on the disks so there is no damage to data. Some of the computer forensics programs available, which will be discussed in a later chapter, can potentially write information to the disk during the imaging process. While the chance of modifying data is minimal, any potential change to the disks should be avoided whenever possible. By providing for write protection at the scene of the seizure, there is even less chance of a mistake being made during the imaging process (i.e., the analyst neglecting to write protect the disk). This is of course not required and is merely a nicety on the part of the officers conducting the search.

Along with floppy disks, CD-ROMs and DVD-ROMs should also be considered during a search. These materials may be located in various places around the house. In the case of simple computer users, the materials may be located near the computer for ease of access. More sophisticated users may be more security conscious, or perhaps paranoid is the better term. These individuals may keep both storage media in traditional CD jewel cases, or the ingenious user may replace these storage media in their favorite DVD movie box. The decision to conduct a search of this magnitude should be based upon the investigator's knowledge of the circumstances surrounding the case in question.

Zip disks and Jaz disks should be searched for in much the same manner as that of floppy disks. Remember that these storage media look similar to floppy disks but store significantly more information. These materials should be treated no differently from any other digital evidence; the materials should be taken immediately to a central individual who will log in the evidence and ensure it is properly labeled. Flash drives are relatively new, and therefore are just beginning to see use in the computer community. These devices come in different designs, but can be recognized by the USB connection that protrudes from one end of the device. Many manufacturers now package their flash drives with neck bands. This means that a suspect may be wearing a storage device around his or her neck. There have been cases of suspects who had redesigned the storage case to look like a container of Chap Stick® or lipstick. Should these devices be encountered, it is important that a thorough examination take place as new methods of concealing the devices are constantly being developed.

Another device that should be considered during the execution of a search warrant is the potential presence of a personal data assistant (PDA) or other handheld organizer. These devices are commonly used to store e-mail, appointments, contact addresses and contact phone numbers, with some personal data assistants today capable of connecting to the Internet. All of the devices allow users to connect the PDA to the owner's desktop or laptop and swap files between the two. PDAs are routinely used to transport files the individual may want to work on during a trip or other time away from a computer. These devices may be located anywhere around the premises being searched. Investigators that routinely encounter technology in their investigations should familiarize themselves with these devices. The majority of these devices are similar in look and design, therefore a small amount of time devoted to gaining a basic understanding of PDAs will be of immeasurable benefit.

Some models of personal data assistants store their data in RAM; because a constant energy surge is necessary to maintain the data, the presence of fresh batteries is necessary. If a PDA without a memory card goes without fresh batteries for an extended period of time, then the data will be lost. For this reason, it is important that when seizing these devices the central evidence technician make a notation to obtain fresh batteries as soon as possible. The worst possible case scenario is for a PDA with important information to be discovered and then left setting in the evidence room until the battery is completely drained. The majority of PDAs that are manufactured by Palm operating system allow the user to quickly and easily check the power status by merely turning the power on. This temporary power on should not harm any evidence; not that the potential for harming evidence would be more important that verifying the battery level in order to prevent all evidence being lost. Should a situation arise requiring the PDA to be turned on, the investigator should make a note in the seizure log to prevent the suspect later arguing that changes were made by law enforcement after the seizure. Along with seizing the PDA, it is also recommended that the connection device be seized. If an investigator fails to seize the connection device, it is still possible for evidence to be recovered, but doing so requires the computer forensic analyst to purchase a connection cable. While this may not be an issue if the analyst has imaged that particular make and model of personal data assistant in the past, it can become a problem if the case is one of first impression. In this case, the analyst will be forced to purchase a connection device that is compatible with the personal data assistant.

Upon completing the search for all storage media, investigators should begin examining the manuals surrounding the computer. There are several reasons for seizing the manuals, but the most important reason is that seizing the materials may help the computer forensic analyst with understanding the various programs on the computer. Despite one's best ability it is impossible to become proficient in every software program. Therefore, the manuals can allow the forensic analyst to learn enough about a program to complete their analysis of a suspect computer. Also, in the past some software programs would require the computer's user to set up the program's passwords during installation. If the user failed to change the default passwords, then the manuals contained the passwords necessary for access to password protected programs. Today, however, many manuals do not contain information on passwords associated with the software program; however, the materials associated with operating the program may still warrant seizure of the manuals. Finally, during the search for manuals it is important that investigators consider the possibility of locating a listing of passwords. Many serious computer users spend hours at the computer. With this in mind, investigators who search under, over, in, and around the area where the computer was stored, may find these passwords taped to a myriad assortment of locations.

Step Seven: Preparing the Evidence for Transportation

Once all of the evidence has been collected, the individual assigned with the task of logging the evidence should verify that the asset seizure log has been completely itemized, so everyone is aware of exactly what items have been seized. A copy of this itemized log should be kept for the records of the law enforcement agency, but an additional copy should be made for the suspect. Once the form is completed, the suspect should be asked to sign off on the copy maintained by the seizing agency. If the individual refuses to sign, then there refusal should be noted and the officer in charge of the form should sign the form. The evidence seized should be listed on the form by lines, with each item seized occupying its own line on the seizure log.

Upon completion of the asset seizure form, the investigator should begin preparing to ship the computer back to the precinct. Some agencies prefer to actually place the computer into a plastic bag and then carry the items out to the car, while other agencies have indicated a desire to box up all of the components and place the box into the car. If the agency desires to use a bagging system, then it is important to remember that hard drives and storage media should be maintained in a static-free bag in order to prevent damage to the contents. If the agency determines to box up the contents, then packing should be used to secure the computer or technological device, but styrofoam should be avoided as it provides for the possibility of static electricity that could damage the computer or the storage media within the device. Additionally, any empty disk drives should have blank evidence disks inserted into the drive to prevent damage during shipping.

Regardless of which packaging method is selected, the computer should not be placed into the trunk of the police unit. The computer should be placed in the back seat and taken to a secure storage facility as soon as possible. There are at least two valid reasons for not using the trunk:

1. The heat—During warm months, or even during cool months, the trunk of a car can become as hot as an oven. If the computer is placed into the trunk and the then there is a delay in getting the evidence back to a secure location, then there is the possibility that the computer could be damaged beyond repair.

2. The electronic discharge of equipment in the trunk—Many police departments place the bulk of their communication control equipment in the trunk of their police unit. This control equipment emits electrostatic discharges throughout the day, and such discharges could be damaging to electronic storage media such as hard drives, floppy disks, etc.

Wrapping Up the Search and Preserving the Evidence

The completion of the search warrant may not necessarily mean the end of the investigator's responsibility. Once all of the evidence is seized, properly logged, and packaged, it becomes important for the investigator to ensure that the evidence is secured in such a manner that it can be presented in court at a later date. To assist in this, the following section will address one of the more pressing issues concerning the preservation of digital evidence: the chain of custody.

Understanding the Chain of Custody

The issue of chain of custody is not a new one for those involved in the field of criminal justice. Anyone studying or affiliated with the criminal justice system has heard the term. While the concept of chain of custody is important in every case, when dealing with cases of digital evidence the chain can maintain extra significance. For example, consider evidence of a traditional crime such as a firearm. If the firearm is left unwatched for an extended period of time then the evidence can be challenged in court. However, can the very nature of the firearm be changed? No. Fingerprints can be wiped off and powder can be cleaned from the firearm. However, the imprints made from the barrel are left unmodified. On the other hand, digital evidence that is left unsupervised can be completed erased and modified in a short amount of time. Digital evidence, therefore, warrants additional care during the preservation phase while awaiting the presentation of evidence during trial.

The chain is normally considered to be the ability of an investigator to provide information on any individual and/or agency that has handled the evidence for the investigator. This "chain" stretches from the time the evidence is seized until it is presented in court, and when the chain of custody is defended in court the judge will look for evidence that "is sufficient to support a finding that the matter in question is what its proponent claims" (*B.A.C. v. T.L.G.*, 1986). In other words proof must provide clearly that the evidence presented in court is the same evidence that was taken from the scene of the crime and that the evidence has not been modified or tampered with in any manner. When prosecutors are attempting to provide proof of the chain of custody, the prosecution may be required to bring in every witness that has touched the evidence since it was seized. Of course there is the possibility that defense counsel may stipulate that digital evidence is the same as that which was seized from the scene of the crime. However, this would be a rare occasion simply for the fact that if the defense is challenging the charges, then they are aware that the computer-related evidence may be an integral part of the case.

Because every individual who has touched the evidence must testify as to the evidence being the original evidence, there are several opportunities for the defense to have the evidence removed if there is a problem with determining who has touched the digital evidence. Along with questioning who has touched the evidence, many times defense counsel may request to know why the individual in question touched the evidence. For this reason it is suggested that an evidence transaction log be maintained when investigations involve the presence of digital evidence. This log can be developed using any of a variety of spreadsheet programs, and contains information related to who removed digital evidence from the evidence storage facility, where was the evidence handled, and why the evidence was removed from the secure area. To better facilitate the storing of this information, it is recommended that the evidence transaction log contain sections for the date, time, location evidence was removed to, the individual's name who removed the evidence, and a brief narrative addressing why the evidence was removed. Another suggestion is that the evidence itself be labeled either by some professional software or by hand, in order to speed up the identification process during trial. There are several pieces of software that will now allow the investigating officer to print out an inventory label as soon as the evidence is collected; many times these programs can be used onsite to catalog evidence seized.

Conclusion

The execution of a search warrant for digital evidence requires a thorough series of procedures. After pre-planning the drafting and the execution of the search warrant, the actual drafting requires investigators to respond to a series of unknowns that are certain to develop. No amount of preparation can ensure 100 percent success without any complications. An investigator may spend months learning a suspect's habits on the computer, only to discover during the search that the computer is running a relatively unknown version of the Linux operating system. It becomes necessary then to ensure that investigators are familiar with the basic procedures associated with seizing a computer or other digital evidence. After all, the search is no good if potential evidence is missed or destroyed during the execution of the warrant.

The first step of the execution process involves removing the suspect from the area of the computer. Whether there is the presence of fast deletion programs or not, the suspect's access to the computer posses a potential threat to the collection of evidence. Once the suspect is under control, the next step is to secure the scene and begin the processing of documenting the search. If possible the use of digital video cameras is recommended. However, for those agencies that cannot afford video equipment, then pictures are certainly an acceptable alternative. Next, the investigator must ensure that there is no possible outside influences. This requires the removal of any and all outside data connection sources. While phone line connections (56.6kb) have historically been common, today's high-speed Internet connection devices are seeing increased use. Failure to properly shut down these communication devices could result in the loss of data.

When the suspect is under control, the scene is under control and the documentation of the scene and the search has begun, it is time to begin powering down the computer. The operating system being used by the suspect will determine the proper procedures for powering down the computer. Some operating systems require a gentle shutdown initiated by the operating system's internal controls, while other systems are capable of surviving an immediate loss of power. Careful consideration must be given to the version of operating system that is running, because shutting down a computer improperly may damage the evidence stored on a computer's hard drive. After shutting down the computer, the next consideration involves the proper packaging of the equipment seized. Careful attention should be paid to the packaging of the materials, and styrofoam or other packaging conducive to static electricity must be avoided. Also of importance is that once packaged the computer equipment should never be stored in the trunk of the transporting vehicle. The presence of electronic communication equipment and the heat generated from being stored in such an enclosed area make the trunks of vehicles dangerous areas to store computer equipment.

The execution of a search warrant for digital evidence does not end with the completion of an evidence seizure log. The chain of custody requires that law enforcement agencies maintain records relating to anyone who touches digital evidence. As a means of ensuring that evidence is not corrupted, nor perceived to be corrupted, the chain of custody form for digital evidence should contain sections related to not only who takes out evidence, but how long evidence is removed, and why the evidence is removed. The securing of digital evidence is different from physical forms of evidence and requires that these additional considerations be given serious consideration during the execution of a search warrant and the preservation of evidence for trial.

Review Questions

1. Why is the removal of a suspect from the computer's controls the first and most important stage of executing a search warrant?

2. Discuss several of the methods of documenting the execution of a search warrant that is mentioned in this chapter.

3. List and discuss the three major operating systems discussed in this chapter. How should each be handled in regards to powering down a computer?

4. Why is the proper powering down of a computer operating system an important consideration?

5. How should a seized computer be packaged and transported? What are some potential problems that may arise if these procedures are not followed?

6. What is the chain of custody? Why is the chain of custody such an important consideration when dealing with digital evidence?

Further Reading

Department of Justice. (2001). *Electronic Crime Scene Investigation: A Guide for First Responders*. Washington, DC.

Mandia, K. and Prosise, C. (2001). *Incident Response: Investigating Computer Crime*. San Francisco, CA: McGraw-Hill Osborne Media.

Chapter 10

An Introduction to Computer Forensics

The responsibilities of the law enforcement agency do not end with the execution of the search warrant and the collection of the computer. The evidence to be obtained from the computer is rarely located within the physical compartments of the computer. Evidence from the computer will more likely be located within the various electronic storage media inside the computer. Once the computer is seized at the crime scene, the next phase is the forensic examination of the computer.

What Is Computer Forensics?

The field of forensic science has witnessed an unprecedented growth in popularity in recent years. This increase in awareness is likely the result of a combination of high-profile court cases that used forensic science evidence and prime time television dramas that have highlighted the positives benefits of forensic science techniques. Forensic science is a term used to describe the application of scientific techniques to the investigation of criminal activities and the presentation of evidence at trial. Computer forensics, then, is the application of computer science to the investigation of criminal activities that use computers. Many people have a misguided belief that once a file is deleted from their computer then the evidence of their activities is gone. The truth, however, is that almost any activity on the computer can be tracked, and evidence that is deleted can often be recovered. Casey (2000) refers to this trail of evidence that is stored on computers and networks as the digital trail.

Individuals who specialize in computer forensics use their training and software applications to recover evidence stored at various points along the digital trail. The field of computer forensics has been around for several years, but recent advances in software technology have provided a recent growth in popularity for the field. Computer forensic technicians are currently in popular demand, not only in the fields of law enforcement but also in the private sector as well. Many large companies employ experts in computer forensics to investigate potential misuses of company computers. These individuals are responsible for investigating cases ranging from embezzlement to viewing pornography on the job. In fact, the employment of computer forensics experts by private sector entities has created a problem for some law enforcement agencies. The earnings potential associated with working for a private company often exceeds the earnings potential associated with working for the government in a law enforcement capacity. Individuals who are interested in conducting computer forensic analyses for law enforcement agencies may almost have their selection of jobs in the future.

How Computers Store Data

To understand how the computer forensics process works, it is first important to understand how computers operate and store evidence. The internal storage device most commonly encountered in computer analysis is referred to as the hard drive or hard disk. When computers were first evolving from the large mainframe designs that took up an entire room to the smaller, more compact designs that take up a tabletop, there was no internal storage device. All information had to be stored on soft, flexible disks that were referred to as floppy disks. These disks came in a variety of sizes, but one of the more common sizes was 5.25 inches. When starting up a computer, a process referred to as booting up the computer, it was required that an operating system be loaded into the computer's memory from one of these 5.25-inch floppy disks. When the idea was put forth to insert a disk inside the computer that would store the operating system, the internal disk became referred to as the hard drive because of its hard casing. The concept of floppy disk versus hard disk has become so developed that even today the small 3.5-inch disks that are encased in hard plastic are referred to as floppy disks.

The physical makeup of a disk, whether one is discussing a floppy disk or a hard disk, consists of several tracks that run around the inside of the disk. Each of these tracks is made of smaller clusters that range in size depending upon the operating system being used. When a file is saved to one of these disks the information is written to one of these clusters. For example, suppose that a cluster consists of 16 kilobytes and a file that is 32 kilobytes in size is saved to the disk. The file would then take up 2 clusters. It is important to note that when a cluster is designated for use in saving data, the entire cluster is devoted to the file. So, in the above example, if the file would have been 24 kilobytes then saving the file would still have required the use of both clusters. Later operating systems have worked to improve the storage capacity of these clusters, in an attempt to avoid "wasting" space.

When a file is saved to one of these clusters the operating system records the location of that file in the file allocation table. The space is then considered to be in use. Returning to an earlier statement concerning the deletion of files, many people still believe that deleting a file results in the removal of the file from the disk. However, if one stops and thinks about the deletion process then it becomes clear that the file cannot be physically removed by mere deletion. Anyone who has ever deleted a file and then realized that they had made a mistake has utilized the recycle bin feature in Microsoft Windows. The recycle bin is where files are "moved" to when the delete command is given. In reality the files are not moved at all. The operating system merely takes note that the file has been selected for removal. The file remains stored in the cluster in which it was originally stored. When a person goes to the recycle bin and indicates that they wish to retrieve a deleted file, the operating system then takes note that the file is no longer deleted and can be accessed once again through the Windows interface. Until a user empties the recycle bin, the recovery of data files is easy—the user just retrieves them from the bin.

Should a user instruct the Microsoft operating system to empty the recycle bin, then the file may no longer be recovered through the Windows interface, but this does not mean that the file has been removed from the hard disk. When a file is deleted the operating system will modify the file's name so that the operating system is aware that the space is no longer being used to store data. The actual contents of the deleted file remain on the disk until the space is needed to save additional data. When files are deleted, the operating system will place the hexadecimal designation "E5" in front of the file name to indicate that the file is no longer needed and the space may be used for future data. The space where these files are stored, but are not being used, is referred to as unallocated space; obviously because the space is not set aside for use and is therefore unallocated.

What happens to the original files when the space is needed to store a new file? The answer is that the new data will overwrite the old data. Let us briefly return to the earlier discussion on clusters. Suppose the operating system uses clusters that are 16 kilobytes and the original file saved is 32 kilobytes. Saving the file will require 2 clusters. When the file is deleted, the two clusters retain the data until the new file, which is 24 kilobytes, is saved to the clusters. The original file was 32 kilobytes and the new file is 24 kilobytes. The new file will require the use of both clusters used in saving the first file. However, the new file is smaller than the first by 8 kilobytes. This means that 8 kilobytes of the original data will remain even after the new file has been saved. The difference between the space needed to store the original file and the new file is referred to as slack space. It is in this area of disk space that valuable evidence may sometimes be recovered.

Internet Activity Stored on a Computer

The above discussion focused on files that were intentionally stored to a computer's hard disk. There is still the consideration of files that may or may not be intentionally stored on a disk when a user is surfing the Internet. Anytime a user logs onto the Internet and visits web pages on the World Wide Web, there is a record of these pages on the computer. Just as many people believe that when they delete a file the evidence is gone, many also appear to believe that once they disconnect from a website or from the Internet, then the evidence of their activities disappear. It is for the examination of these remnants of Internet activity that companies often employ the use of computer forensics analysts.

When a user connects to the Internet and attempts to view a website, the computer will send a request to the server that stores the web pages associated with the website. This request is received by the server and upon approval of the user's request; the data is transferred to the user's computer. In the past Internet connections were much slower, ranging from 14.4 kbps to 56.6 kbps. Websites that contained pictures took more time to load because the data associated with the entire site had to be downloaded before the web page would appear on the screen. To speed up this access, web browsers (such as Internet Explorer or Netscape Navigator) began using what is known as cache memory. The cache folder was where the images from these websites were stored. Once the images were stored on the computer, then should the user attempt to return to a website that had been visited earlier, then there would be no need to download the pictures. The computer would send the request for the web page, the server would download only the new images and text, and then the page would appear on the user's computer screen.

The cache folder is still used today despite the fact that Internet connections are much faster. The premise behind the use of the folder remains the same, and that is to speed up a user's web browsing. Images ranging from borders, headers, text boxes, and the various picture file formats can be found by examining this folder. Should a user realize that these images are being stored on the computer then they may attempt to delete the folder's contents by using a command to instruct the operating system to empty the cache folder. However, when the files are deleted they may not necessarily become unrecoverable Just as in the case of the file saved by the user, the file's name is changed to include the hexadecimal notation and the operating system will consider the space where the image is stored to be unallocated space ready for future use. If the image is recovered before new data is saved over the image, then the user's viewing habits may be constructed.

A second more controversial tool used to speed up web browsing is the use of cookies. Cookies are small bits of data that websites use to recognize returning visitors. The use of cookies is incredibly popular with commercial websites. Take for example Amazon.com, the online book (at least originally) retailer. Amazon uses cookies to track the purchasing habits, as well as the searching habits, of consumers. If you have ever visited the Amazon website and created an account, then when you returned you may have noticed that across the top of the screen was something similar to the following statement, "Welcome back _____; if you are not _____ then please click here." This message is made possible because when your computer requested the Amazon web page, the web server checked your computer and discovered the cookies on your hard drive. These bits of data allow Amazon to not only give you the personal touch when you first access the website, but they also allow the company to make recommendations of similar items on the basis of previous shopping habits. The debate over cookies has revolved around whether a company should have the ability to store and request information from a user without their express permission. In an effort to somewhat address these problems, newer versions of web browsers make the activation and deactivation of the cookies feature even easier.

Internet activity is also stored on the computer when a web page is accessed. When a web page is accessed, the data has to be stored on the computer in order for the user to see the image of the web page. Once the user disconnects from the website and the computer is shut down, the data is deleted and the operating system recognizes that the space is no longer being actively used. Like recovering other forms of data, however, if a computer forensic analyst can get to the data before the space is used again, then the contents of the web page may be recovered and viewed. This technique is useful for recovering evidence from electronic communications that are not stored on either the computer or the Internet service provider's server (e.g., e-mails sent from and received to a Hotmail account). Even if the user did not save the e-mail when they opened the message, or Hotmail no longer maintains a record of the communication, there is still a chance that the data is stored in the unallocated space. This author has personally used this technique to recover communications that were deemed unrecoverable. Consider an example where a suspect is using Hotmail to communicate with a potential victim. Whenever

Mike Flynn, left, and Charles Winegardner of the Indiana State Police work on a computer during a federally-sponsored program designed to set national standards for computer forensic education and certification August 11, 2004, at Purdue University in West Lafayette. The university teamed with law enforcement officers to improve investigation of the new generation of crimes, including computer-aided terrorism, espionage, bank and business fraud, and identity theft. (AP)

the individual uses his/her computer to check their e-mail, the data accessed by the user is stored on the computer. Using the proper tools the entire communication can be recreated.

The Computer Forensics Process

The first step in the forensics process involves duplication of the suspect's hard drive (or other storage media, depending on the case). To ensure that evidence is admissible in trial, it is best that the original storage media not be used during the examination. Should a case involve a hard disk that allegedly contains evidence of child pornography, then it is possible that there are images that have been deleted and have not yet been overwritten. These images may be recoverable from the unallocated space. During a forensic examination where the original hard disk is used, any files or programs saved to the computer could potentially overwrite portions of the evidence. Also, there is the issue of date and time stamping that is conducted by the operating system. Whenever a file is accessed, the date and time accessed is modified. It is recommended that the original media not be used, so that forensic analysts can avoid having to defend themselves from claims that they modified or planted evidence on the computer.

Duplication of the hard drive may take place in one of several ways. First, there is disk duplication capabilities built into some operating systems. Linux, an increasingly popular alternative to Microsoft Windows, allows for disk copying; as does commercial software programs such as Safeback. When a copy of the disk is made, it is important to not use the standard copy commands provided by the operating system. The command to copy a file will result in the operating system copying only the materials associated with the new files. In other words, the operating system will search through the file allocation table and will only copy files that do not contain the hexadecimal "E5" designation. Any data that is left from previous files, such as data stored in the unallocated space or slack space, will not be copied onto the disk. Using the Linux operating commands or the Safeback software allow for what is termed a "bit copy," meaning that every bit of data from the suspect disk is copied to a forensic disk.

In the earlier days of computer forensics hard disks could be backed up onto floppy disks and zip disks. Today, however, while it is still possible for many imaging programs to copy to zip disks, it is recommended that a second hard disk be used to store the copied image. The average size of internal hard disks has increased from 100 Megabytes of data to over 100 Gigabytes of data. Copying a 100 Gigabyte hard disk onto a collection of zip disks would take several disks, where one hard drive to another hard drive is much more efficient in terms of time. CD-ROMs and DVD-ROMs are also sometimes discussed as methods of storing disk images, and while these are capable of storing more information than the typical zip disks, they are still small in size when compared with the typical hard disk. The use of CD-ROMs and DVD-ROMs is better reserved for archiving copies once the forensic analysis has been conducted.

Another semi-recent development that assists law enforcement agencies in handling the image of suspect computer disks is portable computer forensic kits. These units are similar in design to a laptop computer but contain a variety of connection cables that allow for the imaging of a suspect drive at the scene of the crime. The user merely connects the suspect drive to the portable kit and creates an image of the disk that can either be examined on the portable forensic machine, or the disk can be examined at a later time in a secured forensics lab.

The use of such forensic kits may be of great assistance when the computer disk to be imaged is a part of a business computer that is currently being used for legitimate business purposes. If the forensic analyst had to take the entire computer back to the lab to make an image of the drive, then a company could be financially harmed because of the actions of one employee. Many of these forensic kits also take advantage of the ability to image a suspect disk through a network interface card or through a serial port connection. Using the network card or the serial port prevents the analyst from having to take apart a suspect's computer. This in turn prevents, or at the least minimizes, a suspect claiming that their computer was damaged during the process of the evidence collection. Once the imaging process is complete, then the next phase of the analysis involves ensuring that there is proof that evidence has not been tampered with during the analysis.

Verifying the Files and File Signatures

Immediately upon completing the imaging process, the analyst will begin the process of ensuring that no claim may be made concerning the planting or manipulating of evidence on the suspect drive. One method of doing this is to generate a hash value for the hard disk before beginning any analysis of the disk. Because of the volatile nature of digital evidence it is necessary to take precautionary steps that will verify the integrity of evidence both before and after the actual forensic examination. Data on a computer hard disk can be modified and/or deleted with the press of a few keystrokes. For example, when a computer file is opened the access times associated with the file will be modified. Even worse, some access times within the operating system may change when the computer is started up. This is another reason that a forensic backup is recommended whenever conducting an examination. However, it should be noted that legal challenges to the access times will be rare, as the majority of the challenges will likely involve challenges that include data manipulation.

To prevent a data manipulation claim from being successful, it has been recommended that analysts create a hash value for the hard disk. A hash value is basically a 32-character encryption of a disk's contents. If any value on the hard disk is modified then the hash value will be drastically different. A quick comparison of the initial image of the hard disk with the post-examined hard disk should quiet any questions concerning possible data manipulation. There are several logarithms that are used in generating hash values. The most commonly accepted, however, is the MD5 algorithm. The MD5 algorithm works in the following manner:

1. The original disk, or file if you want to only hash a file, is encrypted and a hash value is generated. Many of the current computer forensic packages now allow for a hash value to be generated when the suspect disk is first imaged. The report associated with the imaging of the suspect drive will indicate the date and time the image was made, as well as providing an initial hash value that will be stored in the final report.

2. Once the hash value is generated, then any changes to the file will result in a completely new hash value being generated. Consider if the following sentence is saved into a file entitled activity.doc—The use of computers in criminal activity is wrong!—This file might generate a hash value of "1fcda2ajk 1835c9b3c4328e00k3f9824" Any copies of the file that are made will contain the exact same hash value.

3. If any part of the file is modified, whether a period is added to the file or the margins and spacing is changed, then the hash value would change. So, if sentence in the activity.doc file was changed to—The use of computers in criminal activity is wrong.—(note that this sentence ends in a period and not an exclamation point). This file might generate a hash value of "0beic9akd3195z3m3a4329c87d3a2810" Notice that the two values are not even close to being similar and this is the result of merely changing an exclamation point to a period.

The MD5 logarithm is currently considered to be the best logarithm for creating hash values, but several experts in the field have indicated that it is possible for a better algorithm to be developed in the near future. After all, the use of the MD5 logarithm suffers from the same flaw any other mathematical tool suffers from—the potential for duplication of values. However, when it comes to accuracy, Kruse and Heiser (2002) indicate that the resulting values from the MD5 algorithm are more accurate than DNA tests and DNA tests have been accepted in court as scientific evidence.

Next, it is important to verify the file signatures. When a file is saved, the file's header will contain a signature that tells the operating system what type of file is being saved. This information is then used with the operating system when the file is activated. When a user selects a file to be opened, the header will tell the operating system what program to use in opening the file. Unfortunately, what the operating system reads and what the operating system actually displays may sometimes be different. Returning to the use of Microsoft Windows, have you ever looked at the files on a floppy disk using the Windows Explorer feature (where you click on the icon labeled 3.5-inch floppy and then little icons appear with the names of your files next to the icon). If so, you have noticed that files associated with Microsoft Word will appear with the little document icon, while pictures may appear with a little portrait icon. What happens with these icons is that when a user saves a file they are given the opportunity to save the file in a variety of formats. Many people who are unfamiliar with computers may not even realize that they have this choice, so in an effort to be as user friendly as possible, the default is normally the format associated with the default program. When the file is saved, the format is identified through the file's name extension. For example, a document file that is typed with the Microsoft Word software normally carries the file extension ".doc." When the operating system sees this .doc designation it places the little icon of the tablet next to the file name in the Windows Explorer window.

A problem may arise when a user attempts to mislead the operating system into believing that a document file is in fact a picture file. To do this, the user would change the filename extension to any of the following image formats: ".gif," ".jpg," or "jpeg." Even though the file is a document file and should have the little tablet icon to the left of the image, the operating system will believe that the file is a picture format on the basis of the file extension. Sophisticated criminals who are familiar with computer technology may use this technique in an attempt to hide images and make them appear to be only documents. If a forensic analyst is looking for images of child pornography then they may fail to examine any images that are mislabeled in this manner.

File signature analysis involves the computer forensic software comparing the actual file signature with the header of the file to determine if there is a discrepancy. If the header indicates that the file is an image and the file signature indicates that the file is a document, then a report is generated. The forensic analyst may then physically locate each of the files on the report and examine the files to determine if they are images or documents. Some forensic software packages will actually locate the files for you and then provide a list of the files. The analyst must then only select each of the files on the list and the contents of the file become apparent. This ability to modify file extensions and their appearance it was has led to debate concerning the need to examine every file located on a suspect's hard disk. Because the files can be so easily hidden, perhaps there is a need to examine every file.

The Forensic Analysis

Once the image has been created and the hash value and file signature analysis have been completed, then the actual examination of the computer disk is next. The various computer forensic software programs (to be discussed later in this chapter) come with a variety of forensic tools. The majority of them, however, share in the ability to examine the entire hard disk for images and documentary files. Each also allows the analyst to search the hard disk for keywords, as well as search the unallocated space on the disk for data that has been deleted but has not yet been overwritten.

Many consider the forensic analysis to be the most tedious and unexciting part of the high-technology crime investigation. However, because this stage is also one of the most important stages, care must be taken in conducting the actual analysis. The size of the hard disk will determine the amount of time necessary to conduct a full analysis. Therefore, an in-depth analysis may take anywhere from a couple of days to a couple of weeks. The various integrated search tools available with computer forensics software has made these searches somewhat faster, but there is still a need for the analyst to take their time when conducting an examination. Another factor that will influence the amount of time it takes to conduct an examination is the type of evidence the forensic analyst is searching for. If the evidence is image-based, then the analyst may have to search the entire drive's contents for the necessary images. On the other hand, if the evidence is text-based, then the analyst may have to search the entire drive but there is also the use of keyword searches. A keyword search will allow the analyst to search the entire hard disk for certain words or phrases. Such a search will include not only the actual contents of the files on the hard disk, but will also include the slack space and the unallocated space on the hard disk. Unfortunately, such a search will often be more time consuming than an image search because the hits associated with the keyword(s) may not be the actual evidence that is being sought.

The Forensics Report

Once the analysis is completed, then the forensic analyst will prepare a written report concerning the evidence that was uncovered during the examination. This report may come in a variety of formats. Some of the computer forensic software packages even include a report feature that will allow the forensic analyst to save images, documents and text segments during the actual forensic analysis. Images that are saved can then include narratives that describe where the actual image was discovered—whether the image was still saved on the computer or had been erased or hidden. The final reports can then be formatted to provide an easy to read document including all evidence recovered.

A nice, easy to read report can be used in a variety of ways. First, when it comes time for the prosecutor to determine whether he or she wishes to pursue charges, a thoroughly documented forensic report will go a long way in convincing the prosecutor that the case is winnable. Second, once the prosecutor determines to pursue the criminal charges, a well-documented report may be of assistance when it comes time to discuss a plea bargain. If the seizure of the computer disk and its subsequent search has not violated criminal procedure then the suspect may be more inclined to plead guilty once they have received a copy of forensic report that contains images and/or documents that obviously prove the individual's guilt. Finally, should the case actually go to trial, then the forensic report can be used in the prosecution's case, as well as used by the forensic analyst to refresh his or her memory before their testimony.

The Computer Forensic Software Packages

There are a variety of computer forensic software packages available today. The available packages could be divided into two categories. The first category is considered the more user-friendly because the software utilizes a GUI (Graphical User Interface). GUI is what is used by Microsoft Windows, whereby a user can click on an icon to perform a function. Prior to the release of the GUI feature, users were required to launch software programs from the DOS prompt (the old black screen with the "C:\" designation). Computer forensics software that operates by use of a GUI feature are considered by some to be the best choice for law enforcement agencies that are not staffing full time computer scientists to conduct their forensic analyses. The GUI computer forensics programs are easy to use, meaning that anyone who is willing to learn the software is capable of conducting the analysis. There are two major GUI software packages currently on the market. The first is the EnCase software package manufactured by Guidance Software. The second is the Forensic Took Kit software package manufactured by AccessData.

EnCase

EnCase is considered one of the best computer forensics packages available because of the software's various component programs. For example, users who wish to examine a suspect disk, but do not wish to dedicate the time necessary to make an exact image of the disk, may preview the suspect disk. During this preview session users may conduct any analysis that could be undertaken if an image of the disk was being examined. The latest edition of the software even allows for users to save the progress of their forensic examination conducted through the preview method. The true value of this feature becomes apparent in situations where taking the time to image multiple drives could place an investigation in jeopardy. Consider an investigation involving 15 computers. If each disk requires 30 minutes to image, then the investigator is facing a multi-hour task. However, do all of these disks contain evidence? If the answer to this is uncertain, then first previewing the disk may save hours. In the above example, an investigator could preview the disks, and only image those disks that are important to the case.

A second useful feature of the EnCase software is the ability to image a disk (referred to by users of EnCase as acquiring a disk image) through the use of a network patch cable or a serial cable. While this method of imaging a disk takes longer, the benefit is that the forensic analyst does not have to remove the physical disk from the computer. The EnCase software allows users to create a boot disk that will prevent any data from being written to a suspect's disk during the computer's start up process. Once the computer is up and running, then the forensic analyst can begin making a disk image through either the patch cable or the serial cable. When the image is created, the EnCase software then allows the analyst to search the hard drive by: (1) examining the image files located on the hard drive through a gallery view, (2) examining the files through the use of a hex view (reading the hexadecimal file components), and (3) searching the entire disk for keywords. EnCase also has a reporting feature that allows a forensic analyst to save keyword hits, images and personal comments into an easy to format report that can be printed or e-mailed to attorneys involved in the case.

Forensic Tool Kit

The Forensic Tool Kit is produced by AccessData and contains many of the same features as the EnCase forensic software. Forensic Tool Kit (FTK) allows users to examine an imaged disk by: (1) examining image files through a gallery view, (2) examining files through a hexadecimal view, and (3) searching the disk for keywords. However, FTK also contains a couple of features that are available in the EnCase software but are not as easy to employ. For example, FTK contains an e-mail feature that will automatically search out e-mails stored on the disk and provide the information in an easy to read format. Another benefit to the use of the FTK forensics software is the ability to import image files that are created using a wide variety of imaging software formats. FTK even allows for users to import EnCase image files.

Perhaps the best component of the FTK forensic software is the password cracking component, Password Recovery Tool Kit (PRTK). Many productivity software packages now allow users the ability to encrypt file contents to protect the information from intrusive searches. PRTK is a GUI based utility that will allow forensic analysts to gain access to these files. The password cracking component can be integrated into the FTK package providing a complete analysis kit. A recent version of the PRTK is known as the Distributed Network Attack (DNA), which allows networked computers to work together to crack complex encryption schemes. At this time the password component is the primary difference between FTK and EnCase, although EnCase has made up for the lack of this feature through their in-depth training programs provided users.

Non-GUI-based Software Utilities

Maresware has a suite of command line utilities available for use by computer forensics analysts. The advantage of using command line tools is cost. The majority of the software tools discussed below are available for a fraction of the costs of the above GUI based software packages. The disadvantage to the use of command line tools is the complexity of their use. These utilities are based on an understanding of the DOS command line. Individuals who are not as familiar with computers will likely have more difficulty in using the command line tools. This should not be interpreted to mean that command line tools cannot be used unless the analyst is an expert in computer science, but the utilities doe require more training than the GUI based software packages.

The maresware utility suite contains, but is not limited to the following applications: DISCK_CRC, HEX_SECT, and STRSRCH. DISCK_CRC is a hashing utility that will generate an MD5 value for a particular file or collection of files. Returning to an earlier discussion, this value can then be used to defend against any claims that evidence was altered or implanted. HEX_SECT is a hex editor tool that allows the user to examine the hexadecimal and text values located within a suspect disk. STRSRCH is a keyword search program that will search a suspect disk for keywords and then provide the user with information relating to how many times the keyword appears and where on the disk the information is located.

Another suite of command lines tools is manufactured by NTI. According to NTI there is a GUI based software program being developed, but there is no finalized release date. Some of the utilities available are: CRCMD5, DiskSearch 32, Filter Intelligence and SafeBack. CRCMD5 is a utility used to calculate a cyclical redundancy check value or a MD5 hash value. Both of these values can be used to verify that there have been no changes made to a file or group of files during an examination. DiskSearch 32 is a keyword search program designed to operate on Microsoft DOS systems. Filter Intelligence allows users to locate names, phrases and word groups. According to NTI this program is useful when handling investigations that involve e-mail addresses or electronic communications. SafeBack is one of the most popular utility programs, with users of EnCase and FTK also sometimes using SafeBack. The SafeBack utility allows for the creation of a bit by bit image of a suspect disk. SafeBack is billed as the original imagining utility, but is limited to systems running Microsoft DOS. Users of the GUI based software programs may import an image file generated by SafeBack.

Conclusion

The field of computer forensics is a rapidly developing field. Due in part to the increasing awareness of forensic science as a field, and due in part to the increasing reliance people have on computer systems. Both private and public sector entities are scrambling to locate individuals who are trained in the collection and analysis of digital evidence. Potential evidence ranging from a user's typing habits to their Internet activity is stored on the disks located within their computers. Almost all activity can be examined, and attempts to delete potential evidence do not always ensure that such evidence is not retrievable. There is a variety of computer forensic software utilities available for use, ranging in design from those that are geared toward the everyday computer user to those designed for the more advanced user. Each software utility provides a combination of advantages and disadvantages. The primary consideration is not which software is employed, but rather that a proper methodology is adhered to. Computer forensic analysts must: (1) generate an imaged copy of a disk or work on a protected computer system, (2) conduct a thorough, methodical analysis of suspect disk, and (3) then prepare a well-organized report that documents how the analysis was conducted and what results were discovered.

Review Questions

1. What is meant by the term computer forensics?

2. Why has computer forensics become more important and more discussed in recent years?

3. Briefly discuss the types of Internet activity that a computer forensic analyst may recover.

4. What is meant by the term slack space? What type of information could be located in the slack space of a disk?

5. Discuss the computer forensics process? Why is it important to adhere to an accepted methodology?

6. The MD5 algorithm is considered an important part of the computer forensic analysis. What is the MD5 algorithm and why does it play such an important role?

7. Compare and contrast the two categories of computer forensic software programs (GUI versus command line).

8. What is the advantage of using a GUI based software package? What is the advantage of a command line software package?

Further Reading

Kruse, W. & Heiser, J. (2002). *Computer Forensics: Incident Response Essentials*. New York, NY: Addison-Wesley.

Nelson, B., Phillips, A., Enfinger, F. & Steuart, C. (2004). *Guide to Computer Forensics and Investigations*. Boston, MA: Thomson Course Technology.

Vacca, J. (2002). *Computer Forensics: Computer Crime Scene Investigation*. Hingham, MA: Charles River Media.

Online Resources

Guidance Software—company that manufactures the EnCase computer forensics software package. Available at http://www.guidancesoftware.com.

Access Data—company that manufactures the Forensic Tool Kit and Password Recovery Tool Kit. Available at http://www.accessdata.com.

NTI—company that produces the NTI suite of computer forensics utilities. Available at www. http://www.forensics-intl.com/tools.html.

MaresWare—company that manufactures the MaresWare suite of computer forensic utilities. Available at http://www.dmares.com/.

International Association of Computer Forensics Specialists—organization that trains law enforcement officers in the field of computer forensics. Maintains a very reputable certification program. Available at http://www.cops.org/.

Chapter 11

Legal Issues in the Admission of Digital Evidence

Once the digital evidence has been seized and the computer forensics analysis has been completed, the next step is to introduce the evidence at trial. The entire process up to this point, and more specifically the adherence to standardized operating procedures, has been for the purpose of ensuring that the digital evidence will be allowed at trial. To complete this process there are several considerations, including: issues associated with the admissibility of digital evidence at trial, the integrity of digital evidence and the chain of custody associated with digital evidence.

Admissibility of Digital Evidence

Historically, it was uncommon for a court to allow digital evidence to be admitted into a trial, despite the decision in *United States v. Liebert* (1975). In *Liebert* the defendant was charged with illegally failing to file a tax return for three years. At issue was whether IRS non filer lists could be considered a part of discovery in order to counter the information obtained from computer records. The court felt that computer evidence was admissible in a criminal trial if the following criteria were met: (1) the prosecution could prove that the information obtained from the computer was trustworthy and had not been tampered with, and (2) the defense has been given the opportunity to inquire into the accuracy of the computer system providing the evidence.

The rationale for continuing to dismiss digital evidence was the fact that the Federal Rules of Evidence historically prohibited the introduction of such evidence. There are several sections of the Federal Rules of Evidence that could be applied to digital evidence. The first section involves the admission of digital evidence under the prohibition of hearsay evidence. Federal

Rules of Evidence 801 defines hearsay as, "a statement, other than one made by the declarant while testifying at the trial or hearing, offered in evidence to prove the truth of the matter asserted." Further, a statement is defined as, "an oral or written assertion or nonverbal conduct of a person, if it is intended by the person as an assertion." Hearsay may not be applicable to cases involving digital evidence obtained from acts such as child pornography, but certainly statements between a cyberstalker and their victim might qualify as hearsay. In such a case digital evidence such as e-mails or web postings could be admitted if they are entered in an attempt to counter the suspect's claim that he did not make the statements. Rule 801(d)(1) allows for the introduction of the evidence if the following three conditions are met:

1. the statement is inconsistent with the declarant's testimony, and was given under oath subject to the penalty of perjury at a trial, hearing, or other proceeding, or in a deposition.

2. the statement is consistent with the declarant's testimony and is offered to rebut an express or implied charge against the declarant of recent fabrication or improper influence or motive.

3. the statement is one of identification of a person made after perceiving the person.

By examining number one above, it becomes clear that a defendant being charged with a crime such as cyberstalking could have digital evidence presented at trial to prove that the defendant was in fact making harassing suggestions or making statements that could make the victim develop a fear of being accosted. Likewise, by looking at the number two exception above it becomes clear that a defendant could also use e-mails as a means of proving that his or her statements were not of such a nature that someone could believe they were being harassed or should live in fear of attack. E-mails have in fact been used in several cases, ranging from online entrapment cases where the e-mails where used to show the defendant's predisposition to engage in criminal activity, to online hate speech cases where the e-mails were used to show the defendant's intent to cause fear in e-mail recipients.

Of course, just because the e-mail is admissible under Rule 801 does not mean that the evidence cannot be suppressed under other Rules of Evidence. The issue of authentication involves confirming that the evidence can be validated. The Federal Rules of Evidence Rule 901(a) concerns authentication and states, "the requirement of authentication or identification as a condition precedent to admissibility is satisfied by evidence sufficient to support a finding that the matter in question is what its proponent claims." There are two methods of satisfying this requirement. The first involves Rule 902 and 10 situations where evidence can be self-authenticated. The problem is that there are relatively few, if any, situations where digital evidence could be self-authenticated. This statement is based on the fact that all ten exceptions under Rule 902 require that the evidence be part of a public access system. For example, one of the exceptions is that evidence is self-authenticable if it is a certified copy of a public record. Digital evidence is stored on a technological device and would therefore be almost impossible to certify because it can be routinely altered.

The second, and perhaps more useful method of authenticating digital evidence involves Rule 901, which provides ten scenarios where evidence may be authenticated by a professional who deals with the form of evidence on a regular basis. Of these ten, however, it the belief of this author that only two are directly related to the authentication of digital evidence. The first is Rule 901(b)(1), which provides for authentication by "testimony of witness with knowledge." The second is Rule 901(b)(3), which provides for authentication by "comparison by trier or expert witness." Under these two rules evidence may be authenticated by individuals who work with digital evidence or who have the necessary combination of education and experience to confirm that the digital evidence is equivalent to physical evidence. What exactly constitutes an expert witness will be discussed in the following section.

Rule 801 provides for the introduction of information relating to the admission of evidence that is used as a statement, and Rule 901 applies to authenticated evidence that is either a statement or some other form of digital evidence. Rule 1004 provides for the admission of digital evidence that have been forensically imaged. Generally, the original evidence obtained from the defendant is considered to be the best evidence. This concept is enumerated in Rule 1002, which states, "to prove the content of a writing, recording, or photograph, the original writing, recording, or photography is required, except as otherwise provided in these rules or by Act of Congress." While at first glance it would appear that Rule 1002 does not relate to digital evidence, Rule 1001 provides for digital evidence to be considered under Rule 1002. Rule 1001(1) defines writings and recordings as, "'writings' and 'recordings' consist of letters, words, or numbers, or their equivalent, set down by handwriting, typewriting, printing, photostating, photographing, *magnetic impulse, mechanical* or *electronic recording,* or *other form of data compilation.*"

Rule 1004 continues beyond Rules 1001 and 1002, providing for situations where copies of the original evidence can be admissible. According to Rule 1004 an original piece of evidence is not required when one of the following conditions is met:

1. **The originals are lost or destroyed**—this is an important consideration in terms of digital evidence because of the volatility of digital data. Evidence that is left in the hands of a suspect or even handled by computer forensics experts will be modified because of how computers access files and modify access times, etc. Verifying the integrity of original evidence should be a routine maneuver, especially when one considers that most computer forensics software now allows

for a user to make a verified copy of the suspect's computer storage mediums. This process allows law enforcement to verify that the information on the disk was there at the time of the seizure of the evidence and has not been tampered with in any manner other than that required for examination of the evidence.

2.   **Original is not obtainable**—once a suspect is aware that charges are being brought against him or her, it is only reasonable to believe that they will attempt to destroy the evidence. While there is nothing wrong with returning original storage mediums after an image has been made, to rely upon the original after being returned would result in very little original evidence remaining on the computer storage medium.

3.   **Original in possession of opponent**—here the rules merely state that a duplicate copy of evidence may be used in situations where the original evidence is in the hands of the suspect and he or she has refused to assist law enforcement by bringing forth the evidence. Once again, in discussing digital evidence its volatility lends itself to being allowed under this exception. A suspect who believes they are in trouble may hide or make claims leading an investigator to believe that the evidence was inadvertently deleted.

While the preceding section has attempted to examine the various Federal Rules of Evidence that relate to the authentication and admission of digital evidence, there have been numerous court decisions in recent years that have discussed the issue of digital evidence as well. Some of the court decisions have directly addressed interpretations under the Federal Rules of Evidence, while others have merely attempted to provide additional information concerning the introduction of experts in regards to digital evidence. Other decisions further examine the use of expert witnesses and make mention of the various requirements concerning who may testify as an expert in regards to the use of new computer forensics software.

The Courts and Digital Evidence

When considering the admission of digital evidence as evidence in a criminal trial there are two landmark decisions that must be examined. The first case, *Daubert v. Merrell Dow Pharmaceuticals* (1993), involves the admission of scientific evidence into the federal trial system. The second case, *Frye v. United States* (1923), is used to guide admission of evidence into various state trial systems. In the *Frye* case, the issue was whether or not scientific evidence relating to blood pressure and its effect during the course of telling a lie could be introduced at trial. The court ruled that for scientific evidence to be entered into trial, it must be shown that the process of gathering and analyzing the evidence has crossed the line from experimental process to demonstrative process. It was the court's opinion that because there was no possible way to determine exactly when evidence has crossed this line it would be best to only consider the admission of scientific evidence when the evidence is generally accepted in the scientific community from which it is derived.

The *Daubert* case was a civil case opinion that has been extended into the criminal court arena. In *Daubert* a woman brought forth charges against a drug company, claiming that the birth defects of her child were caused by the medication produced by the company. The company requested a summary judgment and the plaintiffs countered by offering evidence of scientific studies that proved there was a relationship between the drug being used and the presence of birth defects in infants. The court agreed with the company and stated that in order for scientific evidence to be admitted into evidence under Federal Rules of Evidence 702, the scientific method must be shown to have general acceptance in the scientific community (much as the rule described in the *Frye* case). The Supreme Court disagreed, however, stating that there was no requirement for scientific evidence to be generally accepted before it could be entered into evidence under Federal Rules of Evidence Rule 702. Instead, the court ruled that scientific evidence was only required to be reliable and scientifically valid.

Following the guidelines established in these decisions there have been numerous court decisions to address the admission of digital evidence. The first decision to be discussed is *State v. Hayden* (1998). Hayden was charged with the rape and murder of one his neighbors. The victim was found wrapped in a bed sheet containing bloody handprints. Unable to develop a solid fingerprint from the blood prints on the bed sheet, the forensic investigator took a digital photograph of the blood prints. By digitally enhancing the photograph, the fingerprint technician was able to make a match to Hayden. At trial, Hayden argued that the evidence could not be admissible in trial because the process of digitally enhancing pictures was not generally accepted in the forensic science community. Hayden noted that digital enhancement was not new, but that the software used was not designed for forensic examinations. The fingerprint analyst noted that this particular method of collecting prints was unique, but that the science behind the technique was acceptable. The court disagreed, basing its decision on a combination of expert testimony entered at trial and scientific journal articles dealing with forensic imaging.

In the case of *People v. Lugashi* (1988) the defense attempted to have evidence removed from trial on the grounds that the individual who conducted the retrieval of information was not capable of fully explaining how the software program worked. Lugashi was convicted of stealing credit card information stored on computer tapes created from daily backups of credit card accounts. At Lugashi's trial a loss prevention officer testified concerning how the backups were generated. Lugashi, however, claimed that the officer should not have been allowed to testify because she had no background in computer science and therefore could not testify to the accuracy of the hardware and software used in the process. The court disagreed, finding that the officer had worked with the software in her daily activities and was capable of being certified as an expert witness on the basis of her experience and training. The court felt that requiring testimony from individuals intimately familiar with the hardware and software would mean that only those who wrote the software or designed the hardware could testify. Such a requirement would do nothing to further justice, and would only slow down the inevitable. In cases where there are individuals who have worked with the computer program, and is capable of articulating how the software and hardware works, then the individual may be certified as an expert witness. Further, in these situations the evidence obtained from the hardware or software is considered admissible.

Recently, this issue was once again addressed when a court was asked to invalidate the admission of digital evidence on the grounds that the Secret Service agents who recovered the evidence were not experts in computer science. In *United States v. Scott-Emuakpor* (2000), the defendant was charged with participation in a "Nigerian advance fee" scam. Based on the authority of a search warrant, two Secret Service investigators examined Scott-Emuakpor's computer and found evidence of numerous types of files. Scott-Emuakpor argued that the Secret Service agents and their evidence should not be allowed at trail because the two agents admitted that they were not experts in computer science. The court determined that the two individuals could in fact testify and admitted the evidence on the belief that the agents' training in computer forensics was sufficient to warrant qualification as an expert witness. The determination of whether either of the agents were experts in computer science was deemed unnecessary to the court's Daubert consideration.

An even more recent case extended the decision from *Scott-Emuakpor*, discussing the admission of digital evidence obtained from a specific brand of computer forensics software. In the case of *Williford v. State*, both the computer crime expert and the computer forensics software were tested. Investigators were dispatched to a computer repair center after one of the workers discovered child pornography on a customer's computer. The customer admitted to having the image, citing that the image was not illegal because it was available for free on the Internet. After taking the computer back to the police department, the computer forensics investigator made a bit copy image of the suspect hard drive using the EnCase software. At trial the investigator was questioned concerning his background in computer science. The investigator indicated that he had no experience in computer science but that he had received extensive training in the use of the EnCase software. Further, the software itself had been tested repeatedly, and each test confirmed that the software had an extremely high reliability rating. The investigator also testified concerning how several computer science trade magazines had rated the software as one of the best.

Despite these arguments, Williford claimed that the investigator should not have been allowed to testify; and the evidence should not have been admissible as its collection was not the result of a scientifically approved technique. The court disagreed, finding that the officer's training and experience using the EnCase software was sufficient to certify the officer as an expert. The court also agreed that the EnCase software had been sufficiently discussed among computer science experts in the field. On the basis of results from numerous tests and scientific articles related to EnCase and computer forensics, it was the court's determination that EnCase satisfied the requirements for admission of scientific evidence. According to the Guidance Software website (the manufacturers of EnCase), the software has been challenged in several court decisions. Each decision has resulted in the same decision—the admissibility of the EnCase software and digital evidence. Based on these court decisions, it is relatively safe to make the statement that digital evidence obtained from computer forensic examinations will be considered admissible so long as the evidence is obtained through the use of an authenticated computer forensics software package and the user has been trained in the standard methodology of computer forensics analysis.

The Admission of Digital Evidence at Trial

The previous sections of this chapter have addressed the admissibility of digital evidence, but have focused primarily on whether such evidence is admissible under guidelines established for scientific evidence. Even if digital evidence in general is deemed to be admissible there are still additional criteria that must be met before the evidence may be entered. These two criteria are authentication of digital evidence and establishing the chain of custody for digital evidence.

Authentication of digital evidence was discussed in the previous chapter on computer forensics. Many computer forensics software packages now allow for authentication of digital evidence during the imaging process. These software packages will generate a hash value using the MD5 algorithm. Returning to the previous discussion on the MD5 algorithm, the hash value generated by the software is more accurate than DNA testing. Once an MD5 value is generated for each file, or for the entire disk for that matter, then any changes to the contents of the file will result in a drastically different hash value. Investigators can use these hash values to show that the evidence obtained from the suspect's computer is the same as the evidence being admitted into trial. For software programs that do not automatically generate a hash value, there are separate programs that can do this for the investigator. Using this software, the investigator should generate a hash value for the suspect's hard drive before making an image; then, after the image is made, another hash value should be generated and compared to ensure that no changes to the suspect drive have been made.

The second consideration involves establishing the chain of custody. This concept is not unique to computer forensic examinations, as anyone involved in the field of criminal justice is required to understand what the chain of custody is, why the chain is important and what steps should be taken to protect the chain of custody. A basic layperson's definition of the chain of custody is the grouping of people who have handled the evidence in any manner, whether it is to forensically examine the evidence or just to move the evidence to and from a given location. From the time evidence is seized at the crime scene until the evidence is presented at trial and admitted into evidence, the chain of custody must be a constant thought on the minds of investigators.

When a trial begins and evidence is admitted at trial, the chain of custody proves that the evidence presented at trial is the same evidence that was secured from the crime scene. Further, the chain of custody is an important component of proving that the evidence has not been modified since its seizure. Once again, because of the volatile nature of digital evidence it is extremely important that the prosecution can show that the evidence remains exactly the same as when it was obtained from the suspect's disk. To accomplish this, the prosecution will be required to bring in every witness that has touched the evidence from the time of its seizure until the time of its admission at trial. This may become a lengthy process depending upon the number of individuals who participated in the seizure, or the number of people who assisted in the forensic examination. Ideally, there will be one investigator responsible for the collection and one individual responsible for the analysis. However, realistically this may never be the case. The defense can speed up this authorization process by stipulating that the evidence has not been damaged or modified. An investigator should always assume that this will not be the case, as an attack on the chain of custody is an attack on the validity of the evidence. Therefore, a defense attorney is likely going to attempt to discredit the chain regardless of whether proper procedures are followed or not.

In discussing the defense attorney's strategy, it is important to remember that if there are multiple individuals to have touched the evidence, then there are multiple opportunities for the evidence to be dismissed. As each witness is presented to the court and they discuss how they came to interact with the evidence, the defense will be given the opportunity to question why the individual was touching the evidence, what the individual did with the evidence while it was in their custody and whether there was ever a time when the evidence was out of the individual's sight and/or control. Professionals in the field of computer forensics have recommended several techniques or ideas to assist in preventing problems with the chain of custody. The first technique involves the use of a professional labeling process for digital evidence. Casey (2000) recommends that the evidence itself be labeled by professional software. There are several programs that would allow an investigator to input a physical description and then print out an inventory label. At the conclusion of the search warrant's execution, then the program will print out a listing of all evidence entered into the system. At trial this listing may be brought in and the inventory label may be matched with the evidence being admitted and the list generated during the search.

The second recommendation is closely related to the first, and involves the use of a special evidence transaction log. Kruse and Heiser (2002) recommend that an evidence transaction log designed to account for the transfer of digital evidence be maintained by the seizing agency. Using any spreadsheet program a log can be created that includes the following information:

- **The Evidence Inventory Number**—this number may either be manually assigned to the evidence or the inventory number from the electronic logging program may be used.

- **Date and Time**—this section will allow for whoever is requesting the evidence to list exactly what date and time they removed the evidence, as well as a section for what date and time the evidence was returned to the evidence room.

- **Location Removed and Taken to**—this section will allow the individual removing the evidence to identify exactly where the evidence is being taken to; specifically, is the evidence being moved somewhere within the law enforcement agency or is the evidence being transferred to a third party for forensic analysis.

- **Reason the Evidence is Being Removed**—this section is where the individual removing the evidence will indicate exactly why the evidence is being removed

- **Who Removed the Evidence**—this section will be the actual signature section where the requesting individual will officially sign out the digital evidence; additionally, if the evidence is being transferred to a third party for analysis then the third party should be identified and include information on their name, organizational affiliation, address, and contact information.

The use of the above information may seem obvious to some readers. However, the truth is that some agencies do not use detailed transaction logs for their evidence. There have been instances of evidence custodians allowing evidence to be transferred to another individual with only the person's signature. What if the third party is not identified, or even worse it includes only their name. If the case goes to trial over a year later and the primary investigator is no longer working in law enforcement, then how can the third party be identified? The answer to this question depends on several factors, including: how active the investigation has been, how many times has a third party been requested by an agency, whether the same third party organization is always utilized by the agency and whether the third party followed a proper forensic methodology including a detailed report that identifies the investigator and the forensic analyst? If a case has lain dormant for several months and the original investigator is no longer affiliated with the agency, then it may become difficult to locate who conducted the analysis. Of course this is a worst case scenario, but the use of an evidence transaction log requires minimal additional effort and when dealing with digital evidence it is always better to be overly cautious.

Conclusion

The admission of digital evidence at trial has become much more commonplace in recent years with the increasing number of high-technology crimes. While historically the courts frowned upon the introduction of computer-related evidence, sometimes citing the need for the best evidence (the original evidence); today the courts are much more accepting of digital evidence. This evidence, however, must still satisfy certain criteria. To be admissible digital evidence must be relevant to the case at hand, as in the case of digital evidence being admitted to counter an individual's claim that they did not maintain a collection of child pornography. Further, the evidence must be authenticated in order to verify that the digital evidence is in fact reliable evidence. Courts have also begun to back away from the dismissal of digital evidence on the grounds that digital copies are not original. Relying on the Federal Rules of Evidence, digital copies have been deemed admissible because of the volatile nature of digital evidence. When dealing with evidence that can be altered or destroyed it is now accepted that a digital copy may be the best method of ensuring that the evidence is not lost or destroyed before trial.

Another consideration for the courts has been whether to admit expert testimony on computer forensics from individuals who are not experts in computer science. Law enforcement agencies are making great progress in staffing high-technology crime investigation units. However, there are still a great many agencies that have not staffed these units with graduates from computer science programs. The reality is that computer science graduates in many areas can make significantly more money working in the field of computer science than they could working in the field of law enforcement. Recognizing that a computer science degree is not necessary, the courts have allowed for the admission of digital evidence as long as the individual conducting the computer forensics analysis is familiar with standard forensic procedures and is capable of articulating that they followed these procedures. Additionally, when it comes to the admissibility of digital evidence analyzed with a specific computer forensics program it is necessary for the analysts to show two things: (1) that they are familiar with the operation of the software, and (2) that the software has received acceptance among those in the computer forensics field. Satisfaction of the second criteria can be shown if the software has been favorably reviewed in reputable magazines and journals related to the field of computer forensics.

Finally, it is important for computer forensics analysts to be familiar with the chain of custody. The chain of custody is a listing of all individuals who have touched the evidence from the time it is seized until the time the evidence is admitted into evidence in the trial. Through the use of automated labeling programs and a thorough evidence transaction log, the verification of this step of the forensics process should be of minimal inconvenience. However, it should be remembered that while the steps require minimal effort, failure to follow all of the steps can result in the dismissal of evidence and a failure to obtain a conviction should the case actually go to trial.

Review Questions

1. Discuss the three criteria necessary for entering digital evidence (e-mails, statements, etc.) under Federal Rules of Evidence Rule 801?

2. Rule 1004 has been cited as a rule for allowing the admission of digital copies into trial. What are the requirements for doing so?

3. What is the *Frye* case and how is it used in criminal trials? What is the *Daubert* case and how is it used in criminal trials?

4. Discuss how the *Frye* and *Daubert* cases are used to justify the admissions of computer-related evidence.

5. What must a computer forensics analyst show before the individual can be qualified as an expert witness in the area of computer forensics?

6. What is the chain of custody? What are some recommendations for ensuring that the chain of custody is not broken?

Online Resources

Federal Rules of Evidence Online—electronic version of the Federal Rules of Evidence. Available at: http://judiciary.house.gov/media/pdfs/printers/108th/evid2004.pdf.

EnCase Legal Papers—collection of articles on cases involving the admission of digital evidence, and more specifically the admission of evidence collected using the EnCase software. Available at: http://www.guidancesoftware.com/products/legalresources.asp.

Chapter 12

The Future of High-Technology Crime

Having discussed the history and evolution of high-technology crime, as well as the current state of affairs, the future of high-technology crime investigations should be briefly addressed. There are three primary areas to consider here. The first area of consideration is the continuing development of technology-assisted crimes. With the computer and Internet technology becoming more and more a part of everyday life, there are still several areas of criminal activity that could see increased scrutiny in regards to technology-assisted crime. The second area of consideration involves criminological studies that encompass technology-assisted crime. The study of criminology has consistently improved over the last century. However, there have been relatively few studies to attempt explanations concerning why individuals choose to begin or continue engaging in high-technology crime. The third and final area of consideration involves the modification of the legal system. As demonstrated in previous chapters, there have been several legal inconsistencies to develop as a result of attempting to apply traditional physical-realm jurisprudence to the limitless realm of cyberspace. If the legal system must be modified, then what then is the solution? After all, can the realm of cyberspace even be regulated should the government choose to do? Each of these considerations will be examined in a little more detail in the current chapter.

Evolving High-Technology Crimes and Considerations

Cyber Terrorism

Terrorism has become a rather hot topic in the field of criminal justice. The majority of discussion, however, has revolved around physical realm terrorism and not cyber terrorism. In discussing what is meant by the term terrorism, the term has come to refer to politically motivated attacks against individuals or governments that are designed to instill fear into the population. Further, terrorist attacks are preplanned and unlike traditional criminal acts require sincere dedication and a willingness to accomplish the terrorist attack at any cost, including the cost of the participants' lives. Part of the reason that cyber terrorism may not be discussed as frequently as physical terrorism could be that there are far fewer acts of cyber terrorism currently encountered. This is certain to change in the near future as more components of the world's critical infrastructure become intertwined with technology.

Another reason for the lack of attention to cyber terrorism is that much like physical terrorism there is an inability of individuals to associate an exact definition of the word. Recently, there has been a move to formalize a working definition. The USA PATRIOT Act, despite being criticized for its lack of a clear cut definition of terrorism, does attempt to define cyber terrorism. The USA PATRIOT Act has modified the Computer Fraud and Abuse Act to include acts of cyber terrorism, defined as:

> Any conduct that causes (or, in the case of an attempted offense, would, if completed, have caused)—
> (i)   loss to 1 or more persons during any 1-year period (and, for purposes of an investigation, prosecution, or other proceeding brought by the United States only, loss resulting from a related course of conduct affecting 1 or more other protected computers) aggregating at least $5,000 in value;
> (ii)   the modification or impairment, or potential modification or impairment, of the medical examination, diagnosis, treatment, or care of 1 or more individuals;
> (iii) physical injury to any person;
> (iv)   a threat to public health or safety; or
> (v)   damage affecting a computer system used by or for a government entity in furtherance of the administration of justice, national defense, or national security.

In reading the above definition, it should be noted that for an individual to be charged with an act of cyber terrorism it must be proven that the individual could have committed the crime. What this means is that an individual who accesses a government computer that maintains control over some component of the United States' critical infrastructure (i.e. airlines, waste management, medical services, etc.) could be potentially charged with cyber terrorism. Critics of this legislation have pointed out that there is no doubt that the acts discussed above are criminal. However, are all of the acts above worthy of being considered terrorist activity? After all, in examining subsection (i) above, it is possible that some individuals who are accessing protected computers are doing so in an attempt to determine whether or not they can succeed. They should be punished for such activity, but should their acts be considered cyber terrorism? Do these activities work to instill a sense of fear for the public's general safety? Probably not. These acts are criminal but not terrorism.

Some of the subsections, such as two through five are more closely akin to the definition of terrorism. A hacker who infiltrates a city's 911 emergency telephone system and reroutes emergency personnel, ultimately resulting in the deaths of residents, could be considered a cyber terrorist. As could the individual who shuts down the nation's air traffic control system. Each of these scenarios could result in as many or more deaths as any physical terrorist attack.

What Acts Qualify as Acts of Cyber Terrorism?

After reading the exact definition of cyber terrorism provided by the USA PATRIOT Act, the question becomes what acts constitute cyber terrorism. The definition explicitly defines cyber terrorism as any act that caused harm, or could have caused harm if successfully completed. This section will examine acts that hold the potential to be considered acts of cyber terrorism. There have been several accounts over the last few years involving reported acts of cyber terrorism. Oftentimes, however, these individuals provide examples of cyber terrorism that range from completely not representative of the crime to completely ridiculous. Understandings of the types of crimes that are considered acts of cyber terrorism are important for law enforcement personnel, as there is a great potential for a future terrorist attack that is cyber-based.

Even the federal government has accepted that there is a great potential for cyber terrorist attacks. In 1997, 35 hackers were hired by the National Security Agency and were requested to launch simulated attacks on federal computers. The NSA's intent was to determine whether government agencies were taking adequate measures to protect their computers in the wake of rising electronic attacks by hackers and technologically-competent youths. By the test's conclusion, the government's hackers were able to accomplish the following feats:

- The power grids in Los Angeles, Chicago, Washington, and New York were all collapsed, resulting in massive power outages throughout these areas.

- An airliner was removed from the air traffic controller's screen; as a result the plane crashed into a field in Kansas.

- Along with crashing the power grid of Washington, the hackers were also able to collapse the 911 service grid.

- The Department of Defense (DOD) had their entire computer services, e-mail services and telephone services shut down at the exact same moment.

- A United States Navy cruiser had their computer systems shut down.

Operation "Eligible Receiver," as the mock attack was labeled, resulted in the hackers gaining access to over 36 of the DOD's computer networks. This access was root-level, meaning that the hackers had complete control of the computer and could make any changes they wanted to the computer system. There is great potential for danger should a hacker be allowed to gain even a guest user account. Once a guest account is obtained then there are a variety of tools available to help hackers gain a higher level of access. Some damage can even be accomplished from these lower accounts. The fact that the hackers were able to gain root-level access is extremely frightening because from this level the hackers could establish new accounts that would allow them to return at a later date and continue their activities (Christensen, 1999; Overholt & Brenner, 2001).

The plane crash involved in "Operation Eligible Receiver" was a simulated crash, meaning that thankfully there was no actual fatalities associated with the test. However, the fact that the plane could have been destroyed appears to never have been debated. Even worse than the possibility of a plane crashing as the result of such an attack, is the possibility that two or more planes could be removed from the system and crash into each other. What would happen if such an event were to take place? Beyond the loss of lives, there are other considerations as well. One commonly held belief is that the stock marked would suffer immediate and long ranging damage as a result of such an attack. When an event should occur that results in massive loss of human life and involves the use of technology that is designed to make citizens feel safe and not threatened, then it is reasonable to expect some panic.

Such an event as two planes crashing into each other because of a hacker's attack on an airport's computer system could reasonably influence whether people would feel safe traveling by air. When citizens begin to fear travel by air and instead chose alternate means of transportation, or even worse they refuse to travel, it is only a matter of time before the airlines will suffer. After the airlines begin to suffer financial damages, then other industries will begin to suffer as well. For further proof of this one needs to look back no further than the terrorist attacks of September 11, 2001, where the financial markets immediately became unstable after the attacks. Even now, years later, there are some airlines that are still recovering or hovering on bankruptcy because of the financial difficulties brought about because of the attacks of 9/11.

Following the events of "Operation Eligible Receiver" there has been a significant movement toward accepting and preparing for the potential of a cyber attack. Each year the government conducts a computer security examination that deals with how well the networks are secured. For the year 2002 the United States government failed to pass the review for third year in a row. Of the 24 agencies that were tested, only three managed to score a 50 percent on the test. Fifteen of the agencies failed the test, and six agencies received a grade lower than they had received the previous year. Not all agencies failed the examination. For example, while the Department of Transportation failed the test with a score of 28, the Social Security Administration passed with a score of B minus. The administrators of the Social Security Administration claims that their agency scored as well as it did because it trains its people to be proactive in scanning their computers for viruses and Trojan horses. Also, all employees are required to change their passwords on a regular basis in order to deter hackers from infiltrating their computer system.[1]

What Acts Are Not Cyber Terrorism?

Unfortunately, as the level of appreciation for potential cyber terrorist attacks has increased, more and more crimes have been inappropriately termed cyber terrorism. For example, there was a news story concerning a young boy who managed to keep his family under a constant state of "fear" by taking control of several electronic devices around the family's house. Using a combination of electronics skills and computer skills the boy was able to convince his family that the house was under siege by someone who could kill the family at any given time. The media was quick to label the young man a cyber terrorist. The truth is that this was not an example of cyber terrorism. Returning to the definition of cyber terrorism put forth in the USA PATRIOT Act, it can be seen that:

1. There was no financial loss of $5,000 against a protected computer;

2. The boy did not modify or impair the medical examination, diagnosis, treatment, or care of 1 or more individuals;

3. There was no reported physical injury to any persons in the home;

4. There was never any indication that the young boy posed a threat to public health or safety;

5. There was no damage inflicted upon a computer system used by a government entity in furtherance of the administration of justice, national defense or national security

The boy's behavior in the case above was atrocious, and the family probably was scared for their safety. It is even possible that the family may have at some point feared for their lives. Overall, the truth remains that society must be careful not to overextend the definition and labeling of cyber terrorism. Improper classification of the crimes may result in a situation where the crime loses its seriousness because there are so many crimes con-

---

[1]   Please see http://www.linuxsecurity.com/content/view/112930/65/ for a copy of the news article relating to the cybersecurity test and the government's rating.

sidered cyber terrorism. It is important to maintain that only those crimes with serious potential for physical harm are labeled as cyber terrorist acts. Another important reason for properly labeling acts as electronic prank versus cyber terrorist is that the proper preparation for cyber terrorist attacks requires a true understanding of what cyber terrorism is in order to formulate response plans. Can we plan to react and respond to cyber terrorism if there is no consensus on what an act of cyber terrorism is? The answer is no.

Peer-to-Peer Technology and Digital Piracy

Peer-to-Peer technology and the sharing of copyrighted materials are certain to continue plaguing both the criminal and civil justice systems. While these crimes are not as physically threatening as cyberterrorism, they are a serious consideration because of the large number of users who are using the technology to violate copyright laws. Recently it was discovered that the newer Internet2 was being used to share copyrighted movies. Apparently the individuals involved felt that Internet2 was a more attractive choice for their activities because: (1) the speeds involved in the transfer of movie files were so great that full length movies were downloaded in five minutes, and (2) Internet2's newness would prevent the Motion Picture Association of America (MPAA) and the Recording Industry Association of America (RIAA) from monitoring online activities.

These individuals were all students at large universities associated with the Internet2 technology. The students quickly found that they were wrong about the MPAA and the RIAA monitoring the technology. More than 450 civil lawsuits were handed out in an attempt to prevent Internet2 from becoming a haven for criminal activity. Internet2 has been billed as the alternative to the Internet for those who are interested in using the technology to share and conduct research. The RIAA and the MPAA felt that a strong statement was necessary in order to prevent the technology from becoming what the Internet is today—a tool for criminal activity.

Internet2 and its use in the transfer of copyrighted materials will be an interesting area of high-technology crime consideration. However, also of interest will be the development of P2P technology in the wake of the United States Supreme Court decision concerning whether manufacturers can be held responsible for how its technology is being used. At the time of this writing the Supreme Court has just heard oral arguments concerning why manufacturers must be held responsible for the actions of its users. Basically, the arguments supporting this approach claim that if the manufacturers are not held responsible then they will continue to develop technology that helps users circumvent copyright protections and then distribute copyrighted materials. On the other side of this issue are individuals who claim that if the Supreme Court rules that manufacturers can be held responsible for the actions of users, then the future of technology development is at risk.

According to this argument all future software developments will require consideration of whether or not the technology could be used for criminal activity. As a result of this consideration, many software programs that could be of use to the greater society will never be created.

Yet another interesting consideration is how the users of the peer-to-peer programs will respond to the court's decision. As of yet there has been little change in how users view the act of sharing copyrighted files. Despite a large number of lawsuits filed by the RIAA, and more recently an increasing number of lawsuits filed by the MPAA, there appears to be little indication that file sharing can be stopped. In fact there may be as many or more people online sharing files after all of the lawsuits. The more popular file sharing programs are still seeing large numbers of users. Even as the Supreme Court considers the issue of file sharing and liability, there are new peer-to-peer programs being considered.

Evolving Criminological Studies

The future of high-technology crime will certainly involve more advanced criminological studies on why individuals engage in high-technology crimes. Unfortunately there is very little available at this time on this particular subject. There have been studies in the past to address some high-technology crimes such as hacking and identity theft. After all, identity theft is a crime that has been around for decades and only became more prevalent because of technology. In the early days of hacking there were some attempts to also examine hacking motives and develop a hacker profile. On the basis of these evaluations it was discovered that hackers were generally very intelligent, maintained very few close friends and were socially introverted.

The truth is that during the time these studies were conducted this was probably an accurate depiction of a hacker. Computers were not as widely accepted as they are today and those who had computers had to spend a significant amount of time on them because they were not as easy to operate as today's computers. These individuals were normally maintained introverted personalities and few friends either because they spent so much time on the computer, or they spent so much time on the computer because they had few friends and nothing else to challenge them. Either way the individuals were normally smart and very good at computer programming.

Today this is not necessarily the case. Computers are far more popular today and the technology is so much simpler than even ten years ago. Today it is possible for anyone to become a high-technology criminal if they are willing to spend the time searching the Internet. If you doubt this then spend a couple of hours surfing the Internet. There are thousands of websites on the World Wide Web that provide information for beginning hackers, identity thieves and cyber stalkers (even if the website does not mean to provide information on how to stalk someone online). After a few hours anyone can locate some basic hacking utilities and begin launching computerized assaults on targets. If you remember back to the earlier discussion on hacking, individuals who engage in these types of activities are called script kiddies and they are considered by some to be the most dangerous type of hacker because they know so little about computers and how the programs they use could affect computer systems.

For another example consider the crime of digital child pornography. Ten years ago if an individual wanted to manufacture their own child pornography then they had to be very good with clumsy video cameras, still cameras and computer scanners. In order to keep from getting caught these individuals would have had to learn how to develop their own pictures and digitize their own videos. Ten years ago this required a moderate to advanced level of skill. Today, digital cameras are almost as user friendly as they can be. Anyone who has a digital camera is capable of taking pictures and uploading them to their computer. Further, digital video is now infinitely easier with cameras that directly record the footage into .mpeg (video file for play on computers) format for easy storage on computers, CD-ROMs and DVD-ROMs. Anyone who desires to engage in these activities can gain easy access to such technology.

What this means is that today it is almost impossible to develop a profile of a computer hacker or any other high-technology criminal. The man next door with a Ph.D. in Physics is just as likely to be responsible for a high-technology crime as the guy next door who is struggling to acquire his high school diploma. This being said, there are several criminological theories that are considered by this author to be worth further consideration and will possible be addressed by future studies on criminal behavior involving technology. These theories are Sykes and Matza's Techniques of Rationalization and Neutralization, Akers' Social Learning Theory and Cohen and Felson's Routine Activities Theory.

Techniques of Neutralization and Rationalization

In 1957 Gresham Sykes and David Matza developed their theory of neutralization and rationalization techniques. It was the belief of these theorists that juveniles were not always opposed to society's values and beliefs. At the time of their theory there was a belief that juveniles who engaged in delinquent behavior did so because they adhered to a separate system of values. Sykes and Matza disagreed, arguing that these juveniles can be law abiding productive citizens one moment and then the next moment they could become a delinquent. To explain why individuals go back and forth between delinquent and nondelinquent behavior they proposed five techniques of neutralization and rationalization: denial of injury, denial of victim, denial of responsibility, condemnation of the condemners and appeal to higher loyalties.

According to Sykes and Matza, juveniles will use one of these five tech-niques to minimize any guilt associated with their delinquent activities. If the techniques are used before the act is committed then it is a technique of neutralization and if the technique is used after the act is committed then it is a technique of rationalization. Three of the techniques are self explana-tory in their titles. Denial of injury is where the individual will argue that there was no harm caused to the victim of the activity. Denial of victim is where the individual will argue that there is no victim to their acts. Denial of responsibility is where the individual will argue that something made them commit the act—it was someone else's fault that they committed the act. The final two are slightly more complex. Condemnation of the condemn-ers is where the individual will justify their behavior on the belief that the victim is being a hypocrite because he either engages in the same behav-ior or would engage in the same behavior if given the opportunity. Appeal to higher loyalties refers to when an individual will justify their behavior on the grounds that while the act may have violated society's values or rules, the act was not a violation of the values or rules of a subset of society—namely the individual's friends, gang members, etc.

Sykes and Matza's theory was selected first because this author has begun studying the use of these techniques of rationalization and neutral-ization by individuals who engage in the distribution of copyrighted movies and music. These digital pirates, although the title is considered by some to be misleading because the majority of P2P users do not attempt to make a profit off of the technology, are often law abiding citizens by day and copyright violators by night. All types of individuals engage in this behav-ior. Some people may believe that it is only students, but the truth is that anyone is a potential downloader. In fact, this author remembers visiting a small university once for a guest lecture. While waiting for the host I began talking with the secretary and she asked what I was there to talk about. She had a strange look on her face when I said that I was talking about high-tech-nology crime and specifically file sharing. It was then that I noticed that she was attempting to minimize her Kazaa program. I laughed and told her not to worry that I wasn't there to report anyone. After she relaxed again we continued talking and it turned out that nine of the twelve faculty members in their division downloaded files on a regular basis.

After this I began interviewing students who would talk to me about their file sharing activities. After about 44 interviews I began to notice some interesting things. For example a large number of the individuals that I talked to indicated support for Sykes and Matza's denial of injury and denial of vic-tim techniques. It was a commonly held belief that downloading music was not harmful to the recording artists because they still got their money from concerts or from the recording companies. Some individuals even claimed that they used downloading to help them select which CDs to pur-chase. However, ironically these same individuals had purchased very few CDs, if any, over the past 12 months. Others indicated support for newer techniques of rationalization and neutralization that have been developed in the nineties. For example one individual indicated that he was entitled to download music, movies, software and anything else he wanted because he paid $30 a month for his Internet service. Therefore, anything that he could find on the Internet should be a part of that monthly fee.

These results are still exploratory but suggest a need for larger studies with more students, as well as people outside of the university setting. The initial results are frightening, however, because they imply that attempts to regulate P2P through legal action may have an inverse affect on the problem and actually make it worse as more individuals become upset and continue to download.

Akers' Social Learning Theory

Ronald Akers agreed with Edwin Sutherland's differential association theory to some extent. However, it was Akers' belief that differential association was an incomplete theory. Sutherland had proposed the idea that criminal behavior was learned from individuals, but he never discussed the actual mechanisms that aided the learning of this criminal behavior. Akers relied heavily upon behavioral science in reaching his conclusions. Ultimately, he determined that individuals are more likely to engage in criminal behavior when they associate with people who are likely to not only engage in criminal behavior but teach an attitude of acceptance for criminal behavior.

On of the more interesting expansions Akers made with Sutherland's differential association was the belief that individuals could learn criminal attitudes and behavior (including techniques) through the media and other forms of nontraditional communications. Of course the most important forms of association are those that occur on a regular basis and involve encounters with those who are close to the individual (i.e., family, close friends, etc.). With Akers' acceptance that nontraditional communications could provide a forum for communicating definitions and ideas favorable to committing delinquent acts, the door has been opened for studies involving the role of online relationships and the learning of delinquent attitudes.

While this author has found no studies thus far that address this issue, it is still one that is interesting and maintains the possibility for future research. If relationships can explain why individuals develop an affinity for committing delinquent and criminal acts, then online relationships are the newest thing and should be examined. There are thousands of websites on the Internet where people can come together and talk about their interests, their hobbies, even their love lives. It is not unfathomable that an individual who is devoted to this form of electronic communication could become so involved in the online community that Akers' social learning process could develop. There are individuals who devote hours each week to chatting and posting to online discussion forums and virtual communities. Some individuals may spend hours each day engaging in these activities. If these websites and online communities are devoted to activities such as identity theft or other inappropriate activity then it is possible that someone could learn from the Internet. Remember, it was stated earlier that anyone can learn to be a hacker by merely spending a few hours on the Internet. A web community devoted to con artistry and identity theft could allow someone to learn not only the techniques but also the beliefs that such activity is acceptable, justifiable or even necessary in today's society. It will be interesting to see if any studies involving social learning theory and the Internet develop in the next few years.

Routine Activities Theory

Lawrence Cohen and Marcus Felson approached criminal behavior from a different perspective than the previous theorists. These theorists accepted that criminal behavior and attitude is a given. Their theory instead focuses on how activity patterns can affect crime rates and victimization. According to Cohen and Felson there are three factors to consider in whether a crime will be committed: (1) motivated offenders, (2) suitable targets and (3) absence of capable guardians to prevent victimization. For an example of this consider the crime of burglary. An individual who is interested in breaking into someone's home is more likely to break into a home in a community where they feel they have the best opportunity to get away with the crime. In a nice, affluent neighborhood it is more likely that neighbors will take care of each other and report suspicious activity. However, what about a poorer neighborhood?

The burglar wants to break into a home but chooses a neighborhood with a lower median income level. Many of these homeowners may work two jobs in order to support their needs. In this scenario there is a motivated offender who is ready to commit the crime of burglary and just needs some support for his actions. Depending upon what it is that the burglar is looking for, the house has been selected because it likely contains materials of interest to the burglar. Finally, if both family members work then the house is going to most likely be deserted. In this scenario there is a motivated offender, with a suitable target and an absence of a guardian. This home is a much more attractive target than the first home.

In regards to high-technology crime, the crime of hacking should be studied with routine activities theory addressed. Thanks in part to the Internet and the sheer number of computers purchased every year, there are plenty of suitable targets. Hackers are motivated to commit their criminal acts for a variety of reasons—anger, curiosity or just to prove that they can get away with the criminal act. Therefore, there is no absence of motivated offenders. The second requirement is that there must be a suitable target. There are millions of individuals who maintain Internet accounts. The recent move toward high speed Internet accounts with cable and DSL connectivity has made the availability of suitable targets more prevalent. Cable and DSL connections are more desirable than traditional connections because of their speed and the fact that the connections are always on. This means that when the individual is away from their computer the Internet connection is still activated. Each one of these computers is a suitable target for a hacker.

The third factor is an absence of capable guardians. Many individuals have cable and DSL accounts, yet have either antiquated virus protection or no virus protection at all. In terms of computer vulnerability this means that these computers do not have capable guardians to protect them. When all three factors are considered, routine activities theory helps explain why computer hacking is becoming such a frequently reported criminal act. Of course, this is all theoretical but hopefully the next few years will see research studies on the use of routine activities theory and computer-assisted crime.

Evolution of the Legal System

A final area that is certain to see increased change is the legal system. With more law enforcement agencies dedicating staff and resources to the investigation of high-technology crime, it is now necessary for the legal system to provide the necessary assistance. By this it is meant that there must be: (1) adequate statutes addressing the various high-technology crimes and their punishment, and (2) consistent rulings from the courts as to how the law can be applied to high-technology crimes.

In examining point one above, the various states and the federal government have consistently improved in this area. The various high-technology crimes discussed in earlier chapters have been criminalized and/or addressed in the majority of jurisdictions. Some may question whether the penalties associated with the criminal acts are sufficient; and that is certainly an argument that can be made. However, at least law enforcement agencies have a legal basis for responding to crimes such as hacking, identity theft and cyberstalking. Future changes in the statutory law are likely to address the penalties associated with the various high-technology crimes. Deterrence requires serious penalties.

Turning briefly to criminological theory and the deterrence argument, to deter individuals from engaging in criminal activity requires that the punishment be such that an individual would not choose to engage in the act. The entire foundation of deterrence theory rests on the assumption that people maintain free will and make rational choices when it comes to criminal behavior. If people are rational and consider the possible punishment when they choose to behave in a certain manner, then what must the law do to ensure that fewer people want to engage in high-technology crime (there is likely no amount of punishment that could prevent every-one from engaging in certain criminal behavior)?

For example, let us examine the crime of identity theft. Pretend that you are contemplating an act of identity theft that should you be found guilty of you could face up to five years in prison. Does the potential punishment offset the potential gain? If not then it could be argued that a rational person will weigh the potential gain from identity theft with the potential punishment *should* they be caught. The fact that the person will weigh the punishment should they be caught is an important factor. If the person is aware of the punishment associated with identity theft, yet has reason to believe that few individuals are ever subjected to the punishment, then the activity may still appear attractive. Law enforcement agencies and the courts are doing better about ensuring that individuals who commit identity theft are located, prosecuted and sentenced to prison times. The question then is whether the punishment offsets the potential gain from the act? If I can commit an act of identity theft, or even multiple counts of identity theft, and come away from the crime with two million dollars then would the punishment of five years dissuade me from committing the act? If not, then how much time must be added to the punishment before it would dissuade me from committing the act? These are all questions that are likely to come before both state and federal legislatures in the coming years.

Some legal scholars question whether the legal system will be able to handle high-technology crimes in the future. In some areas it seems as though the technology seems to change faster than the crimes themselves. Without denying that the efforts of law enforcement agencies are assisted by statutes criminalizing high-technology crime, there is some merit to the argument that the legal system may not be capable of keeping up with emerging technology. As soon as a statute has been designed that will regulate an activity the technology may change and the statute is either obsolete or no longer covers all possible activities. If the law cannot maintain pace with the technology, then what is the answer to solving the high-technology crime problem?

According to Biegel (2003) the answer may lie in code-based regulation. Under this approach the software is designed to regulate itself and prevent unlawful use. Of course the problem with relying on code-based regulation is that so many crimes involve technology that has been modified or created for the sole purpose of assisting an individual in engaging in criminal activity. If the software is designed to assist in committing criminal acts then there is little reason to believe that the designers would include code to prevent misuse. There are some programs that have been developed for legitimate uses that are now being applied toward criminal activity. For these programs code-based regulation may be an appropriate consideration.

The second area of the legal system that is likely to experience change involves rulings from the courts. Currently, as demonstrated in earlier chapters, there is some discrepancy between how the lower federal and state courts have ruled in regards to applying constitutional law to cases involving high-technology crime. One of the more heavily debated areas involves interpreting the Fourth Amendment in light of technological advancements. Some of the lower courts have ruled that traditional Fourth Amendment doctrines are still applicable to cases involving technology, while other courts have attempted to develop new doctrines to be used in the age of technology.

Whether or not this issue can be solved is one that will remain to be seen. After all, the very nature of the United States court system is such that it creates this area of confusion. When a federal court hears a case for the first time this is referred to as a case of first impression. Let us consider an example. What if the Fifth Circuit Court of Appeals rules on an issue one way, and then the Ninth Circuit Court of Appeals should face a similar issue? Does the Ninth Circuit have to rule in the same manner? No, if the case is one of first impression then it is up to the Court of Appeals to determine how they want to rule on the issue.

If one of the parties is not satisfied with the decision then they have the option of appealing the decision on to the United States Supreme Court. While the Supreme Court is the final answer in terms of constitutional arguments, there remains a problem—the issue of time. When a case is working its way through the various stages of the court system, each step requires a significant amount of time and effort on the part of both sides of the argument. For a case to make it to the Supreme Court may take two years or it may take four years. Not being critical of the Supreme Court, but accepting that it takes time for a case to work its way to the high court, the issue of technology makes the use of the courts problematic. Computers and technology are changing every day. Technology that is cutting edge today may be obsolete in two to three years. Further, the legal issue that is being decided may be moot by the time the Supreme Court agrees to hear the case or before the court may issue a decision.

One example of this would be the case of the Napster file sharing software. The Recording Industry Association of America responded to the issue of file sharing by filing a lawsuit against Napster, claiming that the software's manufacturer was responsible for the illegal use of the software. The courts agreed, finding that the software's design did in fact allow for the company to regulate what files were being shared on the network. However, instead of file sharing software programs beginning to disappear, the new manufacturers merely changed the design of the software. Because the decision in Napster had to do with the central server design, subsequent programs merely removed the central server feature. The software changed and went around the legal ruling.

So, what is the answer to preventing the problem of high-technology crime? The truth is that there is no easy answer. There are several factors that need to be taken into consideration and addressed. The first would be legislation. Attempts to solely control the problem through legislation will not be effective, but there is little argument that there must be criminal statutes addressing the use of technology in illegal activities. Without statutes addressing the activities there is no means of prosecuting the individuals who misuse technology.

Next, is the issue of high-technology crime investigation teams. Law enforcement agencies need to develop a basic understanding of technology-assisted crime and staff a team of individuals to respond to such acts. That being said, the reality is that this consideration is one of the more difficult to address. Clearly law enforcement agencies do not want to be incapable of handling high-technology crime. But having a desire to staff such a team and having the resources are two different things. Agencies may desire to staff a team but find that they have no officers willing or able to staff the team. Investigating high-technology crimes will require that an individual have an interest in computer technology and be willing to undergo intensive training in the area of computer forensics. Smaller agencies may not maintain anyone who is interested in working in such an area. A closely related problem is that even if the agency has someone who is interested in such an area they may not be able to afford the training and equipment necessary to establish the team. In some instances agencies have expressed hesitation to spend money to train individuals in computer forensics because once they have received their training they may leave the agency to work in private security—making more money and working better hours.

Finally, there is the consideration of target hardening. Having teams of trained individuals to investigate high-technology crimes and having statutes to prosecute these individuals once they are located is necessary. Unfortunately, with the nature of the Internet there is no way high-technology crime can be controlled through law enforcement means only. There are millions upon millions of Internet users, and some of the crimes are becoming easier and easier with new technology. This means that millions of users could potentially engage in criminal behavior. The answer may lie in combining the law enforcement response with the process of target hardening, or making potential victims more aware of the crimes and how to protect themselves. Take for example the crime of identity theft. There are more than 500,000 reports of identity theft each year, and this number only represents those that actually reported their victimization. This is just one crime that involves the use of technology. It is impossible to believe that law enforcement agencies can investigate every case of identity theft, so the answer may be trying to reduce the number of victims by making individuals aware about how identity theft works and how individuals can protect themselves. There are an increasing number of organizations dedicated to identity theft awareness and even some law enforcement agencies that maintain officers who alert citizens to potential dangers. Teaching users and companies how to spot potential threats from hackers may help in preventing the takeover and illegal use of computers. All three of these together may be necessary to control, not prevent, high-technology crime.

Conclusion

The rapid advances in high-technology crime over the past five years are sufficient proof that the future is sure to hold continuing problems for law enforcement and the criminal justice system. Digital piracy continues to evolve and could explode depending upon how the Supreme Court rules and how software manufacturers and users respond to the legal system's decree. Of even more concern is society's greater reliance on computers to maintain and operate components of the nation's critical infrastructure. This means that in the future an act of cyberterrorism is more than possible, it could perhaps be characterized as probable. The problem is that many high technology acts are being labeled cyberterrorism. This is problematic because as people read these accounts of high tech pranks that are labeled as cyberterrorism they eventually become immune to the seriousness of cyberterrorism. Therefore, when someone comes forth with a suspicion that a future terrorist attack is going to be cyber in nature many people do not adequately prepare because they are not concerned with the crime. The truth, however, is that cyberterrorism is extremely dangerous and should be a serious consideration for those who develop, implement and staff computer systems associated with the various components of the infrastructure.

Understanding the how is only one aspect of stemming the growing problem of high-technology crime. The other side that must be considered is the why. Why do people engage in high-technology crime? There are numerous studies to address why individuals engage in physical world crime. In the coming years there is a need to begin testing these theories in an attempt to determine which, if any, help explain the actions of high-tech criminals. Once an understanding of the how and the why are obtained, then truly controlling the problem becomes possible. Of course while this sounds simplistic when reading this, the reality is that criminologists still cannot explain the how and the why of several physical world crimes. It is unreasonable to expect miracles in the coming years. Instead, it is important for criminologists to begin studying these problems.

In the past five years the criminal justice system has done an outstanding job of increasing the number of criminal statutes related to high-technology crime. Additionally, more law enforcement agencies have begun staffing teams capable of investigating and prosecuting high-technology criminals. This process, however, is still not complete and there are still problems with applying some of the statutes to high-technology crime. The question that will surely be raised in the coming years is whether or not the legal system can be expected to handle the problem of high-technology crime on its own. Perhaps Biegel's recommendation of code-based regulation is the answer. After all, if the technology is changing too fast for the legal system then perhaps the answer lies in the technology itself. Only time will tell.

Review Questions

1. What is meant by the term cyberterrorism? Are acts of cyberterrorism physically or financially threatening?

2. Discuss how neutralization and rationalization techniques could be applied to any of the high-technology crimes discussed in this book.

3. Discuss how social learning could be applied to any of the high-technology crimes discussed in this book.

4. After reading the definition of cyberterrorism how do you feel about infrastructure protection and computer technology? What recommendations would you make to those who are tasked with securing our computers?

5. Discuss why the answer to controlling high-technology crime may not involve the use of the legal system and statutory guidelines? Is code-based regulation a better answer or do you see problems with this approach?

Online Resources

United States Institute for Peace—website containing information relating to cyber terrorism, the seriousness of the crime and the frequency of the crime. Available at http://www.usip.org/pubs/specialreports/sr119.html.

Social Science Research Council—website containing an article by Dorothy Denning, a well-regarded expert on cyber terrorism. Denning talks about whether the future of terrorist attacks will involve cyber terrorism as a tool of fear. Available at http://www.ssrc.org/sept11/essays/denning.htm.

References

Aftab, P. (2000). *The Parents Guide to Protecting Your Children in Cyberspace*. New York: McGraw Hill.

Akdeniz, Y. (1999). *Sex on the Net: The Dilemma of Policing Cyberspace*. United Kingdom: Garnett Publishing.

Avenger (1991). *Beginning to Advanced Carding*. Retrieved March 28, 2002 from http://www.textfiles.com/anarch/CARDING/.

Bahari, S. (2004). "Online Prostitution Difficult to Police." Retrieved on March 17, 2005, from http://www.mercurynews.com/mld/mercurynews/news/world/9455201.htm.

Bare Bones of Child Pornography (2002). Retrieved April 15, 2002 from http://wwww.safe4kids.org/reports/cporn2.htm.

Berger, S. (2001). "The Use of the Internet to 'Share' Copyrighted Material and its Effect on Copyright Law." *Journal of Legal Advocacy & Practice*, 3:92-105.

Bernstein, N. (1997). "Inmate Accused of Collecting Child Pornography." *New York Times*, (March 28):A16.

Bequai, A. (1978). *Computer Crime*. Lexington, MA: Lexington Books.

Bequai, A. (1983). *How to Prevent Computer Crime*. New York: John Wiley and Sons.

Bequai, A. (1987). *Technocrimes*. Lexington, MA: Lexington Books.

Bidwell, T. (2002). *Hackproofing Your Identity in the Information Age*. Rockland, MA: Syngress Publishing.

Biegel, S. (2003). *Beyond our Control? Confronting the Limits of Our Legal System in the Age of Cyberspace*. Cambridge, MA: The MIT Press.

Blackowicz, J. (2001). "RIAA v. Napster, Defining Copyright for the 21st Century?" *Boston University Journal of Science and Technology*, 7:182-193.

Block, S. (2005). "First Move for Identity Theft Victims." *USA Today*, 03b.

Blue Ridge Thunder Website (2001). Retrieved August 21, 2001, from http: www.blueridgethunder.com.

Bonisteel, S. (2002). "Identity Theft Insurance Going Mainstream." *News Bytes News Network*. Retrieved April 28, 2002, from EBSCOHost database.

Brail, S. (1996). "The Price of Admission: Harassment and Free Speech in the Wild, Wild West." In L. Cherny and E. Wise (eds.), *Wired Women: Gender and New Realities in Cyberspace*. Washington: Seal Press.

Brenner, S. (2001). "Defining Cybercrime: A Review of State and Federal Law." In R.D. Clifford (ed.), *Cybercrime: The Investigation, Prosecution and Defense of a Computer-Related Crime*, pp. 11-69. Durham, NC: Carolina Academic Press.

Brunker, M. (1999). "Streetwalkers in Cyberspace: Oldest Profession Dons High-Tech Cloak." Retrieved on November 19, 2004, from http://msnbc.msn.com/id/3078778/.

Buford, T. (2002). *Your Child and Pornography*. Madison, TN: Tommera Press. Electronic version available: http://www.firesofdarkness.com.

Burstow, P. (2002). "Pedophilia and the Internet." Retrieved April 15, 2002 from http://www.zyworld.com/paulburstow/paedoarticle.htm.

Campbell, D. (2002). "LAPD Slow to Help in Identity Theft." *Los Angeles Times*. Retrieved April 28, 2002, from EBSCOHost database.

Carlson, S. (2001). "Napster was Nothing Compared with This Year's Bandwidth Problems." *Chronicle of Higher Education*, 48(5):a44-a45.

Carlson, S. (2003). "Recording Industry Plans to Accelerate Complaints About Illegal File Sharing." *Chronicle of Higher Education*, (48)17:a46.

Casanova, M. (2000). "The History of Child Pornography on the Internet." *Journal of Sex Education and Therapy*, 25:245-252.

Casey, E. (2000). *Digital Evidence and Computer Crime: Forensic Science, Computers and the Internet.* New York: Academic Press.

Child Molesters and the Internet (2002). Retrieved April 15, 2002 from http://www.kidsap.org/ChildMolestersAndTheIntenet.htm.

Christensen, J. (1999). "Bracing for Guerrilla Warfare in Cyberspace." *CNN Interactive*. Retrieved on May 10, 2005, from http://www.cnn.com/TECH/specials/hackers/cyberterror.

Clark, F., and K. Diliberto (1996). *Investigating Computer Crime.* New York: CRC Press.

Clifford, R. (ed.) (2001). *Cybercrime: The Investigation, Prosecution and Defense of a Computer-Related Crime.* Durham, NC: Carolina Academic Press.

Computer Fraud and Abuse Act. 18 U.S.C. 1030 (1989). Amended 1996, 2001.

Coutorie, L. (1995). "The Future of High-Technology Crime: A Parallel Delphi Study." *Journal of Criminal Justice*, 23:13-28.

Cronkhite, C., and J. McCullough (2001). *Access Denied: The Complete Guide to Protecting Your Business Online.* Chicago: Osborne/McGraw-Hill.

Dearne, K. (2001). "Cyber Crime Costs are Increasing." *The Australian*, 1:36. Retrieved August 21, 2001, from EBSCOHost database.

Denning, P. (1990). *Computers Under Attack: Intruders, Worms, and Viruses.* New York: ACM Press.

Diffie, W., and S. Landau (1998). *Privacy on the Line: The Politics of Wiretapping and Encryption.* Cambridge, MA: The MIT Press.

Dillon, S., D. Groene, and T. Hayward (1998). "Computer Crimes." *American Criminal Law Review*, 35:503-547.

D.K. (1996). "Hacker History." *America's Network*, 100(14):42-43.

Doege, D. (2002). "Milwaukee-Area Officials Say Identity Theft is Lucrative, Rapidly Growing." *The Milwaukee Journal Sentinel*. Retrieved April 28, 2002, from EBSCOHost database.

Donohue, L., and J. Walsh (2001). "Patriot Act – A Remedy for an Unidentified Problem." *San Francisco Chronicle*, October 30, 2002.

Draper, J. (2001). *How Cap'n Crunch Became a Phone Phreaker*. Retrieved May 25, 2002 from http://www.techtv.com/screensavers/supergeek/story/0,24330,334781,00.html.

Electronics Communication Privacy Act. 18 U.S.C. 2510-2522 (1986); Amended 2001.

Electronic Freedom Foundation. (2002). *Privacy, Surveillance and Terrorism*. Retrieved October 12, 2002, from http://www.eff.org.

Elliot, C. (2002). "Identity Theft Becoming More Common, Government Warns." *South Bend Tribune*. Retrieved April 28, 2002, from EBSCOHost database.

Enos, L. (2000). "Study: File-Sharing Stalls Net Music Sales." *Newsfactor Network*. Retrieved February 27, 2003, from www.newsfactor.com.

Estrella, A. (2001). "The Lowdown on E-Mail, Surfing the Internet at Work." Retrieved November 15, 2000 http://pacific.bizjournals.com/pacific/stories/2001/08/27/focus4.html.

Fazekas, C. (2002). "Vigilantes v. Pirates: The Rumble Over Peer-to-Peer Technology Hits the House Floor." *Duke Law & Technology Review*, 20.

Florida Department of Law Enforcement (FDLE) (2002). "LEACH Task Force Agents Arrest a South Florida 'Traveler'." Retrieved December 7, 2002, from http://www.flde.state.fl.us/press_releases/20020405_andrew_hochstadt.html.

Flowers, R. (1996). *The Victimization and Exploitation of Women and Children: A Study Of Physical, Mental, and Sexual Maltreatment in the United States*. Jefferson, NC: McFarland & Company.

Freedman, D., and C. Mann (1997). *@large: The Strange Case of the World's Biggest Internet Invasion*. New York: Touchstone Publishing.

Freedom of Information Act. 5 U.S.C. s/s 552 (1966); Amended 1996.

Freeh, L. (2002). *A Parent's Guide to Internet Safety*. U.S. Department of Justice Federal Bureau of Investigation Publications. Retrieved April 15, 2002 from http://www.fbi.gov/publications/pguide/pguidee.htm.

Fuentes, A. (1996). "Who Opened Their E-Mail?" *Village Voice*, 41:15.

Gill, J. (2001). "One of the World's Most Feared Hackers Switches Sides." *Sunday Business*. Retrieved March 25, 2002, from EBSCOHost database.

Gillen, M., and B. Garrity (2000). "Industry's Anti-Piracy Efforts 'Doomed to Fail' Says Forester." *Billboard*, 112(40):9-11.

Gindin, S. (1999). "Guide to E-Mail and the Internet in the Workplace." Bureau of National Affairs, Inc. Retrieved December 8, 2002, from http://www.info-law.com/guide.html.

Ginsburg, J. (2000). "Copyright Use and Excuse on the Internet." *Columbia VLA Journal of Law & the Arts*, 24:1-45.

Glatt, J. (2001). *Internet Slave Master: A True Story of Seduction and Murder*. New York: St. Martin's Publishing.

Golangelo, A. (2002). "Copyright Infringement in the Internet Era: The Challenge of MP3s." *Alberta Law Review*, 39:891-913.

Goldstein, A. (2002). "Credit-Card Firms Look to Stop Fraud with New Authentication Technologies." *The Dallas Morning News*. Retrieved April 28, 2002, from EBSCOHost database.

Green, S. (2001). "Reconciling Napster with the SONY Decision and Recent Amendments to Copyright Law." *American Business Law Journal*, 39:57-98.

Guidance Software (2004). "Encase." Retrieved October 5, 2004, from http://www.guidance software.com.

Hafner, K., and J. Markoff (1991). *Cyberpunk: Outlaws and Hackers on the Computer Frontier.* New York: Simon & Schuster.

Hallifax, J. (2001). "Inmate Accused Identity Theft Ring." *Associated Press Online*. Retrieved April 28, 2002, from EBSCOHost database.

Hammond, R. (2002). *Identity Theft: How to Protect Your Most Valuable Asset.* Franklin Lakes, NJ: Career Press.

Harrison, W., G. Heuston, S. Mocas, M. Morrissey, and J. Rishardson (2004). "High-Tech Forensics." *Communications of the ACM,* 47(7):49. Retrieved March 30, 2005, from Business Source Elite database.

Hermann, M. (1998) *Search and Seizure Checklists*. St. Paul, Minnesota: West Group.

Hopper, D. (2002). "Reports on Identity Theft on Rise." *Associated Press Online*. Retrieved April 28, 2002, from EBSCOHost database.

Hughes, D. (1998). "How Pornography Harms Children." Retrieved April 16, 2005, from http://www.protectkids.com/effects/harms.htm.

Hurewitz, J. (2002). "Confessions of a Music Pirate." *The Prague Post*. Retrieved on February 27, 2003, from www.praguepost.com.

Jacobsen, H., and Green R. (2002). "Computer Crimes." *American Criminal Law Review*, 39:273-325.

Jenkins, P. (2001). *Beyond Tolerance: Child Pornography Online.* New York: University Press.

Johnstone, D. (2001). "The Pirates Are Always with Us: What Can and Cannot be Done About Unauthorized Use of MP3 Files on the Internet." *Buffalo Intellectual Property Law Journal*, 122-145.

Kaplan, D. (1997). "New Cybercop Tricks to Fight Child Porn." *U.S. News and World Report*, 122:29.

Kerr, O. (2001). "Searching and Seizing Computers and Obtaining Electronic Evidence in Criminal Investigations." *Computer Crime and Intellectual Property Section (CCIPS)*. Retrieved on April 15, 2002, from: http://www.cybercrime.gov/searchmanual.htm.

Kitchen Hand Clicks His Way to Cyber-Fraud History (2001). *The Australian*. Retrieved April 28, 2002, from EBSCOHost database.

Ko, M. (2002). *Porn-Busters, Beware.* Retrieved December 8, 2002, from http://www.marnieko.com/pornbusters.htm.

Kornblum, Janet. (1997). "Mitnick Faces 22-Month Rap." Retrieved July 20, 2003, from http://news.com.com/Mitnick+faces+22-month+rap/2100-1023_3-200750.html.

Kovacich, G., and W. Boni (2000). *High-Technology-Crime Investigator's Handbook: Working in the Global Information Environment.* Boston: Butterworth Heinemann.

Krane, J. (2002). "Cops Chase Drugs on the Internet." March 20, 2002 from www.entheogen.com.

Kruse, W., and Heiser, J. (2002). *Computer Forensics: Incident Response Essentials.* New York: Addison-Wesley Pub.

Kunerth, J., and Gutierrez, P. (2002). "Recent Arrests Show Prostitution Still Flourishes on Web." *The Orlando Sentinel*, July 2. Retrieved from the EBSCOHost database on July 9, 2003.

Levy, S. (1994). *Hackers: Heroes of the Computer Revolution.* New York: Penguin Books.

Levy, S., B. Stone et al. (2000). "The Noisy War Over Napster." *Newsweek*, 135(23):46-53.

Lieberman, J. (2001). *Name Your Own Price . . . for Hookers?!? ebay and priceline.com Muscle in on the World's Oldest Business Model.* Retrieved on July 11, 2003, from http://www.pctyrant.com/mainapril2001.html.

Littman, J. (1996). *The Fugitive Game: Online with Kevin Mitnick.* Boston: Little Brown and Company.

Littman, J. (1997). *The Watchman: The Twisted Life and Crimes of Serial Hacker Kevin Poulsen.* Boston: Little Brown and Company.

Lohse, D. (2001). "IRS Error Causes San Francisco-Area Taxpayers Receive Others' Documents." *San Jose Mercury News.* Retrieved April 28, 2002, from EBSCOHost database.

Masson, G. (2000). "NetPD Tracks File Swapping on Web." *Billboard*, 112(43):8-10.

Mandia, K. and Prosise, C. (2001). *Incident Response: Investigating Computer Crime.* San Francisco: McGraw-Hill Osborne Media.

McCabe, K. (2000). "Child Pornography and the Internet." *Social Science Computer Review*, 18:73-76.

McGraw, D. (1995). "Sexual Harassment in Cyberspace: The Problem of Unwelcome E-Mail." *Rutgers Computer and Technology Law Journal*, 21:491-518.

Meinel, C. (2000). *Uberhacker! How to Break into Computers.* Washington: Loompanics.

Mitnick, K., and W. Simon (2002). *The Art of Deception: Controlling the Human Element of Security.* Indianapolis: Wiley Publishing.

Moad, J. (2001). "Tracking Down the Nasty Guys." *EWeek*, 18:40-41.

National Institute of Justice (2001). *Electronic Crime Scene Investigation: A Guide for First Responders.* Retrieved on August 15, 2002, from http://www.ojp.usdoj.gov/nij.

National White Collar Crime Center (2002). *Identity Theft.* Retrieved August 15, 2002, from http://nw3c.com.

Nelson, B., A. Phillips, F. Enfinger, and C. Steuart (2004). *Guide to Computer Forensics and Investigations.* Boston: Thomson Course Technology.

Nesteroff, G. (1997). *Phreak Show.* Retrieved December 5, 2002 from http://www.peak.sfu.ca/the-peak/97-1/issue3/phreak.html.

Newman, J. (1999). *Identity Theft: The Cybercrime of the New Millennium.* Port Townsend, WA: Loompanics.

Overholt, M., and S. Brenner (2001). *Overview of Cyber-Terrorism*. Retrieved on May 10, 2005, from http://cybercrimes.net/Terrorism/overview/page4.html.

Paradise, P.R. (1999). *Trademark Counterfeiting, Product Piracy, and the Billion Dollar Threat to the U.S. Economy.* Connecticut: Quorum Books.

Parker, D. (1976). *Crime by Computer.* New York: Scribner.

Patzakis, J. (2002). "The Encase Process." In E. Casey (ed.), *Handbook of Computer Crime Investigations: Forensic Tools and Technology*, pp. 53-72. San Francisco: Academic Press.

Penenberg, A.L. (1999). "The Demonizing of a Hacker." *Forbes*. Retrieved June 12, 2002 from http://www.forbes.com/1999/0419/6308050a.html.

Petrova, E. (2003). *Dating Scams: The Real Picture of International Introduction Industry*. Retrieved on July 9, 2003, from http://www.womenrussia.com/who.htm.

Phoenix, J. (1999). *Making Sense of Prostitution*. Palgrave: New York.

Pitta, J. (2001). "Digital Frontier?" *Forbes*, 167(10):60-62.

Platt, C. (1996). *Anarchy Online: Net Sex. The Truth Behind the Hype.* New York: Harper-Prism.

Power, R. (2000). *Tangled Web: Tales of Digital Crime from the Shadows of Cyberspace*. Indianapolis, IN: Que Publishing.

Radcliff, D. (2000). "Vigilante Group Targets Child Pornography Sites." *Computerworld*, 34:40.

Resseguie, D. (2000). "Computer Searches and Seizures." *Cleveland State Law Review,* 185-214.

Richards, J. (1999). *Transnational Criminal Organizations, Cybercrime, and Money Laundering.* New York: CRC Press.

Roane, K. (1998). "Prostitutes on Wane in New York Streets but Take to Internet." *New York Times*, February, 23, 1998. Retrieved from the EBSCOHost database on July 11, 2003.

Royal Canadian Mounted Police. (2001) *RCMP*. Retrieved on March 22, 2002, from http://www.rcmp-grc.cg.ca/html/cpu-cri.htm.

Samaha, J. (1996). *Criminal Law*. New York: Wadsworth.

Sanders, E. (2001). "Children's Online File Swapping Often Yields Porn, Report Says.". *Los Angeles Times*, (July 28).

Savage, D.G, (2002). "Getting Back Your Name." *ABA Journal*, 88(1). Retrieved March 31, 2005, from Academic Search Premier Database.

Schlueb, M. (2002). "Orlando, Florida, Takes Aim at Escort Services." *The Orlando Sentinel*, April 23, 2002. Retrieved from the EBSCOHost database on July 11, 2003.

Section of U.S. Code Covering the Rights of Customs Agents in Regards to Border Searches. Title 19 U.S.C. 482.

Seeger, S., and V. Visconte (1997). *Fourth Amendment Ramifications of Cyberspace Surveillance*. Retrieved on February 25, 2001 from http://wings.buffalo.edu/law/complaw.

Segaller, S. (1998). *Nerds 2.0.1: A Brief History of the Internet*. New York: T.V. Books L.L.C.

Sigal, P. (2002). "AOL Suit Highlights Danger of Internet Theft." *The Philadelphia Inquirer*. Retrieved April 28, 2002, from EBSCOHost database.

Slatella, M., and J. Quittner (1995). *Masters of Deception: The Gang That Ruled Cyberspace.* New York: HarperCollins Publishers.

Stamberg, S. (2001). "Analysis: Sale of State Birth and Death Records Temporarily Suspended in California." *Morning Edition (NPR).* Retrieved April 28, 2002, from EBSCO-Host database.

Statistical Analysis Center (2002). *Information and Technology Capabilities of Mississippi Law Enforcement Agencies.* Retrieved on April 8, 2004, from http://www.usm.edu/mssac/publications/ms_sac_publications.htm.

Stoll, C. (1990). *The Cuckoo's Egg: Tracking a Spy Through the Maze of Computer Espionage.* New York: Simon & Schuster.

Sullivan, B. (2004). *Your Evil Twin: Behind the Identity Theft Epidemic.* New Jersey: John Wiley and Sons.

Suspected Love Bug Creator to Give Up Hacking: Report. Retrieved June 15, 2001 from http://www.antionline.com.

Sykes, C. (1999). *The End of Privacy: The Attack on Personal Rights at Home, at Work, Online, and in Court.* New York: St. Martin's Griffin.

Taylor, J. (2000). "Cybercrime: Explore the Dark Side of Technology." *TechTV Online.* Retrieved on July 12, 2003, from http://www.techtv.com/cybercrime/print/0,23102,3301846,00.htm..

This Eldrick Woods . . . What's He Look Like? (2000). *Los Angeles Times.* Retrieved April 28, 2002, from EBSCOHost database.

Tran, M. (2001). "New Law Forces Police to do an About-Face on Identity Theft." *Los Angeles Times.* Retrieved April 28, 2002, from EBSCOHost database.

Trigaux, Robert. (2000). "A History of Hacking." *St. Petersburg Times.* Retrieved June 15, 2001 from http://www.sptimes.com/Hackers/history.hacking.html.

UNESCO (1999). *Sexual Abuse of Children, Child Pornography and Peadophilia on the Internet.* Retrieved on April 2, 2005, from http://www.unesco.org/webworld/child_screen/conf_index_2.html.

United States House of Representatives (2001). *Children's Access to Pornography Through Internet File-Sharing Programs.* Retrieved on August 15, 2002, from http://www.house.gov/reform/min/pdfs/pdf_inves/pdf_pornog_rep.pdf.

Uniting and Strengthening America by Providing Appropriate Tools Required to Intercept and Obstruct Terrorism Act. H.R. 3162 (October 24, 2001).

Vacca, J. (2002). *Computer Forensics: Computer Crime Scene Investigation.* Hingham, MA: Charles River Media.

Vacca, J. (2003). *Identify Theft.* New Jersey: Prentice Hall.

Van Dam, C. (2001). *Identifying Child Molesters: Preventing Child Sexual Abuse by Recognizing the Patterns of the Offenders.* New York: Haworth Press.

Verton, D. (2001). "Identity Thefts Skyrocket, But Less Than 1% Occur Online." *Computerworld*, 35:7-11.

Wall, D. (ed.) (2001). *Crime and the Internet.* New York: Taylor and Francis.

Wang, W. (1998). *Steal this Computer Book: What They Won't Tell You About the Internet.* San Francisco: No Starch Press.

Wang, W. (2001). *Steal this Computer Book 2: What They Won't Tell You About the Internet*. San Francisco: No Starch Press.

Wayner, P. (2002). *Disappearing Cryptography - Information Hiding: Steganography and Watermarking*. San Francisco: Morgan Kaufmann Publishers.

Weber, G. (2002). *Grooming Children for Sexual Molestation*. Retrieved April 15, 2002 from http://www.vachss.com/guest_dispatches/grooming.html.

Wilson, D. (2001). "Life Is Not a Movie, and Other Hacker Truths." *Los Angeles Times*, (August 19).

Wolf, J. (2001). *Grooming: the Process of Victimization*. Retrieved on May 24, 2002 from http://www.cachouston.org/pressroom/library/feature%20articles/grooming.pdf.

Worley, B. (2004). *Security Alert: Stories of Real People Protecting Themselves From Identity Theft, Scams, and Viruses*. Indianapolis, IN: New Riders Publishing.

Wright, O. (2001). "Identity Theft Drives Wrong Man Into Court." *The Times*. Retrieved April 28, 2002, from EBSCOHost database.

Zaenglein, N. (2000). *Secret Software: Making the Most of Computer Resources for Data Protection, Information Recovery, Forensics Examination, Crime Investigation and More*. Boulder, CO: Paladin Press.

Zillman, D., and Bryant, J. (1989). *Pornography: Research Advances and Policy Considerations*. New Jersey: Lawrence Erbaum Associates.

Court Decisions

Ashcroft v. Free Speech Coalition, 535 U.S. 234, 122 S. Ct. 1389, 152 L. Ed. 2d 403 (2002).

Alana Shoars v. Epson America Inc., No. B 073234 (1994).

Arizona v. Hicks, 480 U.S. 321, 107 S. Ct. 1149, 94 L. Ed. 2d 347 (1987).

Boyd v. United States, 116 U.S. 616, 6 S. Ct. 524, 29 L. Ed. 746 (1886).

Bumper v. North Carolina, 391 U.S. 543, 88 S. Ct. 1788, 20 L. Ed. 2d 797 (1968).

Cales v. Howell, 635 F. Supp. 454 (E.D. Mich. 1985).

Carroll v. United States, 267 U.S. 132, 45 S. Ct. 280, 69 L. Ed. 543 (1925).

Chimel v. California, 395 U.S. 752, 89 S. Ct. 2034, 23 L. Ed. 2d 685 (1969).

Daubert v. Merrell Dow Pharmaceuticals, 509 U.S. 579, 113 S. Ct. 2786, 125 L. Ed. 2d 469 (1993).

Davis v. State, 497 So. 2d 1344 (Fla. 5d 1986).

Frye v. United States, 293 F. 1013 (D.C. Cir. 1923).

Illinois v. Lafayette, 463 U.S. 640, 103 S. Ct. 2605, 77 L. Ed. 2d 65 (1983).

Illinois v. McArthur, 531 U.S. 326, 121 S. Ct. 946, 148 L. Ed. 2d 838 (2001).

Illinois v. Rodriguez, 497 U.S. 177, 110 S. Ct. 2793, 111 L. Ed. 2d 148 (1990).

Johnson v. United States, 333 U.S. 10, 68 S. Ct. 367, 92 L. Ed. 436 (1948).

Jimenez v. State, 643 So. 2d 70 (Fla. 2d DCA 1994).

Matter of Search Warrant for K-Sports Imports Inc., 163 F.R.D. 594 (C.D. Cal. 1995).

New Jersey v. T.L.O., 469 U.S. 325, 105 S. Ct. 733, 83 L. Ed. 2d 720 (1985).

Ohio v. Robinette, 519 U.S. 33, 117 S. Ct. 417, 136 L. Ed. 2d 347 (1996).

O'Connor v. Ortega, 480 U.S. 709; 107 S. Ct. 1492; 94 L. Ed. 2d 714

Parkhurst v. Trapp, 77 F.3d 707 (3d Cir. 1996).

Preston v. United States, 376 U.S. 364, 84 S. Ct. 881, 11 L. Ed. 2d 777 (1964).

Schneckloth v. Bustamonte, 412 U.S. 218, 93 S. Ct. 2041, 36 L. Ed. 2d 854 (1973).

State v. Hammonds, 557 So. 2d 179 (Fla. 3d DCA 1990).

Stoner v. California, 376 U.S. 483, 84 S. Ct. 889, 11 L. Ed. 2d 856 (1964).

United States v. Alfonso, 759 F.2d 728 (9th Cir. 1985).

United States v. Ball, 90 F.3d 260 (8th Cir. 1996).

United States v. Barth, 26 F. Supp. 2d 929 (1998).

United States v. Bizier, 111 F.3d 214 (1st Cir. 1997).

United States v. Blas, No. 90-Cr-162 (E.D. Wis. 1990).

United States v. Bradshaw, 102 F.3d 204 (6th Cir. 1996).

United States v. Burns, 37 F.3d 276 (7th Cir. 1994).

United States v. Carey, 172 F.3d 1268 (10th Cir. 1999).

United States v. Charbonneau, 979 F. Supp. 1177 (S.D, Ohio 1997).

United States v. David, 756 F. Supp. 1385 (D. Nev. 1991).

United States v. Durham, 1998 WL 684241 (D. Kan. 1998).

United States v. Elliot, 50 F.3d 180 (2d Cir. 1995).

United States v. Gray, 78 F. Supp. 2d 5244 (E.D. Va. 1999).

United States v. Haddad, 558 F.2d 968 (9th Cir. 1977).

United States v. Hall, 142 F.3d 988 (7th Cir. 1998).

United States v. Hambrick, 55 F. Supp.2d 504 (W.D. Va. 1999).

United States v. Hunter, 13 F. Supp. 2d 574 (D. Vt. 1998).

United States v. Lyons, 992 F. 2d 1029 (10 .⅃ Cir. 1993).

United States v. Matlock, 415 U.S. 164, 94 S. Ct. 988, 39 L. Ed. 2d 242 (1974).

United States v. Maxwell, 45 M.J. 406 (C.A.A.F. 1996).

United States v. Moorehead, 57 F.3d 875 (1995).

United States v. Ortiz, 84 F.3d 977 (7th Cir. 1996).

United States v. Poulsen, 41 F.3d 1330 (9th Cir. 1994).

United States v. Rahme, 813 F.2d 31 (2d Cir. 1987).

United States v. Ramsey, 431 U.S. 606 (1977).

United States v. Reed, 15 F.3d 928 (9th Cir. 1994).

United States v. Reyes, 922 F. Supp. 818 (S.D.N.Y. 1996).

United States v. Robinson, 414 U.S. 218, 94 S. Ct. 467, 38 L. Ed. 2d 427 (1973).

United States v. Roberts, 86 F. Supp. 2d 678 (S.D. Texas 2000).

United States v. Romero-Garcia, 991 F. Supp. 1223 (D. Or. 1997).

United States v. Ross, 456 U.S. 798 (1982).

United States v. Scheer, 600 F.2d 5 (3d Cir. 1979).

United States v. Smith, 27 F. Supp. 2d 1111 (C.D.Ill. 1998)

United States v. Tank, 200 F.3d 627 (9th Cir. 2000).

United States v. Upham, 168 F.3d 532 (1st Cir. 1999).

United States v. Villarreal, 963 F.2d 770 (5th Cir. 1992).

Walter v. United States, 447 U.S. 649 (1980).

Warden v. Hayden, 387 U.S. 294, 87 S. Ct. 1642, 18 L. Ed. 2d 782 (1967).

West Virginia v. Joseph T., 336 S.E.2d 728 (W. Va. 1985).

About the Author

Robert Moore is an assistant professor of criminal justice at Delta State University in Cleveland, Mississippi. He graduated from The University of Southern Mississippi in 2003 with his doctorate in Administration of Justice. Since that time he has published several articles relating to high technology crime and the legal system's response to technology. Upon request he occasionally provides computer forensics assistance to local law enforcement agencies.

Index